Manic caperings: Cullberg Ballet at the Edinburgh Playhouse

Douglas Robertson

DANCE
Clement Crisp

Aug 30

San Francisco Ballet LAST CHANCE

The San Francisco Ballet ends a visit
today, with two performances (matinée
and evening) of its triple bill of ballets by
the talented Christopher Wheeldon. The
Playhouse theatre is like a morgue but the
dance is lively, well-m

Cu
Edi
CLEM

At last
has com
ideally s
gloom, th
Romaniar
the Playho
Monday ni
from Swede
Strindberg
since ballet
anything on
brief season.
It is an ensen
a movement the
ranges from ma
therapy for the s
disturbed. Its rela
the real world, let
world of academi
to me tenuous. No
(the "ballet"
exec

Clement Crisp Reviews: Six decades of dance

IDWF

Published by
The International Dance
Writing Foundation

First published 2021

© The Financial Times
Limited 2021
'FT' and 'The Financial Times'
are registered trademarks of
The Financial Times Limited

ISBN 978-1-5272-8774-7

A CIP catalogue reference
for this book is avalable
from The British Library.

Editor: Gerald Dowler
Project co-ordinator:
David Wardrop
Designer: Glenn Hilling

Typeset in Trade Gothic
& Joanna

Printed in Great Britain by
Cambrian Printers Limited

Distributed by
Troubador Publishing Limited
9 Priory Business Park
Wistow Road, Kibworth
LE8 ORX, UK
www.troubador.co.uk

Clement Crisp with
Natalia Makarova

Clement Crisp Reviews: Six decades of dance

Edited by
Gerald Dowler

What his friends say...

CLEMENT CRISP IS UNDOUBTEDLY the most eminent ballet expert in the world. Long may he continue to delight us with his great intellect, wit, knowledge and perception.
Lilian Hochhauser

WHAT A TREAT to have this collection of reviews and articles to remind us of Clement's unending passion for classical dance, his rapier wit and his discerning and penetrating eye.
Dame Monica Mason

WHAT A SPLENDID IDEA to bring together the best of Clement Crisp's ballet criticism, his knowledge, understanding, wit and insight to be enjoyed all over again.
Deborah, Lady MacMillan

CLEMENT CRISP IS THE TRUE GURU of ballet criticism. His deep knowledge, appreciation and indeed love of the art of classic dance stands him out from his colleagues. None should ignore his writing; so vivid, so refined, sincere and passionate.
Katya Novikova, Bolshoi Ballet

I LOVE CLEMENT AS A PERSON, his loyalty, truthfulness and generosity. Full of charm, he is a treasure. Clement has the deepest love and profound knowledge of the art of ballet. There is nobody like him, never has been and probably never will be.
Natalia Makarova

COMMENT RENDRE HOMMAGE à Clement Crisp avec autant de talent que celui de son écriture. Merci de sa fidélité, de sa grande connaissance, de notre art, des danseurs et des ballets depuis tant d'années et merci de son amitié et de son humour lors de nos rencontres.
Élisabeth Platel

CLEMENT'S EXPERIENCE of watching dance all over the world is unrivalled – it was always his judgement that meant the most to me.
Dame Antoinette Sibley

With special thanks

Patrons

Lilian Hochhauser CBE

Judy Kleeman

Dasha Shenkman OBE

Linda and Louis Tanner

Sir Michael Codron CBE

Carola and Peter Kleeman

Angela Kane

Anthony Kerman and Joanna Kanska

Spindrift Al Swaidi

and those who have chosen
to be anonymous

Sponsors

Paul Taylor Dance Company
Stuart Steele
Roland John Wiley
Jane Pritchard MBE
Allen Thomas and Jane Simpson
Sir Peter Wright CBE
Imogen Knight

and those who have chosen
to be anonymous

We also thank our supporters
listed on the Foundation's website

CLEMENT CRISP has kept an archive of all his reviews and writings for well over half a century. They lie, carefully cut out and pasted into tome after tome, each review meticulously ascribed and dated and ultimately doing most of the work for a researcher privileged enough to be given access. I have been that researcher, the one to whom the books were entrusted with the words "be careful you don't lose my life's work", half in jest, half in all seriousness. It was a huge responsibility. I subsequently read every review in 'les archives clementines' as I have taken to calling them; that was not difficult in itself, the material so informative and entertaining as it is, and merely required time. The challenge with the writings of a commentator such as Clement Crisp was then to decide which reviews would make the cut to the 'long list' and then onto the 'short list'. Suffice to say that there is enough material to fill several books over, so the following is a very personal selection which I have endeavoured to structure in a fashion which will not only indicate the vast experience and insight of Clement as a reviewer but also give an appreciation of his eclectic tastes and his enduring dance passions.

Introduction
by Gerald Dowler

Through his writings the reader may also get a feel for the man behind the reviews, but that, for so private a man, will only ever be a fleeting glimpse. I have attempted to bring in writings from every decade, and from their differences in tone and focus the reader will appreciate the changes in criticism which moved, as society did, from post-war formality to a freer, more entertaining approach. This book is in no way a biography - Clement has a horror of such things - nor is not for me to dissect Clement's writing style and the nature of his criticism, and so I have included his own description of how he came to love the dance and his examination of what it is to be critic alongside an appreciation of Clement by that great fellow critic and co-author of numerous books, Mary Clarke.

Clement has written for numerous publications the world over but the vast bulk of his reviews have appeared in The Financial Times. He was there at the outset of the newspaper's arts coverage - he always pays tribute to Lord Drogheda, the newspaper's far-seeing Managing Director at the time, for starting it up - and was a constant for some sixty years, reporting with diligence and dedication from the world over. Over the years and decades of writing for the FT, Clement honed the art of newspaper reviewing, not least in what he terms 'the early days' when notices had to be dictated the same night over the telephone to the typesetters at the news-paper's presses; indeed, Clement's own suggestion for a subtitle for this book was

'The Morning After'. The speed with which opinions had to be formed and the limited line space given were 'a splendid discipline' and did much to form his lean writing style - unlike many for whom the limitless blogosphere is their natural milieu; he has never been prolix. What has equally characterised Clement's reviews is the sheer entertainment they give, so much so that many readers of the FT who do not have a particular interest in dance will read his reviews for their delicious wit. So many are the extraordinary turns of phrase and • • •

Carefully cut out and pasted into tome after tome, each review meticulously ascribed and dated

hilarious aperçus that to have included all the reviews in which they appear would have meant a multi-volume book. I have taken the liberty of lifting some from their reviews and scattering them throughout what follows - they are too good not to feature.

Clement's sense of humour does, I feel, come through in his reviews, a slightly off-the-wall view on what he has seen, delivered with a brightly twinkling eye and a keen ear for word-play. Occupying the glorious middle ground between the sheer bravura of these

asides and the couldn't-be-more-serious notice is the 'bad' Crisp review, an appreciation of a performance or an undertaking which simply does not cut the artistic mustard. These are perhaps the most feared notices in the business, embodiments of his own observation "when you shoot, shoot to kill", a selection of which appear in the section I have disingenuously entitled 'someone had to say it'. But the reality is that no-one else could have said it or dared to say it, certainly not in the way that Clement does, with such seemingly effortlessness - they are exemplars of a style of virtuoso criticism which is impossible and therefore unwise to emulate. What accompanies every Crisp review is also a weight of knowledge and expertise that is second to none, which means that his observations are never sour and most certainly never personal - the integrity of art form is what is paramount and everything must be judged accordingly. When his displeasure is incurred, it is with the sharpest of critical stilettos that he carries out the necessary deed, slicing through pretension, mediocrity and vacuity with a surgeon's skill. Naturally, he has his bêtes noires, dance styles or individual choreographers he genuinely believes are misguided in what they seek to do - there have been times with *tanztheater* when Clement has seemed like a lone prophet in the wilderness howling against the storm, but, admirably unshakeable in his beliefs, he has continued to howl.

This book contains his appreciations of the greatest artists he has witnessed, and for them, his praise meticulously identifies what it is that makes them great. Whilst he holds a reverence for the past, he is open to genius manifesting itself in the present, ever alert to the next prodigiously talented artist; for one who has seen and wondered at the likes of Markova, Vyrubova and Lifar, he has ample room to salute Smirnova and Polunin. Clement is keenly aware of the conflicting demands of the dance - creation is its life-blood but it must grow also from what has gone before. He is no museum curator, adamant that works must never change, but is perhaps rather more a guardian - the changes at The Royal Ballet and the dangers of the company severing its link to its own past are fearlessly detailed. His tastes are catholic indeed, from classical ballet and modern dance to traditional Japanese kabuki and Noh, circus and hip-hop - it shouldn't come as a surprise but it always docs.

Preparing Clement Crisp Reviews has been a joy, an education and a privilege. A joy because of the sheer entertainment his writings offer, an education for someone with critical pretensions to see how it is really done and a privilege to be trusted with the weighty tomes and to make my own decisions about content and structure. The motor behind this book has been David Wardrop, a long-standing friend of Clement, who has long believed that such a volume simply had to be produced - he has moved heaven and earth to realise this project and I salute his tenacity and professionalism. I extend my heartfelt thanks to Peter Hollamby and Paul Warren whose encouragement and support have been invaluable. Jan Dalley at the FT has been a great support in getting this book to print; I must express my heartfelt thanks for her guidance. And thanks too to Clement who entrusted me with the project - I thank him for his trust, his faith and, the greatest of the three, his friendship. ▌

11

Chapter 1

Chapter 2

Contents

Chapter 3

Chapter 4

The Choreographers

Chapter 5

The Diversity of Dance

Chapter 6

Chapter 7

Chapter 8

Chapter 9

Chapter 10

Chapter 11

Bons mots

Clement Crisp's reviews would
often reduce his readers to tears of
laughter, bringing welcome relief to
sober reports on other pages of
The Financial Times. Bons mots
taken from many of these are
sprinkled through the pages of this
book, preserved, unlike most of
their misfortunate targets.

**The last image
of the evening...**

is of the women slowly
(because upside down)
going up the wall.
We know how they feel.

Furioso
6th May, 1999

Just Clement

Chapter 1

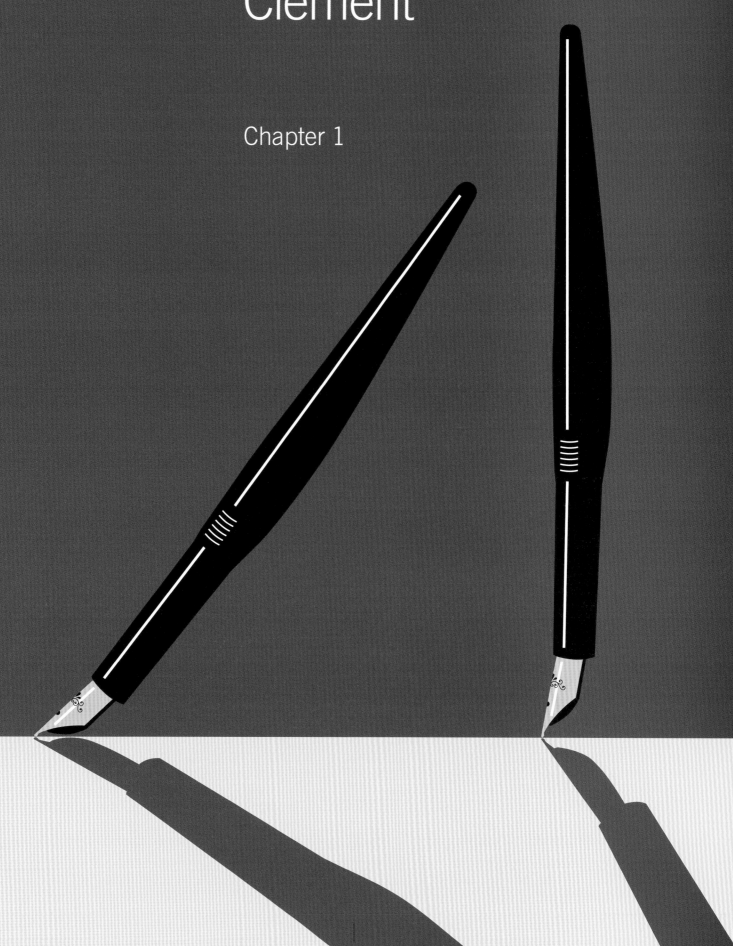

Just
Clement

Chapter 1

'Ballet among the bombs with a bun'

MY BAPTISM IN BALLET had the effect, as Frederick Ashton said about his first view of Anna Pavlova, of "injecting the poison into my veins". I was a young schoolboy; it was 1943; we lived in Surrey and I had nagged my parents, for reasons I now forget, to take me to the ballet.

Tickets were booked for a matinée by the Anglo-Polish Ballet. On the morning of the performance I rose, feverish with excitement. Rather too feverish, as it turned out, since I had a tendency to keel over and was lightly covered with blisters. Chickenpox. Of course. Adieu ballet.

Persistent, I nagged again, and was rewarded with a matinée in London to see the Sadler's Wells Ballet. Bliss was there. How blue the lighting for the second act of **Swan Lake**, and how beautiful Fonteyn. How fascinating the designs in **Comus**, with the blaze of Helpmann's temperament commanding the rout. And then, how people laughed (at the ballet!!) at Helpmann in **Façade**. He wore a natty pinstriped suit, red lined, was wildly beringed and even more wildly funny in the **Noche Español** (a number alas now dropped from the ballet). And Fonteyn, in a red sack dress, was turned upside-down without losing her sweetly uncomprehending smile.

I was hooked. I didn't care that there was a notice in the programme telling us where the nearest air-raid shelter was, and that in the event of a raid we could (but,

inferentially, shouldn't) leave the theatre – though please do not disturb the rest of the audience. No-one ever did leave, and there was no suggestion that the dancers would rush for cover. They stayed. We stayed.

Thereafter my pocket-money could pay for a rail ticket to London on Saturday afternoons, a glass of milk and a bun for lunch, and a seat in the pit for matinées at the New and Prince's Theatres. In a world not without its tensions even for a schoolboy, ballet – and the zest of the then Sadler's Wells troupe – was an abiding joy. the red and gold disease, the mania – it was in the Russian imperial theatres that the word "balletomane" was coined – took hold.

I started to learn not only about dancing but about painting – the company was in its golden age of stage decoration, with design by Edward Burra, Oliver Messel, Leslie Hurry as the norm – and to enjoy unfamiliar music. Constant Lambert, as musical director, regularly included orchestral entr'actes in the programmes: even now I cannot hear "la Calinda" from Delius' Koanga or Lambert's Aubade without being taken back to war-time London.

Osbert Sitwell once declared that he was educated in the holidays from Eton. The best part of my schooling was owed to those early matinées. By certain sensitivities. Remarks about a dancer's physique are forbidden by good manners, and poor interpretations •••

I thought at first
that an etiolated being in white tights (albeit prominently bosomed) was Romeo. It turned out to be Juliet.

Romeo and Juliet
9th December, 1995

must be handled with care, without wounding a dancer's skills. My anger is reserved for incompetent staging, for the traducing of the past, and for choreographers whose works are laden with intellectual pretensions, with flagday generalities, and who deform existing works through insensitivities worthy of Attila the Hun. Here, comment must raise weals.

My heart sang when I learned that a foreign choreographer was so offended by what I have written about his ballets that he refuses to bring his tedious offerings to this country. I had not laboured in vain. ∎

Wartime theatre audience:
'No one ever did leave'

22

"NOTHING PLEASES APOLLO so much as the sacrifice of an irresponsible critic on his altar." I have long treasured this comment by the 18th-century German academic and aphorist Georg Christoph Lichtenberg. In light of a recent court judgment about the rights and wrongs of criticism, the limits of what may pass as comment are questioned. My justification – to myself quite as much as to my readers, should they enquire – for offering something not unlike a hatchet job, goes to the heart of the question of why I am a critic. I speak personally, since I have never discussed my work with any other critic, save to bemoan the stupidity and ignorance of certain commentators.

I wanted to be a critic from the moment, as a child, I was taken to see ballet and started to read books about dancing, and my obsession drove me to seek dancing of every kind, everywhere I could. I was open-minded, ignorant, eager and a voracious consumer of performance and of writings about dancing. Friends somehow guided me into my first attempts at criticism, and it was Andrew Porter – responsible, with Derek Granger, for the creation of this newspaper's arts coverage – who enlisted my early writings. Porter's example was of irreproachable scholarship and elegant prose, and I was inspired by those standards.

My criticism is dictated by a passion for organised human movement, be it Mariinsky classicism or hip-hop or tango, and a need to provide some historical and aesthetic setting for it. Bleakest commentaries are inspired by performances that offer attitudinising rather than steps, by stagings born of publicity rather than fact, and the modish vapidities of Tanztheater, known to me and to my readers as eurotrash. (In reviewing performance, I write as to friends who accept my prejudices and enthusiasms). The extent to which a critic may seek to crush a production or a performance is dictated by certain sensitivities. Remarks about a dancer's physique are forbidden by good manners, and poor interpretations must be handled with care, without wounding a dancer's skills. My anger is reserved for incompetent staging, for the traducing of the past, and for choreographers whose works are laden with intellectual pretensions, with flagday generalities, and who deform existing works through insensitivities worthy of Attila the Hun. Here, comment must raise weals. My heart sang when I learned that a foreign choreographer was so offended by what I have written about his ballets that he refuses to bring his tedious offerings to this country. I had not laboured in vain, and to quote Lichtenberg again: "such works are mirrors; when an ape looks into them, no apostle looks out". I hope, ultimately, I am on the side of the apostles. ∎

Passion... was pointless
- unless the sight of the cast bent in half and clutching their buttocks was a message about the terrors of haemorrhoids.

Momix
21st October, 1994

Clement Crisp
by Mary Clarke

The Journal of the Society for Dance Research
Vol. 21, No. 1

**Summer
2002**

THE WORD 'CRITIC' is often, mistakenly, thought to mean someone who finds fault. but the dictionary definition is 'one skilled in estimating the quality of artistic work, a professional reviewer' – and these words precisely describe Clement Crisp. He has been perfecting his skills ever since his first review was published in 1953 – typically he can remember the date but not the name of the magazine, now defunct, which published him, he never keeps ephemera – but the great body of criticism has been that published in *The Financial Times* since he began contributing to its pages in 1957, first working in tandem with Andrew Porter, who was largely responsible for establishing that paper's distinguished and influential arts page in 1953, and from 1970 as its ballet critic. His FT notices are, by contrast, carefully preserved in large volumes of press cutting books, wonderful records (for he was allowed very generous space) which could be turned into volumes of collected criticism.

He would laugh at the idea but I think he might be persuaded to lodge them, one day, in a library for safe custody. He's never shy about giving advice to other people about their duties to posterity. On this issue, I think we should nag him. As Richard Ralph has said in his introduction, Clement has, over the past fifty years, 'developed an expertise and wielded an influence which are unique'. How did he arrive at such eminence, because eminence in his chosen field is today unchallenged?

I believe the answer lies in the way he has so steadfastly upheld his own standards, standards formulated during his early years of passionately watching ballet and all other forms of great dancing, and strengthened by everything he has seen and valued since. He has had an extraordinary capacity, throughout his long career, to recognise and be enriched by every new development which may further the art of dancing. He may, at times, sigh for what he thinks of as a golden age but the next moment he will have encountered a new choreographer, a new dancer, a new designer, a gifted composer, a great conductor, who must be hailed and commended to his readers for their study and instruction.

His first duty, he always maintains, is to his readers. He cares not a jot for the reactions of the companies about which he writes – although he never shirks opportunities to chastise boards of governors who, he feels, are, through ignorance, impeding the work of the artists he loves. He has, from the beginning, sought to learn about the art of dancing from the artists he admires, from friends among choreographers, dancers, and teachers. He once said that Alicia Markova was 'his university' and he acknowledges an enormous debt to the pedagogue Vera Volkova and, later, to that great mentor, Lincoln Kirstein.

He has a gift, rare among dance critics, to profit from friendships within the profession without in any way being compromised in his judgments on their work. The order •••

Mary Clarke,
editor of *Dancing Times*
(d. 2015)

is important: admiration comes first, then the determination to learn more from his idols. It is this integrity, and loyalty, I believe, which has earned him the respect of the profession. Supreme accolade for a critic. So how did it all come about? Born in Romford, when it was still a country town, he was educated at Oxted Grammar School, then Bordeaux University and Keble College, Oxford, saw his first ballet at the age of ten and from 1942 onwards saw everything he could, first in this country, and specifically London, during the war years, going to the Sadler's Wells Ballet about four times a week (eminently affordable then!), and at the war's end savouring all the great dancers and companies who visited London.

He was lucky (as I was) to have such a cornucopia of dance available from which to profit and learn. Not only the visiting companies, Les Ballets des Champs-Elysees, American Ballet Theatre, Royal Danish Ballet, New York City Ballet – all these before the Bolshoi, the Kirov, the great American moderns came to our shores – but also those marvellous Spanish and Indian dancers who appeared mostly at the Prince's (now Shaftesbury) Theatre, among them Carmen Amaya, Luisillo, Rosario and Antonio, Mrinalini Sarabhai and Chatunni Panicker. It was a splendid time during which an embryo critic could gain experience, simply from watching and understanding, and tribute should also, I believe, be paid to Richard Buckle whose magazine *Ballet*, idiosyncratic although it so delightfully was, did much to educate and excite young readers. The importance of taking stock of all that was happening in the international dance scene, so early inculcated, was to remain a duty observed until today. Never content with an insular view, Clement Crisp has consistently travelled widely, to Paris, New York, Denmark, Sweden, Russia, to observe and record dance activity there.

Before he joined *The Financial Times*, Clement Crisp was ballet critic of the *Spectator*, from 1966 to 1970, and in its pages first established himself as one of the best informed and

liveliest writers on the art of dancing. His style has always been elegant, erudite, well informed about all the component parts of theatrical dancing (he was in his teens a fine pianist), and splendidly wide-ranging. He knows, better than most, that not all 'bad notices'… have to be serious condemnations. He can be stern, very stern, if the occasion demands. 'I shall have to speak truth' he will sometimes say, sadly but emphatically, after a particularly bad evening. But his lively wit and irrepressible sense of the ridiculous have turned many dismissals of silly, unimportant activities into occasions of merriment for his readers. His similes are always apt and often very funny. You are as likely to find a reference to Donald Duck, a ghastly television programme, or the boohbahs in a notice as more erudite examples. He can, if he feels it necessary, perform a job of total demolition, but he is never cruel; there is no malice in his mirth. His gift for easy communication is reflected not only in his writing, as lecturer, as television interviewer or commentator, he is equally fluent, authoritative – and amusing. He has written, co-authored or edited many books about dancing. I have had the opportunity – and the fun – of collaborating on many of them: he insists that at the peak of our collaboration there was a day when we wrote the end on one manuscript and immediately began the first sentence of the next! So I will cite as an absolute model of creative editing *Ballerina* (1975), the book he so lovingly master-minded to celebrate the career of Nadia Nerina.

In 1992 Queen Margrethe of Denmark conferred on Clement Crisp the title Knight of Dannebrog, for his services to the Royal Danish Ballet, and the following year the Royal Academy of Dancing awarded him its most prestigious gift, the Queen Elizabeth II Coronation Award in recognition of outstanding service to the art of ballet. A precept for critics which was set out by Ninette de Valois in her book *Invitation to the Ballet* (1937) is one which I think Clement has, consciously or unconsciously, observed in every review: "Consider whether the performance has that exceptional poise, grace, assurance, and technical strength demanded from the individual, and the unity, order, and vitality from the ensemble, which constant visual experience has trained the eye to expect". In his case the eye has now been in training for over fifty years. He will be the first to insist that training, for a critic, just as much as for a dancer, must never cease. So we may safely wish him (and ourselves) in this Golden Jubilee year, Many Happy Returns. ∎

CLEMENT'S REVIEWS are rarely about companies *per se* – for him they are the setting in which dancers can shine (or not). In later chapters we can read reviews in which the company is seen through the filter of a certain work. When there is a focus on a company it is because it embodies a specific style or school of dancing, so the Mariinsky/Kirov Ballet exemplifies the St Petersburg/Leningrad school and the Royal Danish Ballet demonstrates the Bournonville school of Copenhagen. In these cases, the company is almost synonymous with its school of dance, the exception being the endeavour of the Marquis de Cuevas and his starry ensemble. An exception is the chapter on The Royal Ballet, about which Clement has, naturally for a London-based critic, written the most. It was hard, if not impossible, to find him writing in specific praise of the company because its strengths and qualities are identified in the reviews of its ballets, as in his notice for the first night of Jerome Robbins' **Dances at a Gathering** at Covent Garden in 1970. Matters changed, however, as the century drew to its close where he was unafraid to identify with unflinching precision the perceived loss of the company's style and traditions as he had seen forged in previous decades.

Performing Traditions

Chapter 2

Performing
Traditions

Chapter 2

Bolshoi Ballet -
A 50 Year Love Affair

Royal Opera House,
Covent Garden

**22nd July
2006**

THE NEWS OF A VISIT by the Bolshoi Ballet still sets the pulse racing – our expectations of full-bodied dancing and full-throated emotion speak of an affection and respect for Muscovite artistry that date back to the Bolshoi's sensational appearance at Covent Garden in October 1956. The news broke in the early summer of that year: Moscow's pride, the Soviet Union's flagship artistic ensemble, would give its first performances in the west with a four-week season at Covent Garden. In the freezing climate of the cold war, this was an astonishing and significant move by the Soviets. A sortie had been scheduled to the Paris Opera two years before, but the implications for communist forces of the fall of Dien Bien Phu in Vietnam had caused the French to cancel the visit. Now the Bolshoi would come to London and, in a reciprocal gesture, the Sadler's Wells (soon to be Royal) Ballet would visit Moscow the following month.

David Webster, director of the Royal Opera House and a man of diplomatic finesse, had flown with Ninette de Valois, founder of the Sadler's Wells Ballet, to Moscow in March of that year and supervised the agreement. The Covent Garden booking leaflet printed in red on grey paper; I still have my copy – announced **Romeo and Juliet**, **The Fountains of Bakhchisaray**, **Swan Lake** and **Giselle**, with an ensemble headed by the magical name of Galina Ulanova.

Excitement flared, and not only among the dedicated ballet public. Three days before booking opened on August 27, the queue started: winding down from the box office in Floral Street, crossing Bow Street and making its serpentine way eastwards. Rain fell. Indomitable, waterproofed, chilled – it was a vile end to August – and sustained by gossip, coffee and meals from the market cafes, the queuing faithful waited, slept and hoped. (I, shamefully, was infiltrated into the line at 4am on the day bookings opened by friends already there – people were so zonked with sleep and tiredness that no one noticed). At 8.30am the queue started to move: exceptionally, on this first day, the box office opened early. The first night was "bookable by post only", and there was a ration of a dozen seats for each applicant for the remaining performances. We guessed wildly at casting ("Ulanova will dance the first-night Juliet, and the first **Giselle**, but I don't think she still does **Swan Lake**"). We inched forward and gladly paid the prices (what the hell – baked beans were cheap and nourishing!) Stalls cost £2.15s; the gallery 7/6d. And we settled down to wait for October 3, and the hope that in the flood of requests for first-night tickets, ours might succeed. I trusted on an acquaintance with David Webster, and some very first criticisms in the FT.

And then came Nina and the hats. In early September, a soviet discus thrower, Nina Ponomareva, was alleged to have stolen five hats from C&A Modes in Oxford Street ●●●

**Bolshoi Theatre,
Moscow
(1974)**

provocation made against Nina Ponomareva is not suppressed".

Depressing headlines such as "Bolshoi visit is Off" and a great deal of diplomacy ensued. The daily papers bulged with articles, one astute comment noting that the minister of culture in Moscow had stated that, "the ministry considers the letter was a private expression of opinion". Despair alternated with hope, and such screamers as "Moscow bargains Nina for Ulanova" kept the emotional temperature nicely feverish. On September 25, the minister of culture opined that "all preparations are continuing. We would only be too happy to go but it is necessary to liquidate the current situation". This fine example of Kremlin-speak was followed by the franker "you put Ponomareva on a plane tomorrow and send her home and the Bolshoi will go to London the next day".

On September 27 the headline was "Bolshoi decide visit is On", although the case against Ponomareva was not dropped. (We never heard exactly what happened to her). But the Bolshoi had by then lost weeks of preparation time, and it was not until September 29, five days before the opening night, that the first stage-hands arrived to install the ballet's 80 tonnes of sets at Covent Garden (these had been sitting in the Surrey Docks for a fortnight).

(we faintly wondered what these heavy-duty ladies knew about hats). Moscow's reaction was immediate. The newspaper *Izvestia* published a letter, signed (if not written) by Ulanova and 10 other members of the ballet troupe, declaring that the Ponomareva incident was "provocation", an attack on the Soviet state. "Our performances, which were organised on an exchange basis – the Bolshoi Ballet to go to London and the Covent Garden Ballet to Moscow – we regarded as a great and important event in the cultural life of our peoples… Under the circumstances, we find the provocation staged in London in regard to the well-known soviet sportswoman all the more incomprehensible. Days go by and the

Then came a second drama. The Bolshoi's dancers were scheduled to arrive on October 1, so that the first night might take place as planned, two days later. Their TU104 jets left Moscow at 6.30am but, because of bad weather, landing was diverted from Heathrow to Manston airport, an American military air-base in Kent. The dancers could not leave the aeroplanes until an official from the Soviet embassy in London gave clearance for their stepping on to British soil.

There ensued a further delay of three hours, and then a coach trip to London and arrival at Covent Garden, with its welcoming party, at 6pm. Exhausted and bewildered (Ulanova looked drained and masked herself behind a head-scarf), the dancers were at last allowed to go to their hotel for food and sleep, and for stage-calls the next morning. First night was just 24 hours away.

By now there was a general frenzy to see the company. Appeals for tickets sprouted in the personal columns of newspapers, and touts were there to add to the fun. ("Four times face value, and more for **Giselle**").

And then the first night. I had heard nothing about a seat, but as afternoon darkened into evening, there came a message from the Opera House: A pair of stalls. I blessed David Webster and called a friend. "What are you doing this evening?" "ironing!" "Well, iron your gladrags we're going to the Bolshoi first night".

The Opera House was besieged by crowds, and 200 optimistic souls who hoped against hope that a ticket might fall from Heaven. Inside, I have never known such electricity in a theatre. The curtains parted on the opening trio of Romeo, Friar Lawrence and Juliet – Yuri Zhdanov, Erik Volodin, Miss Ulanova – and the Bolshoi Ballet swept over us like a tide. Dancing of impassioned belief, broad effects and Ulanova's serene truth.

Applause respectful rather than enthusiastic, but ecstatic chatter in the intervals. ("they ought to put David Webster in charge of Suez". "I swear that fat nurse is Nina. Nonsense. You know those women athletes are all men". "Douglas Cooper says the scenery is terrific").

At 11.30pm the curtain fell and the applause swamped the dancers. Years later, Ulanova told me that the cast had been puzzled by our restrained reaction during the performance, but the bravos and the seemingly endless curtain-calls convinced them of our delight.

And so the first Bolshoi visit began, and so it continued. The dancers were adored, the so-different ballets admired, the artistry opened eyes. Paul Czinner filmed Ulanova in **Giselle** during a single night. The season was extended with extra performances in Croydon. Our hearts were won.

And so, I sense, it continues. We have learned to understand and value the Bolshoi's generosity in dancing, its richness in tradition as in artistry. The half-century since that season has brought the unimaginable change to Russia and, inevitably, to the Bolshoi, whose theatre is now under massive refurbishment. And yet, for all these changes in artistic direction, repertory (the company now performs Balanchine, Ashton, Petit) and even in physical appearance (the dancers are leaner), it is the Bolshoi still. And we love it still. ∎

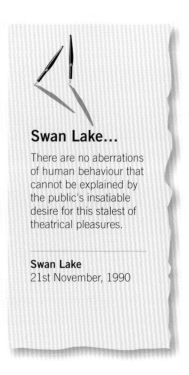

Swan Lake...

There are no aberrations of human behaviour that cannot be explained by the public's insatiable desire for this stalest of theatrical pleasures.

Swan Lake
21st November, 1990

Bolshoi Ballet

FT

FINANCIAL
TIMES

London Coliseum

**17th July
1999**

THE STUD BOOK might describe it as "by Cecil B de Mille out of Stalin" and not be far wrong about the parentage of this specimen of marmoreal politics and choreography. *Spartacus*, which occupies the Coliseum stage this week, is now a period piece and, in its ideology and monumental manner, more than a little dated: brave slaves; proto-nazi Romans (those jumps which make their legs look like swastikas); pure love set against the lusts (both blood and sexual) of Crassus and his courtesan; a military horde opposed to a rabble of shepherds and freed slaves.

The whole thing seems as remote as the over-embalmed Lenin still lurking in the Kremlin. And yet… and yet, see it on the Coliseum stage (a bit small for it) and you sense its power, its beliefs, its cumulative force. Yury Grigorovich's *Spartacus* is still a winner. It was an icon of Soviet art for 30 years, given by Bolshoi artists with a blazing conviction. (How curious that Grigorovich's last big ballet – *The Golden Age* – was an equally strong piece, and imbued with disillusion about how Communism had gone wrong, setting the idealisms of the early 1920s against the social and political actuality known to the audiences to which it played 60 years later. Grigorovich, a far more gifted choreographer than some blinkered Western observers will allow, was clearly attuned to the needs of Soviet art and to the state of Soviet society).

Watching *Spartacus* on Monday night, I felt that it must seem to its cast as remote as *Giselle*, its politics as distant as Romanticism's mists and anguishes. But, as with *Giselle*, the dancers' sense of purpose, their integrity, triumphed over disbelief. The performance was strong, and the sheer emotional drive of the piece, that revving motor of aspiration and despair, bore us along with it. Of the central quartet, I thought Nadezhda Grachova the best Aegina I have seen: beautiful, malign, opulent and alluring in style, and I much admired Mark Peretokin as Crassus, large in scale as in leaps, and as devious as you could wish. Anna Antonicheva was a touching Phrygia – her endless sufferings communicated through her beautiful line – and Dmitri Belogolovtsev was a fanatic Spartacus.

He is lighter in build and temperament than the great interpreters of the past (Vasiliev, Mikhail Lavrovsky, Mukhamedov, all of whom had a bigger physical presence and passions to match), but he convinces by the wiry determination of his manner and the cutting power of his dancing – a rapier to set against the broad-swords of earlier heroes.

The company do their devoted best with every other role – manic shepherds panting with nicely simulated lust (nothing to offend what used to be Mme Furtseva's moral indignation); strutting legionaries; Spartacus's merry men. What I loved especially is the fact that the dancers seem to become stronger, more dedicated to their task, as the evening

34

progresses.the last scenes have more energy than the first. Heroic, ardent playing from the Bolshoi orchestra under Alexander Kopylov: like the dancers, they make us believe. ∎

Dmitri Belogolovtsev (Spartacus)
Ruslan Pronin (Gladiator)
(1999)

Bolshoi Ballet

FT
FINANCIAL
TIMES

**16th September
1994**

THE NEWS FROM the Bolshol Ballet in Moscow has an oddly second-hand air, as confrontation and argument wing round the handsome head of Yury Grigorovich, the director of the ballet. Allegations and counter-allegations have been exchanged during the summer between Grigorovich and the theatre's director, Vladimir Kokonin, with dancers adding their two-kopek's worth. These are the highlights of a very real crisis, the worst for many years in the Moscow ballet's history.

They are, though, par for the course when considering Grigorovich's 30 year tenure as absolute master of the ballet troupe. There have been in the past equally tense confrontations, equally vehement allegations of autocracy, favouritism, and almost any other artistic crime that came conveniently to hand. Maya Plisetskaya, for decades the troupe's most illustrious ballerina, has long inveighed against Grigorovich, as has Vladimir Vasiliev, one of the greatest of Bolshoi stars. Seven years ago, an insurrection was started by Bolshoi dancers dissatisfied with Grigorovich's policies and the dominance of his ballets in the repertory, with much coverage of the struggle in the newspapers. I was in Moscow at the time, and one of the ballerinas told me of the alignments of forces, pro and anti, adding "I am one of Yury Grigorovich's soldiers". Her career depended on this fact.

Yury Grigorovich has been autocratic in his direction of the company. He said to me once: "I have 250 dancers, and that is 250 temperaments!" His view, and in the context of the Soviet society in which he worked it is wholly understandable, was that his decisions must be firm and unchallenged. The pre-Grigorovich Bolshoi, which we saw on its first London visit in 1956, was a marvel, brimming with great dancers, but it was stylistically dated and looked ponderous. Grigorovich, who took command in 1964 at the age of 37, had already produced a series of successful ballets in his native Leningrad. (The first Kirov Ballet season in London in 1961 had shown his stripped-down, innovative **Stone Flower**). As director and chief choreographer at the Bolshoi, such ballets as **Spartacus**, **Ivan the Terrible**, **The Golden Age** and his re-stagings of the 19th century classics, gave the company a leaner, more modern look.

For three decades Grigorovich's Bolshoi triumphed wherever it played, the flagship of Soviet culture. and through the Brezhnev years of "stagnation" and artistic inertia, Grigorovich kept the blood pulsing through the veins of this monolithic organisation. His services to the company, his achievements in the context of Soviet policies towards the arts, cannot be denied – though his detractors (in the West as well as in Russia) have had a merry and mindless time trying to do so.

But with the crumbling of the old order, with the arrival of market forces and the intoxications of free speech and free travel, Grigorovich's absolutism has seemed more like a relic of bad old days. His company ●●●

Good times past.
Galina Ulanova leads a curtain call,
following a performance of *Romeo and Juliet*,
Royal Opera House
(1956)

haemorrhaged stars: such wonderful artists as Maximova and Vasiliev, Semenyaka and Mukhamedov, Ananiashvili, Posokhov, Fedotov, Liepa, have left, and return to their mother stage rarely if at all.

The desperate need to earn foreign currency has sent the troupe on more and more tours, expensive to undertake and prohibitive to watch – and brought the alarming failure of a proposed British visit this summer.

The Bolshoi Ballet, which has just gone into rehearsal for the new season in Moscow, is still Russia's pride, and an example of the highest aspirations of classic dancing, but it is undeniably shaken by events that it seems barely able to comprehend let alone master.

In an intriguing parallel with the dramas now playing at the Opera Bastille in Paris, Vladimir Kokonin, the Bolshoi's general director, is seeking to establish control of the theatre's activities through a contractual system which will engage both administrative and performing personnel on a yearly basis. And so serious and urgent is the situation that president Yeltsin is issuing decrees concerning the future running of the theatre, its opera and ballet troupes. The old autocracy is under threat, and with it Grigorovich's power.

What has not gone, and it is a tragic parallel with so much else in the new Russia, is the other huge problem for the Bolshoi: the lamentable state of the theatre's fabric.

Reports have spoken for years of the subsidence of the building. (There was talk in the mid-80s that the theatre was to be closed for a long period of reconstruction). The electric wiring is known to be antique and fallible. A Moscow friend tells me that it is now thought unwise to go under the stage. Last summer Yevgeny Rudionov, Russian vice-minister for culture and Vladimir Kokonin went to Paris to discuss with Unesco the best means of saving the theatre. Thus far we have heard of no immediate remedies for the situation.

The picture for those who love the Bolshoi Theatre and everything it means in ballet and opera, and in Russia's artistic life, is distressing. It seems symbolic of the state of Russia as it sets about rebuilding itself. And, ironically, what the ballet company needs now is the Grigorovich of 1964: gifted, passionately committed to his art, and able to shape the company for the future. ∎

Ninety years on,
it has all the erotic
charge of a Bath bun.

Scheherazade
16th June, 2000

Bolshoi Ballet

Royal Opera House, Covent Garden

'An Appreciation'

THE BOLSHOI SEASON IS OVER, but not before these superb dancers gave us a final dazzling example of just how superb they are. *School of Ballet*, seen on Friday night, is called a choreographic sketch and it is a tantalising glimpse of something of the Bolshoi training. With the participation of some young Royal Ballet students to show the first steps, Asaf Messerer presents aspects of barre and centre practice, and then gets down to the real business of exploring the achievements of his dancers.

And what dancers they are! The women launch themselves into space and are caught and thrown high in their partners' arms: they turn and leap with that particular Muscovite abandon: the men rocket around the stage in huge jumps, or spin until you think they need never stop. It is a fantastic display piece, less cunningly constructed than Harald Lander's *Etudes* with which it has certain similarities, and with a momentarily cloying use of the children as adoring onlookers; but if there is any flavour of the circus about it the fault lies with the score – arranged and orchestrated by Shostakovich with an unfortunate lack of finesse. However these are minor quibbles: what matters is the dancing, and this is joyous.

The Moscow style as we see it here is heroic, extrovert, almost unrestrained in its exuberance: every step involves the whole of the dancer emotionally and physically, it is a style that excites the gasp of delight and amazement at its muscular prowess (it differs markedly from the Apollonian splendour of the Kirov. For any form of reserve is alien to it). These dancers seem proud and happy to show their physical magnificence; entry on to the brilliantly lit arena of the stage brings them fully to life and they go joyously and easily through their exhilarating paces. ∎

30th July 1963

My stall,
reminiscent of a bucket-seat in an old Dakota, would have pleased an agile midget.

Bolshoi Ballet, Drury Lane
27th August, 2001

Kirov/Mariinsky Ballet

Swan Lake

In 1935 the former Maryinsky Ballet company became the Kirov Ballet, returning to its original name in 1991

Royal Opera House, Covent Garden

11th August 2009

Uliana Lopatkina (Odette/Odile)
Daniil Korsuntsev (Siegfried)
(2011)

WHY IS THE MARIINSKY'S *Swan Lake* unrivalled as a view of this most popular, most traduced of ballets? It is not that its text is especially honourable; the Royal Ballet's version is nearer the original. No, it is lineage – here is a **Swan Lake** from the stage that gave birth to it 114 years ago – and the fact that the tragedies and ideals of Russian history have imbued ballet, and this centrally Russian work of art, with a supra-theatrical identity that transcends its staging.

The Mariinsky's **Swan Lake** is a palimpsest. Beneath its noble physical means are a century's intense consideration about what classical ballet can mean and how best to show its aspirations, actual and spiritual. This may seem highfalutin, but ballet's ardours, not least those defined by Agrippina

Vaganova's teachings in Russia, tell how it can become ritual – proposing an ideal through its insistence on the betterment of the human frame as expressive instrument.

So, the curtain rises (as it did on Friday night) on Petersburg's **Swan Lake** and we see courtiers moving with a kind of supernal ease through a waltz. A skein of swan-maidens arrive at a lakeside, and national dances are transformed into bravura displays of physical panache. We see everywhere a way of dancing that insists on harmony of means and, I suggest, of being. We saw on Friday a ballerina (Uliana Lopatkina) in whose interpretation of the Swan Princess, and her evil double, was the force of Mariinsky tradition, grandly understood, which gave the role dignity, inevitability. Her Odette is the incarnation of

Giselle
Swan Lake
The Sleeping Beauty
The Stone Flower

Kirov/Mariinsky Ballet

Royal Opera House, Covent Garden

FT

FINANCIAL TIMES

7th July 1961

grief revealed in long, eloquent phrasing. Her Odile is hallucinatory – like Siegfried, we may sense that this is Odette still – and the dancing makes us believe without over-zealous bravura.

In all things this is a reading of commanding intelligence and grace. And thus I would describe the marvellous evolutions of the legion of swans, a corps de ballet as protean ballerina, and so, too, the national dances in the ballroom (the mazurka an unfailing marvel) and the soloists. Daniil Korsuntsev was a strong Siegfried for Lopatkina, Andrey Ivanov a brilliant Jester, and Mariinsky style, harmonious, aristocratic in all things, an inspiration. ∎

THE RUSSIANS ALWAYS SEEM to be able to surprise us in ballet: the Bolshoi visit of 1956 was a revelation of dancing and acting fused into an intense expressive style, but when the Kirov visit was announced, we could not have expected a company of equal, though very different, splendour but such is the case: we have now seen all their London repertory, and their impact has been sufficient for us to attempt some sort of an assessment.

Of all the foreign audiences that the Kirov might play to, Covent Garden's can best appreciate the "classics" which have confirmed the importance of our visitors. The Royal Ballet and the Kirov versions of the same classical works have a common ancestry in the Mariinsky productions, and the differences between them offer an interesting commentary on the two companies. Both regard the classics as artistically essential for their dancers, but whereas we are prepared to offer an uncompromisingly artificial display, the Russians seek to "humanize" certain elements. A Soviet writer expressed the matter succinctly: "We preserve the best of Petipa's masterpieces, but give them a new reading". The "new reading" implies such varied factors as the excision of mime passages, and an apparent desire to give the works dramatic logic and perhaps ideological force (both difficult tasks that can dislocate the ballets). The Kirov *Giselle* is less than happy evidence of this: the dramatic emphasis has been shifted so that Hilarion is no longer •••

Anna Zubkovskaya
(Odette)
(1961)

and conflict as more important than the danced means; Leningrad evidently still believes the reverse.

With the possible exception of Miss Zubkovskaya in **Swan Lake** we have not seen one "interpretation" that measures up to our pre-Kirov ideas of what an interpretation should be. **Aurora** and **Giselle** have been presented more blandly than we are accustomed to, and at first it seems as if "acting" has been forgotten, but through the ballets it is possible to observe clear differences in dance-dynamics to suit the dramatic situation. It is this "reserved" manner which places every characterization by a Kirov dancer within the dancing rather than superimposed on it: consider the warmth of movement used by Miss Osipenko or Miss Zubkovskaya as the Lilac Fairy, or the way that Miss Zubkovskaya intensifies her Odette in showing us Odile: the approach to the choreography seems carefully planned for dramatic truth, but after this any further acting is subsidiary to the full exposition of the dancing. Yet when one sees how superlatively these Leningrad dancers perform, this dramatic restraint seems more than justified.

a villain and his death consequently seems gratuitously cruel, Albrecht becomes an unthinking trifler with Giselle's affections, while the absence of Berthe's explanation of the Wili legend destroys an essential link with the second act; all this is seen in a production of some artificiality, with jolly, unconvincing peasants and old fashioned machinery for Giselle's second-act materialization.

DIFFERENT APPROACH

The **Swan Lake** departs significantly in Act I from what we know of the original; in **The Sleeping Beauty** certain variants are more pleasing, others seem less fortunate; but the whole manner of the dramatic presentation of the classics by the Kirov invites serious consideration of what we should expect from these ballets. In **The Sleeping Beauty** the drama is minimized; the ballet becomes almost a set-piece for the display of noble dancing, but it requires from its audience an appreciation of style rather than a desire for dramatic stimulus. Herein lies the long-standing difference between Leningrad and Moscow; the Bolshoi show the expression of character

EASE AND ASSURANCE

Theirs is a style that does not at first reveal itself fully to the spectator, and one of the joys of this season has been the gradual discovery of the richness of the Kirov school. It is an essentially classical art of ease, assurance and harmony, where nothing appears excessive or strained and nothing is skimped. The dancers have great musical understanding, their bearing is always noble, they have extraordinary elevation, with leaps that melt effortlessly into a position; their line is expansive – the strong backs support arms that have an admirable sweep, and among the ballerinas the repertory of beaten steps has an almost masculine force. We may find that they lack something of that diamond brilliance we recognize in certain of our dancers; the compensation seems to be in that feeling the Kirov give of complete absorption in the

42

dancing, and their lyrical control of "legato" movement (as opposed to the more "heroic" Bolshoi style). In effect, this season is showing us a great classical company, where style and interpretation are completely united in presenting the academic dance at its finest. Curiously, the one new work, **The Stone Flower** was the least interesting: its insistence upon dancing rather than drama is promising and marks it as a novelty among the Soviet works we have seen, but it makes less than full use of the company's powers. We can but hope that on a subsequent visit (and may it be soon) the Kirov will also bring modern works which will prove as interesting and rewarding as their classical repertory. ▌

Scotch Symphony
Theme and Variations

Kirov/Mariinsky Ballet

London Coliseum

FINANCIAL TIMES

THE KIROV BALLET is giving only three London performances – the first was on Monday night of one of the most significant programmes it has ever presented in the West. The significance lies in the aesthetic and political implications of a triple bill which comprises two Balanchine ballets, and Oleg Vinogradov's adaptation of Stravinsky's **Petrushka** as a response to the ideas of *glasnost*. By acquiring Balanchine choreography the Kirov lays claim to a genius who left the troupe and school which formed him when he was 20 years old. Argument can rage about the "Russian-ness" of Balanchine's work, which was in essence a staggering New World development, during half a century, of what his Petrograd schooling had given him. The Kirov may see him as a native son (whose art would surely have atrophied under Stalinist aesthetics); America knows him as creator of a 20th century classicism that is still far in advance of dance creativity elsewhere, and out of sight of anything similar in Russia.

How the Kirov deals with Balanchine is, then, a matter of real interest. That the company should open itself to the example of his greatness is admirable, and must surely be a continuing process. That Kirov academism and New York City Ballet classicism are vastly different – the contrast fascinatingly pointed in last year's Holland Festival appearances by the schools of both troupes – merely restates a problem known to any ensemble which borrows from the Balanchine treasury. Speed, musical acuity, rigour in execution, **...**

21st July 1990

mark NYCB's style. By contrast, the Kirov offers aristocracy, a formal dignity, an exquisite variety of lightness and shifts in line and *contraposto*.

Balanchine's **Scotch Symphony** and **Theme and Variations** are well chosen by the Kirov. The first is a tribute to ballet's received ideas about the Highlands, from **La Sylphide** to reels, and on Monday it was excellently done. A pretty set and costumes, Yelena Pankova divinely light as the sylph appearing to Yevgeny Neff's young laird, and Irma Chistyakova so fast and sure as the other female soloist, were part of a staging that looked both Kirovian and Balanchinian: not a compromise but an accord. **Theme and Variations**, which Balanchine made in homage to the world of the Kirov/Mariinsky theatre, came off slightly less well. As polished over the years by NYCB performance, it has such clarity of utterance that the more opulent (and slower-footed) Kirov manner loses something of the rhythmic spring of the dances. There are, even so, real merits to the Leningrad view (and a stunning

set showing the interior of the Kirov theatre): the dance looks luscious in outline through variety of *épaulement*, and dignified. Larissa Lezhnina and Kirill Melnikov were youthfully daring in roles that still ring with the authority of Alicia Alonso and Igor Youskevich, their creators. And, of course, an additional virtue of the Balanchine acquisitions is that they reveal the values of a true modern classical style to dancers whose previous repertory experiences have included the debased manner of Maurice Béjart. ∎

Farukh Ruzimatov
Theme and Variations
(1989)

44

Kirov/Mariinsky Ballet

Mariinsky Theatre, St Petersburg

FT

FINANCIAL
TIMES

29th February 2000

I HAVE AN OLD-FASHIONED – and probably out-of-date – belief that ballets are "about" choreography and its relationship to music. Not so with the new **Nutcracker** which was the main event of the first Mariinsky Ballet Festival, and whose premiere I saw at the Mariinsky theatre in St Petersburg. This is a ballet "about" its designs, and more especially about its designer, New York-based Mikhail Shemyakin. He is admired as an artist, but is not well known as a stage decorator.

Invited to provide sets and costumes for this **Nutcracker,** which replaces the agreeable old (1934) staging by Vasily Vainonen, he has opted for what he referred to as "sane insanity". More particularly this meant a decision to return to the grotesqueries of E.T.A. Hoffmann, whose story of the **Nutcracker** and the Mouse King inspired the ballet. To impose a Hoffmann-esque imagination on this pretty, nostalgic concept, has proved fatal. This **Nutcracker** is, indeed, about Shemyakin – as skilled draughtsman, as surreal fantasist, as dominant and overpowering imagination. The ballet disappears under its designs.

It sinks further out of sight since the choreography has been entrusted to Kirill Simonov, a young character dancer who has little creative experience. An earlier choreographer decided that the task of accommodating dance to such exuberant design was not to his taste, and Simonov has had the unenviable job of making dances, at some speed, round the overriding decorative decisions of Shemyakin.

These are very busy and intractable, and Shemyakin was, so says the programme, "even prepared to show the dancers how to move. He wants to keep everything under control; he alone knows how things need to be done". This can account for the manically fertile range of painterly references: Hieronymous Bosch, Jacques Callot, Grandville, Delvaux come to mind as we see the Stahlbaum dining room dominated by a large painting of a rhinoceros, and such other extravagances as the black snowflakes, a massive rat population, the procession of hats, a colossal fly, and Drosselmeyer as Nosferatu.

This embarrassment of surreal riches sits very oddly upon an action which, albeit entirely respectful of the old Petipa scenario, now makes little sense and even less narrative appeal: none of the characters matters a damn, not even dear Masha (danced with adorable grace by the very gifted Natalya Sologub).

Musically the first performance was fascinating under Valery Gergiev. His sometimes racing tempi, his stunning control of the score's instrumental drama, and his sense of theatre bought many rewards – the snowflake waltz was part of a real Russian winter, the wind whipping the flakes. The production, as you may gather, is elaborate, hectoring and over-active in its decorative manner, and self-evidently expensive. The Kirov's technicians merit every praise for bringing it to the stage, and the Kirov dancers were superb at all times – Natalya Sologub splendidly •••

The back-bends
and the Theda Bara emotings would have won him a contract with D W Griffith.

Farukh Ruzimatov
13th July, 1990

partnered by the elegant Andrian Fadeyev. But this is not a **Nutcracker** that will sit with any comfort in the context of the Mariinsky classic repertory or history. It needs decorative pruning, choreographic re-thinking.

Young Kirill Simonov is an apprentice talent, and well worth encouraging. The music is a masterpiece. The Mariinsky's choice of Shemyakin is understandable: there are polit-ical overtones to the return of such an artist to work at the theatre. The staging can be reworked, sensitively de-Hoffmannised, to its entire benefit. As always with **Nutcracker,** Tchaikovsky should be heeded. ∎

**Natalya Sologub (Clara)
Andrian Fadayev (Nutcracker Prince)**

Royal Opera House, Covent Garden

THERE IT WAS on the Royal Opera House stage, the Kirov's time-machine, **The Sleeping Beauty**, restored as near as dammit to how it looked at its first performance in 1890. Sets and costumes, steps, score, all carefully researched and revived – and not too much revised – and with only one bit missing: the beautiful panorama which traces the prince's journey to the sleeping Aurora, which could not be brought to London because of problems of stage machinery. And, in an age when the old ballets are mugged, de-natured, crippled, how wonderful to see a company which believes that the past, albeit another country, is worth visiting and respecting rather than guying and abusing.

Thirty-nine years ago the Leningrad State Kirov Ballet made its first Covent Garden visit, bringing a version of **Beauty** astounding in its performance style. Now, at the start of a splendiferous five-week ballet and opera season at Covent Garden, the Kirov forces come from St Petersburg's Mariinsky Theatre and bring their greatest ballet, the world's greatest ballet, in what is very nearly its original guise. And what a joy it is. A joy because the score, gloriously played by the Kirov's musicians, is conducted with a passionate belief in its drama as well as in its musical forms by Gianandrea Noseda, and has its colours fresh and exhilarating. A joy because the formal structure of Petipa's dances is clear to see. A joy because an internal logic in the staging, its balances and momentum, are there: each act seems architecturally as

Kirov/Mariinsky Ballet

FT
FINANCIAL
TIMES

**14th June
2000**

well as dramatically complete. A joy because nothing is hustled or skimped or cheated: it is an expansive entertainment made for a court theatre, designed to please an absolute monarch, hymning aesthetically an ideal of imperial order and, most evidently, hymning the order of classical dancing as the *summum bonum* of physical action.

It is a staging, of course, that demands a certain sympathy for its manner, and for its "look". The only begetter of this masterpiece was Ivan Alexandrovich Vsevolozhsky, courtier, diplomatist, director of the Imperial Theatres for 20 years, Tchaikovsky's patron (the composer dedicated the score to him; "Make sure you put his name on the title page" he told his publisher, "he is very proud of the dedication"). Vsevolozhsky decided on the subject, worked on the scenario, designed the costumes. For a powerful court functionary and a worthy amateur dramatist, they are, shall we say, clever – and colourful.

Alexandre Benois wrote that they were "garish in the variety of their colours" (I quote from Roland John Wiley's magisterial study of Tchaikovsky's Ballets, which provides exact and full detail of how these works were first staged). Certainly, in the recreations made by the Mariinsky workshops, they are bright, historically rational, a bit hard to take individually (peasant boys in white blouses and knickers over blue leotards). But as an ensemble of design, against the meticulous revival of the original settings – scrupulous

operatic *verismo* – they enhance the merits of what we see, help us to comprehend the entire basis of the staging.

Petipa's dances are in credible and fascinating shape. These are owed to the Mariinsky's notations of repertoire in the 1900s made in Stepanov notation, and removed from the theatre by Nikolay Sergueyev, régisseur to the ballet, when he left Russia in 1918. They were subsequently to form the basis for several stagings he made in the west, notably in Britain for the Royal Ballet during the 1930s and for International Ballet during the 1940s. Our ballet grew up with much more "authentic" texts than were to be found in Soviet Russia, where editing was rife.

Thus we find Petipa's **Beauty**, much – I'd hazard – as it first came to the Mariinsky stage. I think it wonderful, spacious (and more spacious at the Mariinsky, whose stage is larger than Covent Garden's: there are a few cramped moments, patterns flattened and entirely convincing. The style is old-fashioned, and nothing wrong with that.

The choreography, a lot as we know it, has many sections which are happily amplified or restored. The Kirov dancers sail through it with a lovely sense of propriety, of respect, and a blissful assurance as they •••

**Svetlana Zakharova (Aurora)
Igor Kolb (Désiré)
performing two nights
after the published review**

show off their heritage. Certain performances were outstanding: Veronika Part is a ravishing Lilac Fairy, very beautiful, divinely gracious, and – I note with pleasure – a pupil of Anna Zubkovskaya, a marvellous Lilac Fairy in 1961. I thought Maya Dumchenko dazzlingly good in the second fairy variation of the prologue, and I marvelled at the speed with which the jewel fairies whistled through their tasks in the final scene. Natalya Sologub was a delightful Florine, with Anton Korsakov a fine and airy Bluebird.

The Aurora was Diana Vishneva. Brilliant in technique, lovely, she seemed a little over-eager to dazzle us, and a certain simple grace and an unaffected authority that should be Aurora's, were lacking. I find it less than easy to accept her exaggerated extensions. In a staging which strives for century-old authenticity, extremes of modern technical trickery seem anachronistic. Her cavalier was Igor Zelensky: he is a princely dancer.

Thus *Beauty*. How wise the Russians are to reclaim and restore their inheritance: I recall with what love and skill the war-destroyed palace at Pavlovsk has been made new. There are still more balletic treasures to be reclaimed. Forward, onward, to that glorious Petersburg past. ∎

Tuesday night's pair

behaved as if they were struggling out of a broom cupboard.

Moszkowski Waltz
8th September, 2000

**Apollo
Orpheus
Scènes de ballet
Allegro Brillante**

State Theatre, New York

NEW YORK CITY BALLET is celebrating its Golden Jubilee this season. No fewer than 100 ballets have been scheduled for performance, of which the majority are by George Balanchine. The result is not merely a celebration of a noble ensemble which was the instrument of his genius, but an unprecedented assemblage of the work of the greatest choreographer of our century, and an astonishing survey of the creations and achievements of the most significant classical ballet ensemble in our century.

For 20 years, Maurice Béjart called his Brussels troupe "the ballet of the 20th century" What he was offering was vulgar dancing (lots of bare-chested boys and crutch-sprung girls) as a flatulent illustration of 20th century (and his 20th century at that) obsessions and politically correct ideas. His dances and his dancers were out there on the streets and in opera houses, in arenas, tents and the Boboli Gardens, drumming up support for whatever good cause – down-with-pollution; sexual freedom: the brotherhood of man – he could philosophise about, and happy hordes of young idealists hailed the Master and his not-so-merry men and girls. But classical dancing as an art of the 20th century? Not a hope or a clue. This was ballet as a flagday or a ribbon to pin on your lapel.

Meanwhile, back in New York, ballet was – and is – alive and well on just the terms (if not the manner) of Béjart's troupe. George Balanchine had brought the classic art of his

FT

FINANCIAL
TIMES

**1st June
1999**

native St Petersburg to America in 1933, at the invitation and insistence of Lincoln Kirstein. With the unfailing support of Kirstein – himself one of the most influential of American patrons and polemicists for the arts – Balanchine reformed the academic dance on fresh and eager bodies through his School of American Ballet, founded in 1934. He reshaped the dynamics of the academy, cleared away the emotional and theatrical clutter of the Ballets Russes, set the grand traditions of Petersburg Ballet upon democratic bodies unclouded by the attitudes of the Old World, laboured for 15 years for his and Kirstein's various ensembles, on Broadway and in Hollywood, and set about making classical ballet an American art. When in 1948 a new Balanchine/Kirstein troupe was invited to take up residence at the New York City Center, City Ballet was born.

What they – and ballet-lovers worth their salt – celebrate during this season is the very fact of a classical art that remains true and vital when, almost everywhere else today, it is haunted by regrets, out-of-date repertory (the curse of **Swan Lake** – though, ironically, the troupe has this season staged **Swan Lake** for reasons hard to comprehend), by under-funding, by political and artistic uncertainty. Ballet in Russia fights for financial life. I find it hard to think of even a handful of "classical" choreographers whose work is worth the time spent watching it. Looking at New York City Ballet last week, I saw dancing that was content to be dancing, born of ...

Alexandra Ansanelli
Allegro Brillante

its music, flowering through bodies whose honesty and clarity of means honoured everything they showed us.

There are, of course, prophets of doom, guardians of the flame, specialists in nostalgia, who would have it that without Balanchine – and he has been dead for 15 years – the company is no longer What it Was. Indeed. Impossible to recapture the devotion of artists to a man to whom they owed their very artistic existence and identity, especially when that man was one of the supreme geniuses of our century. But the treasure-house of his repertory remains; the Jerome Robbins ballets are there; and Peter Martins, director since Balanchine's demise, has provided a body of work – well-made, albeit conscientious – that feeds the troupe's need for novelties. And the merits of the company style, its brightness of attack and speed, its musical acuity, all virtues that Balanchine urged upon his artists both as teacher and choreographer, are still there. Some sense of daring, of dancing on a fine line of bravura, is lost with certain artists, but *Agon* – that NYCB icon, that miracle of dance in the 20th century – remains as vivid as ever.

I saw parts of two of the mini-festivals that have been designed as the structure of this season's celebrations. The Stravinsky homage ranged from Balanchine's *Apollo* and *Orpheus* to a brand-new piece by Christopher Wheeldon for the students of The School of American Ballet set to *Scènes de Ballet*. The *Apollo* was led by Peter Boal, whom I think among the very finest interpreters of the young god. He gives such vitality to the dance, marks so clearly the musical and dynamic shape of each phrase, that the piece seems newly conceived for him. It is a reading of huge authority, but never pompous or aware that this is a Masterpiece. Boal inhabits it with complete freedom, and with a loving sense of its drama as well as its movement.

Extraordinarily good. The *Orpheus* remains one of Balanchine's most hieratic and style-conscious works, imbued, it seems to me, with the shapes and formal devices of Isamu

Noguchi's magnificent design. With Helene Alexopoulos as Eurydice and Charles Askegaard as the Dark Angel, narrative and dance were clear. Alas, Nilas Martins as Orpheus looked no more than a cypher, and the ballet suffered thereby.

Christopher Wheeldon is one of the few, the very few, young choreographic talents able to use the classic vocabulary with any sense of adventure and grace. His new *Scènes de Ballet* is a clever oddity. Made for The School of American Ballet, it employs students of all ages in a work whose caprice is that the stage be divided vertically so that each half is a mirror-image of the other – a ballet barre is the separating line. Lumberingly set in what looks like a Bulgarian railway station buffet, the dance relies for much of the time upon the old trick of dancers reflecting each other's actions. The very young enter, and scamper attractively enough, and then older students are seen, dancing well. (One girl, alas, suffers from Guillem's disease, and tells us that it is an eternal six o'clock). A female tot is seized with the cutes and gazes in sticky adoration as an older student enters to embark on a duet. Wheeldon redeems this homage to Shirley Temple by closing the work on a very astute sequence of dance patterns, and his choreography – though he is obliged to duck some of Stravinsky's more sophisticated ideas – is ingeniously made for the young.

In the Tchaikovsky-fest which followed the Stravinsky week, I was able to see one extraordinary interpretation. *Allegro Brillante* was set by Balanchine to the single movement that is Tchaikovsky's third piano concerto. It contains, said Balanchine, "everything I know about the classical ballet" – in 13 minutes. It is a marvel of choreographic wit and economy: a ballerina and her partner, four supporting couples, and the music made flesh as Tchaikovskian bravura sets the dancers problems which they must solve with radiant ease.

I have seen and loved it over many years, and in Alexandra Ansanelli it has found a new and

It's a case of
"never mind the drama; feel the clichés".

Tocororo
18th July, 2003

wonderful interpreter. Ansanelli, still very young, soars, sparkles, cuts each choreographic gem with brightest facets, and seems to rejoice in every challenge that the dance sets her. She fires the movement with a vitality, a musical rightness, that are exactly the qualities that Balanchine sought for his artists, and she is a joy. That she has range in her artistry I also saw in Jerome Robbins' **The Cage**, that chilling view of femininity that is the second act of **Giselle** performed by wili-insects, Ansanelli was the novice who must copulate and kill. Her performance was as menacing and emotionally powerful as that of Norah Kaye who created the part in 1951. The only disappointment I found in these Tchaikovsky performances was my first view of the company's Aurora's Wedding from **Sleeping Beauty**. The stage picture was flimsily vulgar (gimcrack design by David Mitchell) and performances seemed superficial: little dignity, but much facile efficiency in technique. Not quite what is needed if Petipa is to make sense.

Little matter, I suppose, when one has been saturated with so much of a choreographic elixir of life. This celebration, taking place as our century ends, must be seen as a summation of what classic dance has done – most significantly in the past 50 years. Here in New York, we can see it as an art of our century. Of what other troupe or country can we say the same thing? ∎

Square Dance
Other Dances
Stravinsky Violin Concerto
Symphony in C

New York City Ballet

Royal Opera House, Covent Garden

THE CURTAINS OF THE Royal Opera House parted last night and there were a dozen dancers of the New York City Ballet, simply clad, posed against a cyclorama. We were at the start of what I would hazard is the most important season the company has ever given on a foreign tour, a visit prodigal in ballets – 30 works are to be seen during the next three weeks – by a company of unique importance. Watching NYCB we see an ensemble shaped exactly as the instrument of the master choreographer of our century. In training and in repertory NYCB presents the image of the classic academic dance as it has been formulated in the United States, developed and extended by Balanchine, burnished, purified so that classicism itself has acquired its truest identity for the last quarter of our century. And it is glorious.

There will be much to enjoy, and much to report, during the course of this season, but last night's programme suggested a good deal about the variety and richness with which Balanchine and his associates have endowed dance. The opening **Square Dance** used to feature the baying of a "caller" super-imposed upon high baroque concerti of Corelli and Vivaldi. He has now been happily suppressed, without loss of the original conceit: that the formal devices of American social dance, its promenades and inter-weavings, could adapt to balletic convention. The piece works well, especially with Merrill Ashley as its diamond heart. • • •

5th August 1979

Ashley is a marvel of speed, precision, and that noble simplicity that now informs so much of NYCB's dancing. In **Adagio** she is purity itself; in **Allegro** she moves so fleetly that the eye can barely comprehend the quickness of muscular reflex. And at every moment the dance looks easy, serene. Her partner, Sean Lavery, is a notable artist, and to him falls one of Balanchine's most exciting male variations. Oddly accented, sometimes introverted, it looks like a solo for a prince in some 19th century spectacular

**Merrill Ashley
and Sean Lavery**
Square Dance

that has kept pace with time and acquired fresh impulses without losing its original dignity: it is beautiful and beautifully danced.

In Jerome Robbins' **Other Dances** which followed, Mikhail Baryshnikov was joined by Patricia McBride. I reported on their interpretation from Copenhagen last summer: its difference from the original Makarova/Baryshnikov casting is in a certain loss of Russianness. No longer such an exhibition of Kirov temperament, it remains a joy, albeit a cooler one, with McBride superlatively assured, and Baryshnikov teasing and flirting with the dance – the mazurka rhythms ever present in his movement.

The two other works in the programme stand at opposite ends of Balanchine's creative style. **Stravinsky Violin Concerto** (Manoug Parikian a fine soloist) is framed by two brightly fragmented ensembles, sportive in manner, very quick in pulse. At the ballet's core are duets to the two arias of the music. The first is for Karin von Aroldingen and Bart Cook, angular, uneasy, a pair whose physical relationship is strained and contorted. It makes grand capital of Von Aroldingen's sometimes harsh style, stressing the abrasive and dominating force of her presence, and ending in a pose of dark poetry as Cook lies on the stage facing the back-curving figure of Von Aroldingen. There could be no greater contrast, despite some choreographic similarities, than with the lyricism of the second aria for Kay Mazzo and Peter Martins. In this, as in **Duo Concertant** Martins seems a creator working with his muse, guiding and watching Mazzo's lovely evolutions: the effect is of a tender reflection of the earlier duet. From all four artists magnificent dancing.

The final **Symphony in C** is Balanchine's brilliant response to Bizet's youthful symphony. It is a cascade of dances, sun-lit, warmed by a feeling of buoyant happiness. It brought the only appearance in the evening of Suzanne Farrell, in a performance quite miraculous. Her entry in the adagio showed a ballerina who seems to dance from some still point

of classic grandeur. If Balanchine had stayed in Leningrad, this is how the Kirov would now dance. This, indeed, is rather how the greater Kirov dancers do dance, with a physical dignity informed by just such intensity of emotional concentration. In a tremendous evening, this was, for me, the most satisfying and thrilling interpretation; ideal physique deployed with superb assurance and musical understanding of unerring grace. ∎

Umewaka troupe

The Burden of Love

FINANCIAL TIMES

Queen Elizabeth Hall

21st September 1991

Traditional Noh theatre mask

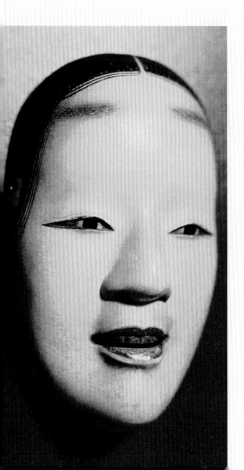

IN MUCH OF JAPANESE ART we can sense how aesthetic contemplation has shaped both form and expressive means. The flow and weight of the brush-stroke in painting or calligraphy; the rigorous line of a pot; even the abstraction of landscape and figures in a print, all tell of a concern with an essential identity through concentration of experience.

Just so in Noh theatre, where the masks worn by the principal actors are the outward signs of a spiritual truth. With Noh we have to acknowledge seven centuries of tradition that have refined and stylised the nature of the players and their texts. There results drama at once intensely pure and dense with the weight of its own wisdom.

Watching the illustrious Umewaka troupe on Thursday night, at the opening of their brief season at the Queen Elizabeth Hall, I found myself wondering not at the infinite strangeness of the style – with its whooping and gargling vocalists, its absolutely other time scale, its arcane rituals – but at the communicative power of each incident, each moment. Where nothing seems to happen, everything happens, as stillness reveals the heart of the drama. Where dimensions of activity are circumscribed by centuries of performance, and verbal meaning can be lost even to Japanese listeners, there is yet established a world of most potent and often ferocious behaviour, whose force strikes unerringly home. You have, I believe, to surrender to Noh; once that decision is taken, then you remain its grateful prisoner for life.

The Umewaka troupe's first programme contains the by now usual two Noh dramas separated by a Kyogen farce. Both plays deal with the supernatural – as do many such texts and the world of demons and ghosts gains in terror through the conventions of the style. In **The Burden of Love** an old gardener, the *shite* (principal) role, falls in love with a court lady. She rejects him, testing him by asking him to lift a heavy burden. He dies, and his reproachful ghost taxes the lady with her cruelty before forgiving her. ∎

**Sagi
The Lady Aoi**

Umewaka troupe

Dome Theatre,
Brighton

**18th May
1970**

THE NOH STAGE, with its unvarnished timber and clean lines, sits there defying the fussy interior of Brighton's Dome Theatre by its antique simplicity. A flute sounds off-stage, and the drama begins – or it should have begun thus on Friday night at the first of two performances by the Tokyo Noh Theatre as part of the Brighton Festival. But we were treated first to a well-meaning and distinctly long-winded explanation of what Noh is about which effectively duplicated the material in the programme book. However, with this out of the way, the splendours of Noh took their customary course.

Here is a form of total theatre so stylised, so intense that it seems as if history, emotion, life itself, has been purged of all excess and transformed into an essential ritual that combines dance, music and drama. Time is suspended as the performance discloses the unrivalled power of a deliberate, utterly purposeful manner which extracts the maximum force from every movement, every sound. It is all centred upon the *shite*, the focal figure of the tale, whose presence governs the whole action which builds up to the final dance that is the crown of the drama, and we were fortunate to see two superlative interpreters of *shite* roles in Friday's programme. In the first play, **Sagi** (the Heron), Mr Manzaburo Umewaka appeared as the eponymous bird which so delighted an emperor that he invested it with court rank. Gorgeously clothed, the emperor and his attendants watch the bird dance before it flies away; Mr Umewaka

moved with majestic serenity through the ancient ritual of the heron's dance. The interplay of elaborate white costume, fan, and unhurried gliding steps, made poetry from the simplest-seeming actions: really I suppose that this notice should take the form of *haiku* – those brief poems that transfix a moment's delight – for nothing else can convey the magic of the performance.

As a traditional interlude we next saw a *kyogen* farce, the statutory comic divertissement that features common folk as a contrast to the celestials and aristocrats of Noh. This introduced Mr Sengoro Shigeyama as a marvellously funny and totally expressive melon-stealer who gets his come-uppance.

The second Noh play of the programme was **The Lady Aoi**, based on an incident in the amorous adventures of Lord Genji. It makes use of the rich traditions of Japanese ghost-stories, and here the *shite* was Mr Maklo Umewaka appearing as the spirit of the Lady Rokujo, a former mistress come to attack the Lady Aoi, Genji's current favourite. The Lady Aoi is represented simply by a folded robe laid on the stage; a priest, a high official and a young priestess arrive to exorcise the jealous spirit of Lady Rokujo. Superbly caparisoned – as are all the players – Mr Umewaka first enters wearing a calm female mask, but revealing a terrible ferocity with each turn of the head, each movement of the fan. The priest intervenes, and the ghost reappears hooded beneath a golden-orange robe which •••

falls to the ground to disclose a fearsome mask, horned and tusked which tells everything of the spirit's evil nature. The duel between the priest and the demoniac lady Rokujo is the culmination of the drama, the demon armed with a wand, the priest rubbing his prayer-beads incessantly together. The spirit is finally appeased, but not before we have been able to appreciate the incredible formal power of gesture and movement – a sharp turn of the head, a hand raised slowly to the eyes have the force of a Racinian tirade – which make Noh so immense an experience in the theatre. ∎

A chap

in an actionable red velvet outfit that made him look like a sofa in a bordello.

Gaité Parisienne
28th September, 1999

Shuteika Bugaku

Royal Albert Hall

GAGAKU is a word made up of two characters which tell everything about it: Ga means elegant, Gaku music. Between the 7th and 10th centuries music and dance from the Asian mainland were imported into Japan, and the musical and movement ideas developed from them became the palace entertainment of that time in the Imperial Court. Preserved there, Gagaku today is a unique survival, a living tradition of performance whose text has stayed unchanged and which is handed down from generation to generation of interpreters who form part of the Imperial household. It is in no sense a "popular" art, but even to the Western observer it is of the most stylised and grave beauty.

We saw a single performance by the Gaguku troupe five years ago, and yesterday they returned to the Albert Hall for a matinee. The setting, placed in front of the organ loft, is a raised green stage, framed by a red lacquer surround. The first part of the programme features Gagaku music; the second part is the companion art of Bugaku dance.

The Gagaku Ensemble is a true chamber music group, comprising the stringed *biwa* and *koto* drums, and a battery of wind instruments which include three different kinds of flute, and, most important, the *sho*, a mouth organ (in the true sense of the word) with seventeen pipes. These pipes have metal painted mouthpieces, very sensitive to moisture, and during performance the *sho* is kept tuned by being heated over a charcoal

Gagaku

**25th October
1976**

fire – we see the players rotating them over the mouths of porcelain jars containing the coals.

The sonorities are delicate, haunting, and yesterday's performance, in addition to the ancient Gagaku music, included a new work specially composed in this traditional mode by Toru Takemitsu. This piece – **Shuteika** – is fascinating, and to a Western ear sounds an authentic development of Gagaku procedures.

The second section of the programme is made up of Bugaku dances. Gorgeously caparisoned musicians sit behind the stage, and in the first number no less splendidly robed dancers move with exquisite slowness through a ritual in which two pairs of men face each other and move in unison. The movements are simple-seeming: expansive sweeps of huge-sleeved arms form a counterpoint to feet pawing and stamping the ground, but the cumulative effect is extraordinarily powerful. Even more so, the succeeding solo for a most splendidly dressed figure who impersonates a prince so beautiful that in order to frighten his enemies during battle he wore a grotesque golden mask. The final dance is for warriors, who demonstrate the ultimate stylisation of battle as they move holding sword or lance or shield.

The effects, as throughout the whole performance, are hieratic, infinitely remote, and yet utterly gripping. An ancient Bugaku guide to performance advises the dancers to become like "tinted leaves blown about in a storm on a mountain in autumn". The impression left by these noble performers is exactly that. ▮

Chikamatsu troupe

Love Suicides at Sonezaki

FT

FINANCIAL
TIMES

Sadler's Wells

**5th June
2001**

THE PLACE IS OSAKA. The year is 1703. A 19-year-old prostitute sits on the veranda of a tea-house, hiding her lover from the other women and their clients. The lover has been dishonoured, unjustly accused of theft. The girl, Ohatsu, extends her foot, and her lover slowly draws it across his throat. He intends, we must understand, that they should commit suicide.

The machinery of a Kabuki drama has drawn us to this moment, ritualistic, prodigious in intensity, absolutely foreign to our understanding, and absolutely communicative. Ohatsu is played by Nakamura Ganjiro III, who is 69, and whose marvellous talent has earned him the title of Living National Treasure. The lover, Tokubei, is taken by his son, Nakamura Kanjaku V. The text is by Chikamatsu Monzaemon (known as "the Japanese Shakespeare"), and Nakamura Ganjiro III has devoted his long career to the rehabilitation of these dramas. And if our crowded London year of dance offers more telling and profound performances than these, I shall be very surprised indeed.

Nakamura Ganjiro III has brought his troupe to Sadler's Wells as part of a year-long celebration of Japanese arts. We are seeing Kabuki at its most earthy and most refined – wonderful how the commonplaces of life are intensified by the rituals of Kabuki playing, in just the same way that the storms of love and despair and anger acquire an irresistible force.

Everything in these performances tends towards abstraction, towards that distillation of feeling and experience that Frederick Ashton called "a pill". Visible yet "Invisible" attendants. Musicians and narrators on stage as chorus. A vocal technique of swoops and wails and faint keenings that become ravishing to the ear, their music insidiously revealing of emotion. Costuming that is both extravagant in its beauty and also – Ohatsu dressed for death in white robe and purple sash over a red under-robe – self-explanatory. The journey to and from the stage along the *hanamichi,* the flower-path which bring the protagonists across the audience: the seeming simplicity of the stage itself (but examine the contrasts of pattern and shape in woodwork and screens): all this is part of a theatre which I find utterly satisfying. (And this season benefits from an admirable translation system, so that nuances of the drama are made clear).

As you may judge, I think this evening, which also includes a comic piece, superbly good. Nakamura Ganjiro III has devoted his life to playing *onnagata* (female) roles. The subtleties of his interpretation are prodigious – there is a heart-tearing moment when Ohatsu learns of the false accusations against Tokubei. Immobile, she lets fall a fold of her red robe: it is as if trumpets had sounded. The death scene is done with such spiritual focus, such grace of carriage and expression, that nothing matters in the world except this burning moment. For Nakamura Kanjaku V,

Nakamura Ganjuri III
(Ohatsu)
(2001)

no less praise. His account of Tokubei's disgrace, weeping, protesting, suddenly reduced to a despair that only death can erase, is marvellous: as his storm of protestations passes, he kneels, slowly folding a paper which is his proof of a debt owed.

The curve of his body, the slow actions of his hands, tell everything of his sense of injustice and disgrace. His progress along the *Hanamichi*, head hidden in a vast straw hat, is a Hokusai print brought to life. The world in a few lines. It is grandest, simplest, most heart-tearing art. We are privileged to watch these two great actors. • • •

The evening opens with a farcical tale of a lord and his servant who visit a temple and fish for wives, and are rewarded, after a fashion. It is very cheery, and Nakamura Ganjiro III plays the servant. He is a joyous droll, especially when his new wife is revealed as a ballooning and hideous coquette. His clown's face, his drunken dance, his sheer horror at what he finds he has caught with his fishing-line, are marvellous to behold. ∎

Keisei Hangonko

Théâtre du Châtelet, Paris

'Captivated by Kabuki'

FRANCE HAS MARKED 1997 as "Japanese Year", with exhibitions, concerts and theatrical performance. In a final burst of glory, after visits from Bunraku puppets and Noh Théâtre, the Festival d'Automne is presenting a season of Kabuki drama and dance at the Théâtre du Châtelet in Paris. And for theatre lovers the occasion, as the guide book puts it, *vaut le voyage*. Most especially so in that the show stars two of Japan's greatest actors, both honoured as Living National Treasures - Jakuemon Nakamura V, who is the supreme player of *onnagata* (female) roles, and Tomijuro Nakamura V, to whom fall the heroic characters. Both are astounding in artistry, in subtlety, in power and – beneath the ritualistic mask of Kabuki – in passion.

Kabuki is a "popular" theatrical form, its dramas encompassing the darkest as well as the lightest in the theatre. It is, to western eyes, ravishing in aspect. If we miss the minutiae of the action, we are still drawn into its world of exquisitely dressed figures – the colours almost intoxicating in their effects – and into the dramas as vividly expressive as the robes and maquillage and the clangour of the accompanying musicians. For the Châtelet visit, surtitles prove a tremendous help in making clear the action of the first part of the evening.

Keisei Hangongko deals with Matahei, a painter with a ferocious stammer, who is seeking

Chikamatsu troupe

FT

FINANCIAL
TIMES

**19th November
1997**

promotion from a master-painter but is passed over. As played by Tomijuro Nakamura we understand the extreme tensions which exist between the comic aspects of his disability (his wife must always speak for him) and the tragedy of a man trapped in his inability to express himself.

The *onnagata* role of his wife, Otoku, is taken by Jukuemon Nakamura, whose portrait features copious wifely explanations (a wonderfully convincing babble) and in the play's most illuminatingly beautiful moment, her willingness to die with him and her astonishment when a painting he has made on a fountain permeates the entire stone. Irresistible is the passage when Matahei tries to put down the brush with which he has painted, and cannot, and gently Otoku releases each finger in turn from the handle. Great art. Great theatre, wonderfully framed by the supporting company of actors and musicians. And the dance scene, which completes the programme, is quite astonishing.

It tells how Vanya-kyubei, a rich young man maddened by a dissolute life, sees a vision of Natsuyama, a courtesan whom he has loved. In his dream, they relive their passion. Here is dance at its most refined, most telling, most ritualistically true. Jukuemon Nakamura is 74 years old, and as Natsuyama, gloriously robed, exquisitely poised, he is the very essence of a beautiful woman. Tomijuro Nakamura is 68, and he becomes the embodiment of hallucinated and sorrowing

youth. If I mention the ages of these two superb artists it is to stress how much these years have given to them in perceptive power, in grace and economy of means. The love scene is astonishing in its discretion – hands touch; the young man puts on the courtesan's robe (and we feel a frisson of eroticism) and the swoops and steppings of the dance are more potent and more thrilling than western dancers roaring through the "Black Swan" duet. A theatrical marvel. ∎

**...it looks like
Dame Edna
Everage's boudoir**

The first act might have
been done by Fragonard
during a nervous
breakdown.

Sleeping Beauty
28th July, 1988

Beijing Dance Academy

**The Red Detachment of Women
The Yellow River Concerto**

FT

FINANCIAL
TIMES

Peacock Theatre, London

**31st Ocotber
1998**

THE TRADITIONAL CHINESE THEATRE is as rich in physical bravura as it is in subtleties. Chinese acrobats – like Chinese athletes and gymnasts – are astonishing in virtuosity. And Chinese ballet dancers have, since the 1950s, shown something more than a prodigious aptitude for the classic dance. There is something in their temperament, as in their physiques, which enhances all the traditional attitudes of the Academy: Chinese ballet dancers – be it in the political blatancies of **The Red Detachment of Women** or in the nuances of Bournonvile or Petipa – are superb. The Beijing Dance Academy is a school which trains artists in both ballet and the demands of national dancing. A "national" style, clearly underpinned by classic training but also exploring the pyrotechnics and the exoticisms of traditional theatre, has emerged during the past four decades, as we saw on Tuesday night when a fine group of young dancers from the Academy opened a week's season in London at the Peacock Theatre.

It must be said at once that these young dancers are admirably gifted. The girls ravishingly pretty, seem mistress of a large, exultant style (big jumps, high extensions) as well as of those tripping, beguiling activities (all floaty draperies and sweetest smiles) that have lingered from the manner of old opera stagings. They offer sleeve-dances of immense charm, and at moments seem to be verging on the sort of winsome trippings that featured in the production number that

ended the second act of a musical comedy (Our Miss Wu perhaps?) in 1912.

The men are strong, handsome, daring beyond any call of bravura, and produce marvels of acrobatic steps: barrel-turns, fizzing outbursts of *coupé jetés*, as well as lightning-bolt energy. In a scene celebrating a battle in the second century before Christ – it is the best thing in the evening – they offer a ferociously bold cross between Spartacus's army and the Polovtsian warriors. (This last is a ballet which would suit them admirably well). Tremendously good.

The rest of the programme ranges from the politically proper to the determinedly quaint. A girl cradled on the back of a yak, adorable as she seemed, and clever as were the two chaps playing the yak (either side rather than back and front), is not calculated to win my heart, nor is a desperately cute number about young people learning Chinese opera (though Pin Yang and Huang Doudou are splendid advocates for it). The up-dating of an ancient dance with modern technique – which seems to lie at the heart of what the Beijing Academy does – was illuminating, and good. About a realisation of that famous piece of orchestral kitsch, **The Yellow River Concerto** (Saint-Saëns out of his skull on rice-wine), I must report that a large cast was ideologically sincere, emotionally clear, technically devoted, and the whole thing reminded me of those official Chinese paintings of the 1970s which were lately on view in Bilbao

in the Guggenheim Museum's wonderful show of Chinese art: brave peasantry honouring their native soil in many and unrelenting ways.

The dancers are the thing: And they are superb. I have taken a bet with myself that a vital part of the future of classic ballet lies with Chinese dancers and teachers. There is not just a magnificent physical aptitude; there seems also a sincerity and dedication (and without loss of individuality) which promises marvels.

A propos: I can report with pleasure that Chi Cao (a very gifted danseur with Birmingham Royal Ballet) has lately won a gold medal in the Varna Ballet Competition. ∎

The Red Detachment of Women
**National Ballet of China
in dress rehearsal,
Lincoln Center Festival
New York
(2015)**

National Ballet of China

Romeo and Juliet
Pink Floyd Ballet
Raise the Red Lantern

FINANCIAL
TIMES

Tianqiao Theatre, Beijing

5th January 2007

ANYTHING TO GET AWAY from the interminabilities of the English Christmas, or as we probably have to call it, 'The Xmas Winter Break". So, China. The prodigies of sci-fi architecture in Shanghai: the insane traffic (why wait when you can walk or, improbably over-burdened, bicycle against eight lanes of traffic?); the vastness of Beijing, already in the grip of Olympic anticipation; the Great Wall: the endless prodigies of art in the museums. And the present prodigies of the National Ballet of China during its season in Beijing.

I make no bones about my admiration for the National Ballet, and my belief that great things in classical ballet have already been achieved, and that greater innovations and artistry will come from China. In its less than 60 years, including those marked by the politicisations of the Cultural Revolution, Chinese ballet has made strides no less amazing than those of the Royal Ballet from its first tender shoots in Ninette de Valois' 1926 Academy of Choreographic Art.

Chinese classical dancers are admirably well-trained, dramatic, musical, vivid in performance, their academic style marked by exceptional clarity in line, and that harmony of proportion which is the ensign of any true classic expression. (In Wang Qimin they have a young ballerina, as I reported three years ago about her performance in **The Nutcracker** in Hong Kong. Of rarest gifts: exquisite physique, no less exquisite articulation of ballet's language, and that mystery which can mark

a burgeoning talent – I felt it on first seeing the young Ludmila Semenyaka and Altynai Asylmuratova. Ms Wang is of that calibre).

I attended three revealing programmes during the National Ballet's December season at its home theatre in Beijing. These suggest the extent and the openness of the National Ballet's repertory – it contains all the usual Russian classics and the company's own "classic" stagings that tell of historical antecedents (**The Red Detachment of Women**); modern work from the west (MacMillan, Petit, Rudi van Dantzig, with Pina Bausch's **Rite of Spring** promised soon and Natalia Makarova's **Swan Lake** with its fourth act by Ashton). The December repertory comprised Cranko's **Romeo and Juliet**, **Raise the Red Lantern**, adapted from Zhang Yimou's film, which the troupe successfully brought to Sadler's Wells three years ago; and Roland Petit's **Pink Floyd Ballet**. They were danced with verve and a fine appreciation of style, from the Chinese historical and theatrical traditions in **Lantern**, by way of Cranko's brightly dramatic neo-classicism, to Petit's fizzing showbiz extrava-gance, which was irresistible.

The **Romeo** was given with designs proposed by the Cranko estate: a veristic set and rather fly-by-night costumes from the Canadian designer Susan Benson, which dutifully frame but do not inspire. I saw the piece twice, delighted by the energies of the company and the expressive force of the principals. Both Zhang Jian (a head-strong girl) and Wang

Qimin (borne on a wave of emotion) were Juliets to treasure; Hao Bin (all ardour) and Li Jun (obsessed by his love) were their excellent Romeos. Everything about the company interpretations seemed to me exact, honouring Cranko.

Lantern remains as hugely theatrical as I remembered it from the Wells' performances. It is most noteworthy for its ability to combine the dramatic forms of Chinese theatre with the conditions in 1920s Chinese life. Concubines, and the sexual tensions implicit in their lives, fire the drama: male brutality shapes its darkest moments: searing pictorial imagery (rape shown by means of a vast red silk cloth; an execution squad smacking red paint on a wall, and creating thereby an abstract painting that would not disgrace an art gallery) burns the action on our retinas, it was stunningly done at two performances I saw: first by Zhu Yan and Sun Jie as the hapless concubine and her lover, a Peking Opera actor, and then by Wang Qimin and Hou Qingfeng. If my heart was torn, yet again, by Ms Wang's artistry, I must also salute the anguished power of Zhu Yan as the heroine, and of the two male dancers. And then **Pink Floyd Ballet** and an audience very different from the somewhat staid public of the preceding nights explained perhaps by ticket prices that can stretch a local household budget. For Petit's delicious extravaganza, with its ranks of white-clad dancer-gymnasts (Zhou Zhaohui an ebullient marvel) and its indefatigably witty sequence of dances, there

was a pop-concert audience, with girls screaming at every feat of bravura by the chaps on stage. It is a knock-out show of inventive ideas, brilliant lighting, Petit pulling tricks and reminting the coinage of his years making brilliant shows in Paris theatres for Zizi Jeanmaire and never failing to give the songs their due. It was danced with a wit, an elegant Olympic bravura from the men that was irresistible.

But then, I find the National Ballet of China irresistible in its integrity, artistry and huge potential. ∎

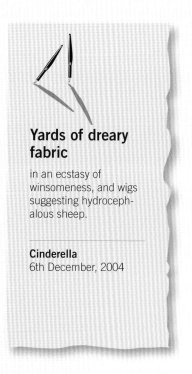

Yards of dreary fabric

in an ecstasy of winsomeness, and wigs suggesting hydrocephalous sheep.

Cinderella
6th December, 2004

National Ballet of China

FT
FINANCIAL
TIMES

Royal Opera House, Covent Garden

**30th July
2008**

THE NATIONAL BALLET OF CHINA has arrived for a week's season at Covent Garden, bringing **Swan Lake** as its opening gambit on Monday night, and following it on Friday with **Raise the Red Lantern**. This repertory ploy is astute: We are to see not only that the Chinese troupe is a fine classical ensemble in the most sacred of balletic fare, but that the company is also able to make works that reconcile the demands of its national identity and theatrical traditions with the exigencies of the western dance-manner it has embraced.

The company is, as we saw with this **Swan Lake**, and as I have had the pleasure of reporting over the past decades, a strong, assured ensemble. These dancers have not put

on the academic manner as a convenient disguise: the style is theirs by right, and they speak its language with authority.

You have but to watch Wang Qimin, the Odette/Odile on Monday night, to know that you are in the presence of an artist of marvellous gifts, exquisite voice, unerring sensibility, most refined physique. The role lives and flowers in her performance. (Only in St Petersburg, I would venture, are you likely to find another young ballerina so grandly suited to the most extreme demands of the classical style). The placing of the dance on her body, the articulation of a phrase, the ravishing onward flow of movement and the perfect outlines of a gesture as it lingers on the air, are tribute not just to her own astonishing gifts but to the academic disciplines that have shaped the entire ensemble. The white flurry of swan-maidens in the second and fourth acts (this last in Frederick Ashton's elegiac version) is a marvel of schooling and disciplined intelligence: the inner world of **Swan Lake**, with its mysterious aspirations and despairs, and the shaping of this dreamworld in the language of the academy, is admirably done by the company.

The production is Natalia Makarova's, with its stylistic intelligence, its ardours and its sense of mystery – drama as hallucination – framed by Peter Farmer's darkly brooding designs.

**Wang Qimin (Odette)
(2008)**

Raise the Red Lantern

National Ballet of China

Royal Opera House, Covent Garden

FINANCIAL TIMES

5th August 2008

THE ADVANCES MADE by Chinese ballet over the past three decades – from the time that the Cultural Revolution ended – can be clearly understood by considering *The Red Detachment of Women*, an iconic work of the 1970s, and *Raise the Red Lantern*, staged in 2001, with which the National Ballet of China closed its London season as last week ended.

The Red Detachment is a vehement political statement, immediate in its concerns and still significant. *Raise the Red Lantern* is no less political in showing Chinese urban society 80 years ago, and in the message that it gives to audiences. Yet it is able to examine the past (rather in the way that Grigorovich's *Golden Age* did as Soviet communism stagnated in the 1980s) and offer its public a clear-eyed view of women's social identity (or, rather, their non-identity). It also, and here's the most intriguing aspect, uses Chinese theatrical conventions to find an artistic, as opposed to a doctrinaire, voice.

In the Covent Garden performance on Friday night, the shaping of the central tragedy – a new concubine's illicit love is betrayed and she and her lover and her betrayer (another concubine) are killed – in the context of Peking Opera performance and life in the household of a wealthy warlord is astutely done.

We savour the customs of this distant world, are teased by a certain exoticism of means (Chinese opera performance is part of the action) and must be harrowed by the **. . .**

The Chinese dancers respond throughout with entire devotion. Ensembles are coherent (if tending towards the lightweight in the ballroom's national divertissements, though this is a failing with every troupe save at the Mariinsky) and everywhere you can see the clarity of means, the sense not of best behaviour but of best manners, which touches everything this company performs.

This was also evident in the playing of the National Ballet's orchestra under Zhang Yi. Individual roles were done with finesse: Hao Bin was Siegfried, his dancing clean and assured, and the first act trio was elegantly stated by Yu Bo, Cao Shuci and Zhang Siyuan.

Looking at this first appearance in our national ballet house, we have to recall that ballet in China is the fruit of 60 years of aspiration and endeavour (and those years terribly scarred by the decade of the Cultural Revolution).

As with so much from China's four millennia of artistic creativity, we marvel and rejoice. ▌

implications of hanging red lanterns that signify which concubine may expect the attentions of her Lord on any evening.

The dance language mixes ballet and Chinese theatrical means. The design is brilliant and the effects of the score, of the dramatic playing, are bold. The heroine is raped, an act hidden beneath a vast sheet of red silk; the betraying concubine rebels and destroys the red lanterns.

The tragedy moves to a ferocious climax: death by beating is explicit in the procession of the warlord's soldiery making bloody weals on a wall with red paint on their staves.

The performances are wholly communicative: Zhu Yan as the heroine, and Sun Jie as her lover, Meng Ningning as the jealous concubine, demonstrate every virtue as dance-actors. It is an assured and imaginative example of Chinese ballet. ∎

Zhu Yan (second concubine) and Sun Jie (her lover) (2008)

Cloud Gate Dance Theatre

Sadler's Wells

RICE. MORE RICE. Tons of rice – raining down on a motionless man for over an hour, piling up on the stage, flung about, glittering in the air like a firework display, scattered, gathered, cascading down with the density of monsoon rain, pushed about in a triumph of lethargy. Thus the Cloud Gate Dance Theatre from Taiwan, appearing for the first time at Sadler's Wells in a spectacle lasting 75 minutes, and entitled **Songs of the Wanderers**. The producer/choreographer is Lin Hwai-min, and the message of this dramatic risotto is that Life is a Journey. Frankly, if it means trudging at snail's pace through this Gobi of rice grains, I'm going to wait for a taxi.

The staging plays as its trump card the idea of oriental slowness of means. So characters – pilgrims on Life's Way – trail over the stage, each bearing a staff – decorated with a tiny bell (ah, the significant tinklings), and all working hard on the idea of inertia as art. If the production aims for some religious significance, its mélange of Buddhist contem-plation and Hinduism, against a soundtrack of doleful Georgian male singing, has an unlikely air. The language is part old-fashioned modern dance, part Tai-chi, and all portentousness. Rice-coloured costumes – cunningly tattered – are by Taurus Wah.

The sight of these oh-so-slow performers changing position, grouping and clambering over each other with all the merry vivacity of a sloth, is intriguing for about five minutes. Bowls of fire are brought on, and everyone

seems to be terribly serious about this, but the point (other than an indication that something might be cooking – could it be a paella?) escaped me.

There are moments when angst takes hold of the players: the women tend to swish their hair about and claw at the air; the men go in for anguished scufflings in the rice-piles and grunt a bit. Meantime the rice goes on pouring over the immobile Buddha-figure, whose powerful concentration and stillness is the most remarkable thing the evening. It is, ultimately a performance having one tune to play, and as Gertrude Stein nearly said – rice is rice. ▮

15th March 1999

"Rice. More rice. Tons of rice – raining down on a motionless man for over an hour......" (1999)

Royal Danish Ballet

Coppélia

FT
FINANCIAL
TIMES

Royal Theatre, Copenhagen

8th October 1993

Niels Bjørn Larsen at 80

NIELS BJØRN LARSEN was born on October 5, 1913. His entry in ballet dictionaries identifies him as a Danish dancer, balletmaster, choreographer, artistic director of the Royal Danish Ballet for more than a decade, and "the company's most distinguished mime". What must now be added to this curriculum vitae is that on Tuesday night, to celebrate his 80th birthday, he once again stormed the "Old Stage" of the King's Theatre as Doctor Coppélius. And he was marvellous as ever – as a devoted observer of his art, I would venture "more marvellous than ever" – in a role he has danced for 48 years.

The tradition of mime performance is one of the glories of the Royal Danish Ballet. The Bournonville repertory has ever depended upon a framework of "natural" observation to set off the grand dance sequences. The life of a location, its bustle and character, its crowds and the bright interplay of personalities, fascinated Bournonville, and his ballets were often souvenirs of places he visited – Paris, London (he made a piece about the Crystal Palace exhibition), Bruges, Moscow, and, supremely Italy, which he adored. (His **Napoli** is as true an aspect of Danish nineteenth century art's fascination with the sun-lit South as the paintings of Marstrand).

It is in showing this local colour to us that Danish dancers and mime artists have, across the years, become so expert, so truthful in their playing, and Danish ballet itself has gained so greatly in distinction. (That the Danes also dance with such joyous grace is the other vital part of Bournonville's bequest to his heirs).

Niels Bjørn Larsen has been one of the exemplars and beacons in this tradition of dance-acting. We were fortunate in London, during Peter Schaufuss' years with English National Ballet, that Larsen was a frequent guest - his Madge in **La Sylphide** is, for me, the definitive reading of the role, terrifying in malevolence and power, and with a nice edge of venomous humour. We first saw him in London 40 years ago, when the Royal Danes made their first big tour: then, as now, he gave his role a weight, an intensity of observation, so that character seemed wholly and marvellously alive.

For his 80th birthday performance – and it is certainly not a farewell: he has much to do, and much still to show us – he returned to a role he has made his own. The Danes' staging of **Coppélia** tells a credible story of peasant love in a believable setting – this might well be Galicia, rather than the usual Ruritania. It is also unlike other versions in text: the choreography has developed over the years from a Copenhagen production at the turn of the century. It is, in its present happy revival by Frank Anderson and Anne Marie Vessel, jolly and coherent in its folk style – you sense that these villagers have seen a plough, unlike the usual droves of balletic toilers whose hands have been dirtied by nothing more than a window-box.

The production is wise, and heart-warming. (The celebrated sequence when Swanilda tests her beloved Frantz' fidelity by the rattle of seeds in an ear of corn, is replete with feeling). Henriette Muus and Lloyd Riggings were the lovers on Tuesday night – sprightly and sweetly sincere in feeling. But, of course, we were there to see Niels Bjørn Larsen, and he was tremendous. The characterisation treads, and with what finesse, a narrow path between eccentric comedy (the old chap – Coppélius, that is! – is forgetful, and given to antic bursts of activity) and wild dreams of magic. At every moment Larsen speaks to us. His playing is a marvel of timing, each gesture phrased and placed with subtlest understanding, each moment bright with a psychic energy as lively as his still astonishing physical resource. He tells us the truth, both comic and, at the last, tragic, about Coppélius. It is rare theatrical art, and as with the motto over the proscenium of the King's Theatre – "Not for pleasure alone" – it has moral dignity, because of the humanity that inspires the reading.

At the end of the evening there were cheers, flowers, presents, hats thrown in the air, embraces. We were saluting a superb performer who has embodied the ideals of his theatre throughout an illustrious career – and, most happily, continues to do so. ■

Niels Bjørn Larsen (Madge)
(1994)

Royal Danish Ballet

Napoli

FINANCIAL
TIMES

Royal Theatre, Copenhagen

**25th April
2007**

**Royal Danish Ballet
in the classic production
directed by Frank Andersen
(1988)**

NAPOLI IS ONE OF the great masterpieces of dance. It was staged by Bournonville in 1842, just after he returned from a long trip to Italy. He was enraptured by Neapolitan life, and he captured it in dance with marvellous skill. The passing years have brought a few changes to the text. (The second act, known for years as "the Bronnum's act" after a restaurant in which balletomanes used to seek refuge from its longueurs, is set in the Blue Grotto at Capri, where Teresina, the heroine, has been abducted by a sea-sprite and is rescued by her beloved, Gennaro, a fisherman, with the aid of a holy amulet and has been much tinkered with). But the dances in the last act are uniquely wonderful in their buoyant physicality, and *Napoli* remains a joy in the world.

It is also, and this explains my return to Copenhagen at the weekend, a fascinating study in the life of Danish dancers. My excuse was a celebratory performance to mark the Jubilee of Eva Kloborg, dancer, teacher, producer, who was marking the 40th anniversary of her entry into the troupe. Given the enduring traditions of the Royal Danish Ballet, it is easy to chart her career from the varied roles she has danced in *Napoli*.

Like many a child from the ballet-school, she stood on the bridge that spans the decor in the last act, waving, clapping, gazing down at the artists who fizz over the stage. Accepted into the company, she danced in the pretty sextet of girls who weave through the first act, became a naiad soloist in the Blue Grotto,

Royal Danish Ballet

Royal Theatre, Copenhagen

5th December 1979

and then knew the demands of the solos in the last act, which unfailingly intoxicate audiences, the dance alight with happiness. The final accolade was Teresina, a role I recall Eva Kloborg playing with a lovely elegance, and bright-cut footwork.

Retirement from dancing meant teaching, producing and inheriting those character roles that Bournonville made so interesting, and which Royal Danish artists make so rewarding. (Amid the bustle of **Napoli's** first act, a Lemonade Seller, a Macaroni Seller, a Ballad-singer – with attendant drummer! – are great gifts, and on Saturday night, Flemming Ryberg, Poul Erik Hesselkilde and Mogens Boesen were irresistibly good). So Eva Kloborg appeared as Teresina's mother, Veronica. The role calls for charm, and a passage of tragedy when it seems that Teresina has been drowned: Kloborg made it gracious, vivid, and in its dark moment, piercing in grief.

The evening was, of course, of the happiest, and led by Thomas Lund and Gudrun Bojeson as the lovers with finesse in step and feeling. The entire troupe seemed on its most exuberant behaviour, and on a dynastic note, I record that Eva Kloborg's son, Sebastian, was very sparky in the last act's sextet. ∎

THERE IS A MOTTO above the proscenium arch of the Royal Theatre in Copenhagen which runs: *Ej Blot til Lyst* – Not for pleasure alone. This declaration of moral intent seemed both apposite and wrong during the week's festival dedicated to the work of August Bournonville one hundred years after his death. That dance lovers from all over the world had come to Copenhagen to see the Royal Danish Ballet was tribute to that special and civilised pleasure which Bournonville alone affords. Yet the festival, more than any other in recent years, gave a chance to assess the achievement of a choreographer whose work has increasing popularity and increasing value, not least because the theatre's motto was the theme behind his creative life.

Of course Bournonville believed that dancing should give pleasure. "Dancing is essentially an expression of joy", he asserted. "Every dancer ought to regard this painstaking art as a link in the chain of beauty, a necessary decoration for the stage which, in turn, is an important factor in the spiritual development of the nation". But he desired to see dancing an honourable and honoured profession, and dance no less distinguished than the creativity of the Danish writers and artists – Thorvaldsen, Hans Christian Andersen, Oehlenschläger – who were his models and friends. His concern that ballet be accepted as decent and influential, his determination – a severe integrity of purpose – that it eschew the frivolous, the indecorous, were lofty •••

ideals at a time when ballet had entered upon its decline into mindless virtuosity and empty show.

In the six performances that made up this festival, offering almost the entire canon of Bournonville choreography as it has been preserved and edited in Copenhagen, this rectitude of creative principle was especially noteworthy, as, too, the way in which his training system – his "school" – honours and respects the human body. Yet if we recognise Bournonville as an advocate of 19th century bourgeois probity, scrupulous in all things concerning his art, and a passionate patriot (despite being half French and half Swedish), we can also hail him as a choreographer of genius, a poet who forged a language of rare beauty for dance.

Very properly the first programme of the festival began with *Konservatoriet*. This is the key to the Bournonville style, for it enshrines his memories of the class of Auguste Vestris in Paris in the 1820s where he studied, and learned everything about dancing which was to feed his later career and shape his understanding of movement. It would be unjust to say that the performance was as assured as some we have seen, though Fleming Ryberg showed himself an exquisite stylist; but the lovely ease and buoyancy of Bournonville dancing was everywhere present. And in the succeeding *Flower Festival in Genzano* duet, the soaring sweetness, the radiant and heart-lifting grace of Bournonville's manner, were ideally shown by Heidi Ryom and Ib Anderson.

These two young dancers, part of a grand new generation in the company, seemed the embodiment of Bournonvillian merit. Their dance is quick, airy, imbued with that delight in movement that is the hallmark of the school.

They show an entire honesty of utterance, without false nobility or daintiness; their virtuosity is that true brilliance which means that difficulties do not seem to exist – rather than being seen to exist and being triumphantly overcome, which is the cheaper and more common way of bravura dancing in Europe. Their bodies have a happy, frank aspect which speaks of moral as well as physical virtue.

However, our view of Bournonville, even in Copenhagen, is incomplete. He has been spared the fate of Petipa – grossly traduced and deformed by succeeding generations of producers – but much has been lost, notably of his grandest spectacles of Nordic myth and history. And with the remaining half-dozen full-length works there is some tendency to accelerate productions, excising mimetic and narrative bridges, suppressing the breathing space between scenes and acts, to satisfy current taste for speed and excitement of incident. Thus *Kermesse* and *The King's Guards on Amager* go helter-skelter along, and even the great *Folk Tale* seems more hurried than when we first saw it at Covent Garden in 1954. *Napoli*, *La Sylphide*, retaining their first shape, became more convincing as narrative because action has room to develop, and its progress can be savoured by the audience.

What has not been lost, though, is that rectitude of feeling, both spiritual and physical, which is so essentially Bournonville's. The two-act *Far from Denmark*, which dates from 1860, is a unique survival of the vaudeville-ballet. It tells of a Danish frigate anchored off the coast of the Argentine. Lieutenant Vilhelm falls under the spell of Rosita, daughter of the Danish consul. There is rivalry with her suitor, Don Alvarez. Vilhelm forgets his beloved in Denmark, and Rosita manages to obtain his engagement ring. At a ball on board (Act 2), Vilhelm recovers the ring and restores Rosita to Alvarez, Thus the dramatic skeleton which Bournonville fleshes out with a great deal of pantomime, and a general divertissement to bring the piece to a merry conclusion. The first act in the Consul's house is given over to *parlando* mime recitative – superlatively done by the Royal Danes – in which sentiment is unabashed, and emotion directly communicated. Bournonville provides genre pictures of Argentinian life and ship-board festivities of great charm; more significantly, he shows the virtues of patriotism – a key moment comes when a young sailor kisses the Danish flag – and the necessity to resist temptation. Vilhelm's infatuation for Rosita must pass and he must return to a real world implied by a letter from his Danish sweet-heart – unlike James in *La Sylphide* who is lost to reason and reality, which is why *La Sylphide* is in essence the least typical of Bournonville's ballets, an exercise in that Romantic extravagance which he so mistrusted. Like Gennaro in *Napoli*, like Junker Ove in *A Folk Tale*, Vilhelm is put to a test (he even has to dive into the sea to recover his engagement ring): the happy outcome of each ballet is the result of loyalty to a sane ideal of love that avoids the lure of the exotic or the other-worldly.

About the performances of the masterly *Folk Tale*, of *Kermesse in Bruges* and *La Sylphide* I shall hope to write later. What must be said is that at every festival performance the Royal Danish Ballet looked stronger, happier, than for several years. It is a matter for envy that the company can field so many superb male dancers at every level, from grand senior artists like Niels Bjørn Larsen, Fredbjorn Bjornsson and Kjeld Noack, to the tremendous Niels Kehlet, a consummate dance-actor in *Kermesse* and *A Folk Tale*, and still the ideal Gennaro in *Napoli* through his verve and joyous élan. The newest incumbent of heroic roles is Arne Villumsen; he has the romantic air for James and Junker Ove, and a big speedy style, excellent for Gennaro. Ib Anderson is the latest darling of the Copenhagen public, brilliantly gifted, a true virtuoso: but the company also boasts the exemplary Flemming Ryberg, the sparkling Frank Andersen, the dashing Johnny Eliasen, and a promising new talent in Bjarne Haecht. And more.

Among the women there is also much to delight us, not least the continuing presence of the ever-beautiful Kirsten Simone, now seen in maturer roles, and quite irresistible. And there is one new talent – Lis Jeppeson – who seems to me the most touching and most exciting young dancer I have seen in 20 years. Her performances as the sylphide and as the heroine of *A Folk Tale* had a mysterious, other-worldly grace that makes entire sense of the most frayed clichés of the romantic dance. ∎

The Kirov monstrosity

combines the worst features of Hellzapoppin and Vampire Lesbians of Sodom.

Coppélia
23rd December, 1995

Royal Danish Ballet

Konservatoriet

FINANCIAL
TIMES

Royal Theatre, Copenhagen

**4th April
1995**

LOVERS OF BOURNONVILLE'S ballets – those ancestral treasures of the Royal Danish Ballet – always lament the fact that so many of his works have been lost. He produced more than 30 works during his half-century (1829-1879) as ballet master, dancer and teacher in Copenhagen. Of these, the Danes have kept half a dozen full length pieces in continuing performance since their creation, together with a few shorter items. They provide a portrait of a man whose dance genius is still potent, still communicative of a joyous delight in movement, a sterling sense of theatre, and a moral integrity that saw art as a guide to man's highest aspirations. Our view of him is necessarily partial, since ballets significant in their time – historical dramas, tales rooted in Nordic mythology – have fallen from the repertory. Latter-day attempts at "reconstruction" have been well meant but less than likely, as we saw with stagings of the long-lost epic **Lay of Thrym**, and **Abdallah**. What audiences adore and want is more of Bournonville as provider of joyful dance and no less joyful drama.

Now, splendid to report, an echt Bournonville work has been rescued and revived. Last week the Royal Danish Ballet gave the first performance in 60 years of **A Newspaper Courtship** – part of which is known to us as **Konservatoriet**. This latter is a hallowed Bournonville fragment, a scene set in the Paris Opéra dance studios of the 1820s, where Bournonville learned to dance under the tutelage of the greatest teachers of the

age. His training – that elegant French schooling – was the basis of his later achievements as a pedagogue, and his style, the Bournonville school we see today, is still shaped by that instruction. **Konservatoriet** or **A Newspaper Courtship** was made in 1849 as a ballet-vaudeville, the happiest of comedies. It told how the director of the Paris Conservatory, M. Dufour decides not to marry his house-keeper, Mlle Bonjour, and instead advertises for a bride, whom he will meet at a restaurant at St Germain en Laye. How his pupils contrive to trick him by dressing up as prospective brides, and how everything is happily resolved, is the matter for two acts of the most charming, sunny dance and mime.

How the ballet has been restored to the stage is a no less happy, and characteristically Royal Danish story. The Danes (unlike certain companies nearer home) know that dancers as they age become valuable as teachers, mime artists, exemplars of past traditions and values. So the Bournonville repertory has always been enriched by mime, by small dance roles, that are gloriously performed by artists no longer able to bound with youthful joy through the most exacting steps. Respect for dramatic playing has always been part of the Royal Danes' identity. I reported last year on Niels Bjørn Larsen's jubilee perform-ance – aged 80 – as a grand Coppelius. And it is Larsen who is one of the rescue team for **Konservatoriet**, together with his daughter, Dinna Bjørn, and the eminent dancer and teacher Kirsten Ralov.

Konservatoriet was last seen in its entirety in 1934, when Larsen appeared as a waiter (but had his eye on the role of M. Dufour) and Kirsten Ralov was the little girl whose aspirations to become a dancer are part of the plot. Together they have now restored the lost second act and the dramatic scenes which frame the celebrated classroom sequence in Act One. Their task might seem formidable after 60 years, but continuity of Bournonville performance by the company, the living example of how dramatic scenes must be given in other Bournonville works, and the Danish Ballet's respect for its own traditions, mean that **Konservatoriet** as I saw it last week has an authentic "feel". This is not a dinosaur reconstructed from one vertebra – however careful or loving in restoration – nor an approximation. It is the real and splendid thing. The narrative is happy, the dancing bright, the playing flawless. Chief praise must go to Tommy Frishoi as M. Dufour – pompous, vain, wholly credible and wonderfully engaging. No less praise for Kirsten Simone as Mlle Bonjour. Forty years ago, when I first saw her, Mme Simone was the loveliest young dancer in the company. She is beautiful today, and her dramatic skill – the subtle shifts of emotion, the pouts and mock fainting and upbraidings and sweetness of character – give the role a wonderful richness of feeling. The rest of the company are entirely at ease in the comedy as they are in the dancing. Lloyd Riggins, as leading dancer and inspirer of intrigue, pulls off a delicious Charley's Aunt impersonation and Lis Jeppeson is no less

Kirsten Simone (Mlle Bonjour)
Tommy Frishoi (M. Dufour)
(1978)

merry as a masked beauty. But joy, as so often with Bournonville, fires every step, every action. It touches, sublimely, the work of Johan Kobborg as a soloist in the hallowed classroom sequence. This young artist provides dancing as near perfect as we are meant to see in a Bournonville ballet: he shows us the old master's *joie de vivre* and *joie de danser*. ▮

FT

FINANCIAL
TIMES

Royal Opera House, Covent Garden

5th December 2008

ONDINE HAS RETURNED to the Royal Ballet, and to my eyes it remains one of the most mysterious and satisfying works in the company repertory. Ashton made it 50 years ago as a tribute to Margot Fonteyn, enshrining in its dances those gifts he had discerned during the 20 years of their collaboration, and those qualities that he had encouraged during that time. It is, of course, a ballet that is dominated by Ondine, but it is equally a ballet that displays Ashton's masterly way of showing water on stage: the dance is fascinated by the movement of streams and rivers, and even the Mediterranean.

It is, I think, a masterpiece, blessed with a wonderful Henze score and by superlative design by Lila de Nobili, as potent as Ashton in suggesting an aqueous world.

What I love about **Ondine** is its uncertainties, as if the emotional ground moves under our feet, and we traverse a dream-world of the unexplained. Ondine is child-like, but becomes a tragic figure in the final scene. Who is Palemon, a hero riven by romantic frenzy and indecision? Is Berta's passion for him mere jealous pique? Set in a dramatic scheme as uncertain and dangerous as water itself, the tragedy is borne along on an impulse as irresistible as a river in flood. All these images resonate through the ballet, pulling us along with them in marvellous fashion.

And in Wednesday night's performance they were superbly shown by Tamara Rojo and Edward Watson. Rojo's debut as Ondine a couple of years ago was a marvel of intelligence, and of what seemed entirely natural sympathy with the role. (I own to finding her more credible in the part than Fonteyn). Now, she draws the character and the dance with heart-stirring grace, with that simplicity and fluency that are the mark of great artistry: the role and the dance are hers, and exquisitely so. Watson is a magnificent Palemon: haunted by passion, vivid in response to every emotion, it is a reading that is hallucinatory, ideally romantic. Ricardo Cervera as Tirrenio, Genesia Rosato as Berta, are their worthy colleagues. ∎

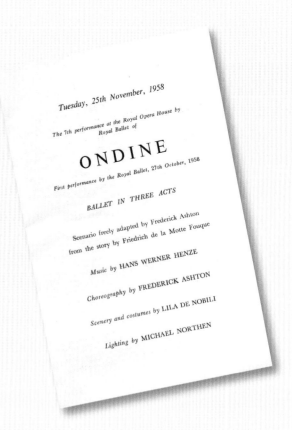

Tuesday, 25th November, 1958

The 7th performance at the Royal Opera House by Royal Ballet of

ONDINE

First performance by the Royal Ballet, 27th October, 1958

BALLET IN THREE ACTS

Scenario freely adapted by Frederick Ashton from the story by Friedrich de la Motte Fouque

Music by HANS WERNER HENZE

Choreography by FREDERICK ASHTON

Scenery and costumes by LILA DE NOBILI

Lighting by MICHAEL NORTHEN

Tamara Rojo (*Ondine*)
(2005)

The Royal Ballet

Dances at a Gathering

FINANCIAL TIMES

Royal Opera House,
Covent Garden

**20th October
1970**

I AM INDEBTED to an American friend for the most succinct comment upon Jerome Robbins' **Dances at a Gathering**: "It makes you feel good for a month after you've seen it". And after last night's first London performance by the Royal Ballet I am prepared to bet that our lives will be permanently enhanced by this beautiful work. The basic premise seems almost too simple; take ten dancers and eighteen solo piano pieces by Chopin (played last night with fine musicianship by Anthony Twiner), set them in simple costumes against a sky cloth, and you have sixty minutes of unalloyed delight. But there is more to **Dances at a Gathering** than this. It was staged last year in New York for the City Ballet, and it marked Jerome Robbins' return to the classic dance after some years working on a theatre project; it must seem to us that he has poured into this ballet a pent-up store of knowledge and love of the academic dance.

The result is a glorious flood of dancing – solos, duets and ensembles – that are rooted in the Chopin music, that flower from it, expressing both its innermost feelings and its formal structure. The ballet begins with a mazurka which brings on Rudolf Nureyev in a solo whose technical flavour owes much to the steps of the mazurka itself, and this I suspect sets the key of the whole ballet. It seems to me to be a work as filled with a feeling for Poland as is Chopin's music; the cast are like a group of aristocrats disporting themselves on a summer day, revelling both in their nobility and their sense of national

identity. Just as Chopin's music uses national dances and transforms them through an extremely cultured sensibility, so does Robbins take the steps of the mazurka and set them in the classic vocabulary, which becomes the equivalent of Chopin's pianistic manner.

But Robbins does not restrict himself to mazurkas, though they figure largely in the musical framework; he uses some of the studies, and waltzes, plus a scherzo and a nocturne to close the piece. He presents us with a sequence of dances that explore both the music and the personalities of its interpreters – it is quite remarkable how the characters of the dancers are revealed, and how Robbins can give an inner dramatic impetus to what is, superficially, a series of lightly-linked dance incidents.

After Nureyev's first solo, David Wall and Monica Mason are seen flirting together; then follows a lyric duet for Sibley and Dowell, which leads into a *pas de trois* for Ann Jenner and Laura Connor with Nureyev, that finds the girls competing for the man's attentions. This in turn becomes a quintet of radiant good humour, to be followed by a duet for Lynn Seymour and Nureyev, a *pas de six*, and a splendidly showing-off waltz for Michael Coleman and Monica Mason.

It would be pleasant, though impossible for space reasons, to detail the later development of the work; all I need say is that Robbins' invention never slackens, that delight follows

80

on delight, and that the dancing springs with complete rightness from the music. The Coleman/Mason waltz is dazzling in the way it mirrors the brilliant filigree of the piano writing in movement; there is a delicious humour here that bubbles throughout the work, reaching its high-point in a sequence for Seymour as a girl mad about dancing who is offered positively no encouragement by three successive partners – it might have come from that earlier and hilarious Robbins/Chopin piece, **The Concert**. The ballet builds almost imperceptibly through a series of climaxes: a wonderful waltz sextet, a pyrotechnic study for Nureyev, leading up to the penultimate scherzo, darker in mood than anything that has gone before. Finally, with the last nocturne the whole cast gather on stage in a moment of quietude. Nureyev touches the ground from which both music and dancers have sprung, the couples link arms, and move away, and the curtain falls.

Dances at a Gathering is a ballet by a master choreographer; it is superbly crafted in its matching of music and dance on the highest level of understanding. At times it is daring in its realisation of the score, but it is the daring of genius, and for me it shone new light both upon the Chopin music and on the art of the classical dancer. Yet nothing is strained or awkward; the choreography seems an effortless extension of the score, and as with **Les Sylphides**, I feel already that no other interpretation of the music is possible.

**Jerome Robbins
with First Cast members
(1970)**

It is hardly necessary to add that the performance, by the most stellar cast the Royal Ballet has assembled in years, was magnificent: to Antoinette Sibley, Lynn Seymour, Monica Mason, Ann Jenner, Laura Connor, Michael Coleman, Anthony Dowell, Jonathan Kelly, Rudolf Nureyev and David Wall, best thanks. To Mr Robbins, our gratitude for a ballet that will enrich our lives for years to come. ∎

Jerome Robbins with First Cast members, Antoinette Sibley, Lynn Seymour, Anthony Dowell, Rudolph Nureyev, David Wall, Laura Connor, Michael Coleman, Monica Mason, Jonathan Kelly and Ann Jenner

The Royal Ballet

FT

FINANCIAL
TIMES

Royal Opera House, Covent Garden

**8th May
2010**

AN EVENING, or rather two-thirds of an evening, of rarest pleasure with the Royal Ballet on Wednesday, but the rest of it – Mats Ek's interminably fatuous *Carmen* – was despicable.

The first cause for delight was the choreographic debut on the main stage by Liam Scarlett (aged 24 and a member of the company) announcing a talent for making dances of true classical style, musically apt, and assured. An added joy was the return of Christopher Wheeldon's **Electric Counterpoint**, a brilliant capriccio proposing the most intriguing adventures in ways of showing and perceiving dance.

But pride of place must go to Scarlett for a creation, *Asphodel Meadows*, that merits its place without apologies for youth or

inexperience. The score is Poulenc's double piano concerto, music of elegance, fizzing energies, manic changes of mood and irresistible charm. Its three movements are led by Marianela Nuñez and Rupert Pennefather, Tamara Rojo and Bennet Gartside, and Laura Morera and Ricardo Cervera, all splendid, with an attendant group of seven couples.

And what they do is what the music does. There is somewhere an argument hinting at an underworld, an afterlife, its title taken from a poem by CW James, which I found easy to ignore. What we see is dance sprung from its score, cleanly shaped, suggesting that Scarlett has a sense of formal integrity: he has looked at MacMillan choreography, yet with a sure sense of his own gifts.

Patternings for the attendant group are handsome, stated without fuss; writing for the three leading couples is imaginative, fluently set in its music, albeit Poulenc's references to his own world are too varied to capture entirely. What delighted me was the sensitivity with which Scarlett coped with the score's changes of mood or metre: the dance is its companion. Here is a notable debut.

The work is, inexplicably, laden with hyperactive design by John MacFarlane a setting like some monstrous barcode, intermittently obscured by black screens – and costuming of stupefying dowdiness. ∎

**Marianela Nuñez
and Rupert Pennefather
(2010)**

**Steptext
La Ronde
Firstext
Rhapsody**

The Royal Ballet

Royal Opera House,
Covent Garden

FT
FINANCIAL
TIMES

**1st May
1995**

IN ORDER TO SEE "fearful sights", an Elizabethan herbal recommended anointing the temples with lapwing's blood. There is no need for such recherché treatment this week: a ticket for the Royal Ballet's new triple bill will provide all the fearful sights a dance-lover needs for this year, or any other.

Thursday's first performance had the over-ripe Limburger whiff of awfulness as we entered the auditorium. Curtain up. Stage open to its deeper recesses, with stage-hands and various worthies watching while bits of scrim went up and down amid the litter. Faint twittering of a violin and occasional clankings. A tiny projection of the words *The organisation of culture*. (What about the organisation of the production, we thought). Inky darkness as every light went out – and part of the audience struggled to find seats in the blackness. The edges of the stage briefly ringed with flames. If the place burns down, I thought, at least we shan't have to suffer any more of this arrogant nonsense. Then the house-lights up to half-power, Sylvie Guillem stretching and eeling about the stage in boneless contortions, with five other dancers dressed as for private athletic exercise in grey. And we are off into Forsythe-land, a place of stones, with dim light and dimmer intellectual pretensions.

William Forsythe is an inescapable presence in almost every balletic repertory. His current brand of angry, dislocated action (he once made feat classic dances and strong dramatic pieces, as we recorded) has that portentous air which gulls audiences into thinking that something significant is happening. His dance works are acquired by all and sundry. At his home-base in Frankfurt, he is greatly admired, as he is in Paris which has given him an annual season at the Châtelet. His kick-boxing steps, the menacing sense of ill-concealed psychic violence that pervades his stagings, has captured audience imaginations. His two works acquired by the Royal Ballet, **Herman Schmerman** and **In the middle**, are typical of his recent manner – the apotheosis of the brutal and insolent – and benefit from the presence of Sylvie Guillem, who has the bravura and allure to make them seem interesting.

Invited to make a new piece for this programme, Forsythe cried off, claiming that he could not work away from his Frankfurt team. An existing work, **Steptext,** was offered as substitute, and then a new piece, **Firstext** was also manifested as a collaborative effort with Dana Casperson and Antony Rizzi from his Frankfurt ensemble. And this is what the Royal Ballet offered as the opening part of a new and fearful triple bill – which, once again, can be laid at the door of Baron Frankenstein as an example of the butcher's craft. **Firstext** is played with houselights up, then down, with no sound track save for faint violin tweetings and the occasional thunderous clatter by Thom Willems, as of sheet-iron dropped from a great height. (The programme, with straight face, calls it "music") Mlle Guillem leads the rout, •••

and is fascinating because so lithe. Her colleagues wriggle and writhe, too, and are less fascinating. Nothing happens, bursts of manic activity being as dreary as bursts of inactivity.

When **Steptext** arrives – unannounced – the violin arrives, crudely amplified, and we hear the Bach Chaconne fragmented for Forsythe's barbarous ends, while Deborah Bull and three chaps behave with a good deal of uninvolved energy towards each other. The language is less extreme – the piece is ten years old, and Forsythe's academic distortions have a more rational air – and is yet another banquet of Dead Sea fruit. The need for this arid tosh in the Covent Garden repertory escapes me. Let the Royal Ballet be the one troupe in the world not performing Forsythe: to succumb to such modishness is indicative only of uncertain policies.

To follow this interminable affair with a revival of Glen Tetley's **La Ronde**, suggests an entire lack of understanding of what a ballet programme is about. **La Ronde** was first seen, and not wholly admired, with the National Ballet of Canada. As I reported at its premiere last season, it is a version of Schnitzler's *Riegen,* a chain of copulations of exquisite tedium, and A flings it to B, who flings it to C, and so, as one might say, on. It takes skill to make sex boring, but Tetley pulls it off, aided by the turgid nonsense of Korngold's *Sinfonietta,* a score actually written by Richard Strauss's hairdresser. Ten dancers deserve what they get for involving themselves in this hymn to the dangers of the pox, and look befuddled by Tetley's writhings. My sympathies are with the marvellous Darcey Bussell, cast as a prostitute whose unenviable task is to end the ballet by wriggling on the ground with all the amorous ecstasy of a grass-snake on heat.

La Ronde was a bad repertory choice, and is now an inexplicable revenant. That its constant set changes – another of its winning little ways – mean interminable intervals, suggests how ill-advised is the programme-building at Covent Garden.

And as a *coup de grace* on an evening of memorable awfulness, a re-dressing of Ashton's **Rhapsody**. This was his tribute to Baryshnikov, a late and cunningly made hymn to a great artist and a great virtuoso. (Baryshnikov matched with Rachmaninov's view of Paganini – triple transcendentalism). Its original designs by Ashton and William Chappell were mimsy, but at least allowed the dance to breathe and glow. For whatever reason – perhaps incipient dementia praecox – the Royal Ballet has opted for new designs, and has chosen Patrick Caulfield. (He, it may be recalled, provided thumping decoration for Michael Corder's **Party Game** at Covent Garden ten years ago).

For **Rhapsody** Caulfield has donned the mantle of Clarice Cliffe. The stage, hectic in red and aquamarine, is an Art Deco fantasy of seriously distracting shapes. The choreography survives, but only just. Costuming is inelegant – what do painters know of stage dress? – the men in vaguely military jerkins which help them to look neckless, the girls in dull, bi-coloured frocks with troubling sequinned fins at the wrist. Viviana Durante (in Lesley Collier's original role) has a yellow outfit for which I hope she is claiming danger money. Tetsuya Kumakawa, accepting Baryshnikov's challenge, looks vaguely like the Jack of Diamonds. He dances with prodigious bravura, though without Baryshnikov's elegance of manner. Durante is pleasing. The sextet of men are fine; the girls a bit anonymous. And in the desperate company that it is keeping, **Rhapsody** is even more of a joy. It has steps, logic, form, ideas, craft, assurance of means. It has – perish the thought – choreography. But what an evening to sit through in order to see it! To Philip Gammon, the pianist in **Rhapsody**, continuing admiration for the distinction and felicity of his playing. ∎

Darcey Bussell
La Ronde
(1995)

Horseplay
Dream of Angels
Highly Strung
Words Apart
In the Middle, Somewhat Elevated

The Royal Ballet

Lyceum Theatre, Sheffield

FT

FINANCIAL
TIMES

'Bad, bad, ballet'

**7th March
1998**

IT IS DIFFICULT to guess what the good burgesses of Sheffield made of the Royal Ballet's latest *Dance Bites* venture in last week's matinee. Outside the Lyceum Theatre, blue skies, sunshine, balmy air. Inside, the Stygian experiments of four hapless dance-creators, rattling round a half-empty auditorium. It is harder still to imagine what the Royal Ballet supposes this ill-conceived event will do, save lose it more "face" with the Great British Public.

There are two Dance Bites shows currently on mini-tours. As in the past three years, the sacred ideas of innovation, experiment, opportunity for creativity, are the banners under which the affair sails. It is a flag of the direst convenience. What I have seen in previous years, and abundantly more awful on this occasion, is pretentious and unguided creative muddle, and bad, bad ballet.

To itemise the pieces on show in Sheffield seems nugatory. What excuse is there for the dull prancings of four men – looking far below their best – in Tom Sapsford's **Horseplay,** or for Matthew Hart's thin jape in which the fascinating but immature Jerry Douglas involved himself with two violins and attempted coition with a 'cello, while the *andantino* from Debussy's string quartet went unconcernedly on?

What malign fate decided that Irek Mukhamedov, one of the greatest dancers of our time, should be trapped in a triumph of Balkan tailoring and William Tuckett's **Dream of Angels,** as the father of Sarah Wildor (expiring in First Communion frockery) and be required to exchange mimetic nullities with Zenaida Yanowsky? And why did 10 dancers in green scamper and pose, before Deborah Bull and Christopher Saunders embarked on a ham-fisted, ham-footed duet in Cathy Marston's **Words Apart**?

After these four little humdingers, I took to the hills – the closing Forsythe **In the Middle** is no antidote to what had gone before. The afternoon was pernicious – in the Royal Ballet's assumption that a regional audience should pay to see such inadequate stuff, in the company's condoning such enfeebled creativity, in allowing such limping inadequacy on the stage.

One would think our national ballet would make an effort to show part of its great repertory on a regional tour. These fly-by-night creations only deserve exposure on an experimental stage – and there are enough of those in London. Programmes such as this cast even more serious doubts upon the Royal Ballet's creative policies, which have lately brought us such triumphs of the nul as *Amores*, *Mr Worldly Wise*, and *Dances with Death*. It is not just a home that our national ballet lacks. ∎

The Royal Ballet

Castle Nowhere

FINANCIAL
TIMES

Royal Opera House,
Covent Garden

**28th March
2006**

THERE ARE A GOOD MANY questions to ask about *Castle Nowhere*, a new ballet by the Canadian choreographer Matjash Mrozewski, having its first performance in a triple bill (with *Polyphonia* and *Requiem*) on Saturday night. The first and most immediate is: why stage it at all?

We are presented with four women in hideous Edwardian dresses, hugely bustled. (Subsidiary question: "Does my bum look big in this?". "Yes. Vast!") With them four men who have been forced to make their own evening suits, and look like disaffected undertaker's mutes. (Clothes by Caroline O'Brien). Skied over them a hail-shower of throw-outs from a failing antique shop – a candelabrum, busts, picture frames, and assorted junk. (Design by Yannick Larivée). From the orchestra pit a clanking score by Arvo Pärt that is nowhere in the programme identified as to title. (Necessary, surely, if one hopes to avoid it in future).

And what do the dancers turgidly classically do? They do what such people always do in such affairs: they look agonised, swoop about, grapple, enter and exit inexplicably, and behave as if they were in a bad copy of an Antony Tudor ballet. (Tudor made sense of this manner in the late 1930s by creating vivid characters in taut situations. Mrozewski makes no sense at all).

Trapped in this apotheosis of the danced cliché are Zenaida Yanowsky and

Edward Watson, who – if we are to pay attention to a page of clotted prose in the programme – are unable to love each other. Since, as characters, they have all the depth and weight of tissue paper, the only emotion aroused is pity for two fine artists offering their profiles to us, and striking Anglo-Saxon attitudes in a rising tide of banalities. ∎

**Swan Lake or
Swan Fake...**

There is, I often think,
only Swan Lake.
"Give them anything"
says the box-office
"but call it Swan Lake".

Swan Lake
22nd September, 1993

Don Quixote

The Royal Ballet

Royal Opera House, Covent Garden

FT
FINANCIAL
TIMES

'Postcard from the Costa del Miscasting'

THE ROYAL BALLET'S STAGING of **Don Quixote** is a dismal thing. It is one of Nureyev's several views of old Barcelona, but not his last (nor his best), which is the Paris Opéra version. This production, on loan from the Australian Ballet, might cause a bit of excitement on a sheep station, but in the harsher conditions of an opera house, and treated with our national troupe's sang-froid, it remains a souvenir of the Costa del Miscasting. Jollity by numbers and a determined daintiness in dancing make for dull viewing. The piece has returned as tourist-bait at Covent Garden this week, though why not show the trippers something authentically national and worthwhile: **Fille** or **Cinderella** or **Manon** or, perish the thought, a triple bill of local choreography. • • •

24th July 2002

Marianela Nuñez (Kitri)
Carlos Acosta (Basilio)
(2002)

But no. Russified, ossified Spain it is, and deadly it looks. The production lacks focus in performance, clarity in dancing, force in characterisation, vitality in spirit and style. It lacks design: the sets are dowdy enough to have served for a production of **Carmen** in Harbin in 1925: the costumes are tired to the point of exhaustion. The Royal Ballet's dancers, lost in a style for which they have no experience, behave with the grim delight of people who sense they are entertainers on the Titanic. Only the leading couple on Monday night – Marianela Nuñez and Carlos Acosta – had the measure of the occasion and the light hearts to make something tasty of these funeral-baked meats. Nuñez is a most promising soloist with an already fizzing technique – great facility on turning steps – and a charming way with a character. Her Kitri is not too saucy and the dance flows prettily and freely. Her reading has to battle against the surrounding sogginess and she does not – as yet, as she will one day – set light to the stage, but the skill and the sparkle are there, and I hope she may be given a better production in which to realise fully her attractive soubrette manner.

Carlos Acosta clearly knew on Monday night that it was Up To Him. So, relaxed charm, bright presence and brighter steps, and – as the final *pas de deux* at last arrived – bravura and breathtaking tricks, and a joy in dancing (and an ease in that joy) which galvanised this corpse into a semblance of theatrical life. Huge aerial pyrotechnics. New adventures with pirouettes – almost as many as Eglevsky with his famous 14 turns – and, most appealing, a sense that there was power to spare and happiness in reserve. Stunningly good.

Merely stunning was the orchestral playing: even Minkus can sound better than this. And Barcelona itself had all the murky moments that we associate with Inverness as the winter day dies. Lighting, seemingly by the Prince of Darkness, and a scene-change replete with scurrying figures. (The best scene-change for these sets would be from an incendiarist). ∎

In the Middle, Somewhat Elevated
Por vos Muero
Carmen

Royal Opera House, Covent Garden

'Eurotrashing a troupe's historic heritage'

THE ROYAL BALLET'S new triple bill is the worst, the most dispiriting, I have ever seen at Covent Garden. It brings the return of Forsythe's **In the middle** (electroconvulsive therapy for dancers); the low Spanish jinks of Nacho Duato's **Por vos muero**; and the acquisition of Mats Ek's **Carmen**, a work of the most exquisite awfulness which has, I suppose, been brought in to provide Sylvie Guillem with a role in which she can wear a red dress, smoke cigars, and behave badly.

Ballet companies are born with a genetic make-up as potently formative as that of any human. The Royal Ballet was given beliefs by Ninette de Valois: about a school and a theatre, about roots in the nation's arts and in an older repertory, which would encourage choreography. These ideals were realised in the work of Ashton, Cranko, MacMillan. The Royal Ballet conquered the world with a distinctive manner of dancing and dance-making. It is increasingly difficult to reconcile today's Royal Ballet with its past. Is it, with preponderant foreign principals, still the Royal Ballet? Why has the company's school failed to produce talent as impressive as Tamara Rojo, Alina Cojocaru, Johan Kobborg, Ethan Stiefel? Why no house choreographer, no musical director?

We are halfway through Ross Stretton's first year as director, and his plans for the next season are announced. The schedule of ballets

The Royal Ballet

FT

FINANCIAL
TIMES

**12th April
2002**

has shrunk; between October and May next year, the Royal Ballet offers a mere 10 programmes – seven full-evening works (of which only a revived **Sleeping Beauty** is new) and three triple bills, containing one creation. Other novelties are bought-in. The Royal Opera, meantime, proposes 22 productions, of which nine are new, and one a world premiere. Stretton's acquisitions for the current season have been for the most part ill-considered. Cranko's **Onegin** was welcome. The invitation to Christopher Wheeldon to make a ballet was excellent news: he is a classicist, Royal Ballet-trained. But what are we to make of the **Don Quixote** with its provincial designs and entire lack of appeal to Royal Ballet casts? Stephen Baynes' **Beyond Bach** looked feeble; Antony Tudor's **The Leaves are Fading** was a dew-sodden antique, and Forsythe's hyperactive dances head down a Cresta run to frenzy. Ek's **Carmen** is the latest and worst stage in this dégringolade.

Stretton favours a European choreographic manner that erodes classic rectitude with dank emotionalism and turgid dance. From Stockholm to Madrid you can find this Euroglum style, company after company offering the same choreographies, the same clichés. Duato and Kylian (whose bustling **Sinfonietta** is promised next season), are part of this pandemic, as is Angelin Preljocaj (whose **Le Parc** also looms). Ek is a further name in this cheerless catalogue: I think his assaults upon classical ballets defile the stages on which they are played.

If we seek a happier future, Stretton must look to the company's past and to creativity from within its ranks. It is unthinkable that a national troupe should not honour its own history, that dancers and audiences should be ignorant of their artistic past, from Fokine and Balanchine to de Valois, Ashton, MacMillan. Next season's MacMillan Tribute is more remarkable for its omissions than its revivals. We shall see box-office blockbusters, but none of those short ballets in which his questioning talent was so bravely shown. Why no **Requiem**, **My Brother My Sisters**, **Le Baiser de la fée**, **The Invitation**, **Different Drummer**, **Rite of Spring**?

There are dance-makers here who merit Opera House interest. Michael Corder is a gifted classic creator; Matthew Hawkins, Russell Maliphant, Jonathan Burrows, Matthew Hart – all, like Corder, formed by the Royal Ballet – work away from what could intriguingly be their base. All are worthy of the time and money that is expended on Stretton's choice of miscreants. There is a world shortage of choreographers who explore the academic manner. Wheeldon offers hope for the future; elsewhere much new classic writing is skewed, inept. The Royal Ballet is a classical ensemble, and should be addressing this problem. Stretton must consider the facts of the company's personality – its historic identity and its neo-classic potential. Otherwise, a fog of Euro-tedium threatens, in which our national ballet may swiftly become invisible. ∎

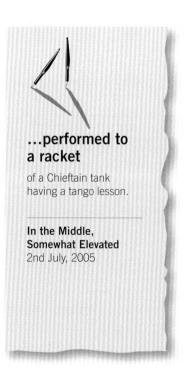

...performed to a racket of a Chieftain tank having a tango lesson.

In the Middle, Somewhat Elevated 2nd July, 2005

The Royal Ballet

FT
FINANCIAL
TIMES

Royal Opera House, Covent Garden

13th April 2014

WITH A PLAY HAVING so complex and so "inward" a narrative as *The Winter's Tale*, the translation of spoken text into dance-theatre is a vexed matter. The character of Leontes is fascinating; the terrible effects of his jealousy and demented imaginings are all too inviting of danced expression, as indeed are the contrasting worlds of Sicilia and Bohemia. But the sustaining dramatic structure is not, as in *Romeo and Juliet* – that lure for danced Shakespeare – built upon incident that invites (let alone admits of) strong realisation in movement.

It is to the credit of Christopher Wheeldon that his realisation of *The Winter's Tale* as a three-act spectacle for the Royal Ballet, seen for the first time on Thursday night, is as well managed as it is. And in everything he is sustained by Joby Talbot's vividly responsive score. The linchpin of the staging is Edward Watson's portrayal of Leontes and his descent into a nightmare of jealousy and manic suspicions, which must give the narrative its momentum. Of course, Watson is superb, his body contorted by shapes entirely revelatory, his anger and his anguish in Wheeldon's imagery profoundly disquieting, and ever inviting of understanding. It is a wholly real, masterly portrayal, and the austere embod-iment of his lost conscience is admirably well taken by Zenaida Yanowsky's grand, commanding Paulina.

These seem the poles of Wheeldon's dramatic scheme, her noble stillness set against his

madness and fevered unreason and, in the last act, his lacerating remorse. Faced with the need to display the pastoral jovialities of Bohemia in the second act, Wheeldon produces a cascade of peasant activity of the most determined verve, with Steven McRae brilliant as Florizel and Sarah Lamb enchanting grace itself as Perdita. But, dear Heaven, how they all do go on, skipping and leaping, and round-dancing and wearing quaint outfits and being jolly. And (like all "folk" performers) never, ever knowing when to stop. That well-known country implement the pruning knife is needed.

Absolutely splendid are Bob Crowley's designs throughout, giving Leontes' realm a monumental grandeur (not unlike one of Gordon Craig's massively austere settings), and producing the ultimate summertime fantasy, centred round a glorious tree, for Sicilia. His references to Caspar David Friedrich, his dazzling evocations of sea-storms and a shipwreck, are everywhere admirable, dramatically resonant, brilliantly done. The staging is a visual triumph, potent, evocative, eye-delighting.

The final act, as dramatic knots are untied, is both the most successful as drama, and the briefest in playing time, with a satisfying sense of calm at its close as Hermione (a serene Lauren Cuthbertson) is restored to Leontes. At curtain fall, we can sense both the skill of Wheeldon's adaptation and something of the problems he has faced in bringing the

narrative to the dance stage. The contrasts he
stresses between Bohemia and Sicilia,
between the increasing darkness of the first
and the sunny exuberance of the second, are
vital to the ballet's progress, albeit there is a
sense of too much activity for the ballet's
own good, of a need for editing. ∎

Sarah Lamb (Perdita)
The Winter's Tale
(2014)

The Royal Ballet

FT

FINANCIAL
TIMES

**7th December
1985**

'The Past Coaching'

THE DEDICATION of the opening
performance of the Royal Ballet's new *Giselle*
staging to Dame Alicia Markova on the occasion
of her 75th birthday this week was a happy
tribute. Markova was one of the greatest
Giselles of this century, her interpretation –
first seen in the infancy of our national ballet
in 1934 – acknowledged as a supreme
example of the ballerina's art.

Markova is essentially Russian. In training her
teachers including the grandest names of the
classic dance. Her career was international
from its beginnings with Diaghilev, with
years spent as ballerina of the Ballet Russe de
Monte Carlo and Ballet Theatre, albeit her
presence in Britain. In the 1990s with the
Vic-Wells, Rambert, and Markova-Dolin
companies, and her later work with Festival
Ballet and the Royal Ballet, identify her vitally
with the mainstream of our national dance.
(But what other British dancer has had roles
created for her by Fokine, Massine, Nijinska,
Balanchine, as well as Ashton, Tudor, de Valois?)

With a phenomenal memory for style and
step, Markova is a balletic treasure-house. It is
this richness of her experience which seems
to me typical of the assets wasted by our
national ballet. It should be an accepted fact
of British dance that great artists hand on
their wealth of understanding about technique,
and the implications of their roles, so that
young aspirants may comprehend the vital

aesthetic and technical life of the repertory.
They would thus learn of the traditions, of
the subtleties as well as the practicalities, of
performance, of pacing and shaping an
interpretation, that their mentor had gained
through long theatrical experience, and had
garnered in their turn from instruction and
coaching by their forebears. It is this chain of
interpretation that brings continuity of
wisdom, and richness of meaning, – to every
major role. Yet this has all too rarely seemed
the Royal Ballet's way, and our national
company – and its school – are the poorer
thereby. Hence our present shortage of young
ballerinas who can, with proper command,
reveal the life of the classic repertory, instead
of taking the stage like perpetual debutantes,
conducting (as was said of George Moore)
their education in public.

They order these things differently in Russia.
A vital substructure of Soviet ballet is the
transmission of knowledge from one generation of artists to another through extended
coaching in the niceties and the lore of the
role. (It was a tradition of the Imperial Ballet,
too). Thus a young Kirov or Bolshoi ballerina,
making a first appearance as Odette or
Giselle or Aurora, is prepared by a ballerina
celebrated in the part. The newcomer takes
the stage, eventually, armoured with the
decades of her instructress' experience,
technical and emotional. So Ulanova coached
the young Maximova for Giselle, handing
on all her prodigious knowledge. So Makarova
was taught both by Natalya Dudinskaya and

Tatyana Vecheslova (concerned respectively with text and dramatics) for her first Giselle. And so she could speak of being sent to Marina Semyonova, most illustrious of Soviet ballerinas, for coaching in **Swan Lake**.

Soviet dancers speak with reverence and affection of their mentor; acknowledging at every moment throughout their careers the invaluable gift that has been bestowed on to them. Dame Alicia Markova can speak of working as a 'very young dancer' on the **Swan Lake** adagio with Mathilde Kschessinskaya, the first Russian Odette in 1901, and successor to Legnani, the role's creator at the Mariinsky. She has worked with Fokine, Nijiska, Massine on their major ballets; with Lyubov Egorova to whom Diaghilev sent the young Markova to study the Bluebird duet since Egorova was acknowledged the role's notable interpreter at the Mariinsky. But will any of our aspirant ballerinas speak, in years to come, of learning with Markova about the roles she so illuminated? Will they, in their turn, be able to pass on the received wisdom not just of their own careers but also of so grand a preceptress? Not unless a change in Royal Ballet attitudes takes place, and the company views the classics, and its own repertory, notably its priceless endowment of Ashton works, as part of a chain of theatrical example and interpretative wisdom.

This year's detestable revival of **Ballet Imperial** told of the depths of parochialism and complacency to which the company could

sink, when none of the artists who shone in the original Covent Garden staging – Moira Shearer, Beryl Grey, Michael Somes, John Field, Kenneth MacMillan – was, as I understand, invited to pass on what Balanchine had given them, and hideous design was imposed that went counter to everything the ballet should mean. The Royal Ballet has a store of eminent former ballerinas and danseurs, creators of important works and exceptional incumbents of the classic repertory, whose wisdom, like Markova's is effectively a wasted asset. I hear of no lengthy periods of coaching and consultation set aside to prepare young dancers for the greatest challenge of their art, through study with celebrated interpreters of these very roles. (It is an ironic exception that we still honour the advice given by Tamara Karsavina about **Giselle** and **The Firebird** and **La Fille mal gardée**). Our national ballet can claim some parentage with the old Russian ballet through its canon of classics bequeathed by Nicholas Sergueyev. It would do well to consider that there are obligations owed to these ballets – as to the native Ashton repertory – concerning text and style, which are implicit in this priceless inheritance and this irreplaceable link with the past. ∎

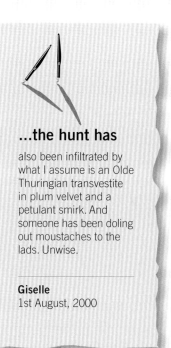

...the hunt has also been infiltrated by what I assume is an Olde Thuringian transvestite in plum velvet and a petulant smirk. And someone has been doling out moustaches to the lads. Unwise.

Giselle
1st August, 2000

The Royal Ballet

Song of the Earth
Afternoon of a Faun
In the Night

FT
FINANCIAL
TIMES

**Royal Opera House,
Covent Garden**

**2nd June
2015**

"JUST DANCE THE STEPS, DEAR!" "Why don't they trust the choreography?" These comments by two great choreographers about their dancers came to mind during Friday night's performance of MacMillan's **Song of the Earth**, which brought the debuts of Lauren Cuthbertson (returning to the stage after a long absence owed to injury) as the Woman, and Ryoichi Hirano, replacing Rupert Pennefather as the Man.

That Edward Watson gave an ideal interpretation of the Messenger goes without saying: he trusts the choreography, and the dance grandly lives. So, too, with Cuthbertson. Nothing was forced, self-consciously emotional. The Woman's role probes deepest feelings of loss with an austere dignity – anything false in the dancer will fatally show. Cuthbertson told the truth; the choreography lived, and eloquently so. (The great sequence of eddying steps that signs the role near the ballet's end was heart-stirring).

Hirano was admirably honest, and the dance spoke. Watson cut to the heart of MacMillan's creation, and is as sublimely true as was Egon Madsen, who first danced the role in Stuttgart nearly 50 years ago. Staggering artistry.

This programme also brings two cunning emotional capriccios by Jerome Robbins: **Afternoon of a Faun**, which re-imagines the steamy Nijinsky original as an encounter between two young dance students in a New York studio – audience as the fourth wall of the set observing the faintest stirrings of attraction (well done by Sarah Lamb and Federico Bonelli); and the Chopin-born emotions of **In the Night**, as three couples expose passions innocent, aware, anguished. It is dance artful, impeccably made, rewarding to perform, and the Royal Ballet's lovers – the enchanting Emma Maguire and Alexander Campbell, the commandingly beautiful Zenaida Yanowsky with Nehemiah Kish, the tempestuous Marianela Nuñez fleeing and yet seeking the arms of Thiago Soares – were fine. It is kitsch, but admirably done. And I salute yet again Campbell, whose dancing here, and in **Song of the Earth**, as in other recent performances, has a clarity, a musical and theatrical verve, which enhance every role. ∎

Ryoichi Hirano,
Lauren Cuthbertson
and Edward Watson
(Messenger of Death)
(2015)

Le Grand Ballet du Marquis de Cuevas

Summer 2005

LE GRAND BALLET du Marquis de Cuevas was a delight to ballet-goers. It possessed that most precious of attributes, theatrical glamour. Its performances seemed always to have a frisson of excitement to them. It was rich in star dancers, artists who thrilled by their bravura as by their emotional command over their roles, and their audience, which made even the most dubious creations seem oddly exhilarating. The company boasted a varied and often stimulating repertory: Fokine, Balanchine, Massine, Lichine, Nijinska, Taras, Dollar, Ana Ricarda, Antonia Gobos, Edward Gaton, Eglevsky, Rosella Hightower, and George Skibine were among its choreo-graphers. Looking at the de Cuevas troupe, and I was blessed in being able to see the extent of its performances from 1947 until its last gasp in 1962, was always exhilarating: you breathed a theatrical ozone more heady, more intoxicating, than the quieter airs inhaled during the usual run of dutiful performance on home ground, or even with such visiting luminaries as New York City Ballet and American Ballet Theatre. When the Russians arrived – the Moscow Bolshoi in 1956, the Leningrad Kirov in 1961 – there came the same (though very different) sense of watching more intensely, experiencing more vividly.

There comparison had better end, for some small number of the de Cuevas offerings were ill-advised, more vehicular for stars than serious as art objects. But the sense of enjoy-ment, the vivid records in studying such superlative artists as Nina Vyroubova, Rosella Hightower, George Skibine, Serge Golovine; of catching the late and still dazzling glow of Riabouchinska, Toumanova, David Lichine, Andre Eglevsky, and Leonid Massine in serious revivals of Ballets Russes repertory, were inducement enough to return time and again to the de Cuevas company. It made ballet-going even more addictive, more intoxicating, than it already was. Can this, I wonder, be said of any troupe today – even including the Moscow and Petersburg ensembles?

The eighth Marquis Georges de Piedrablanca de Guana de Cuevas – or, to give the shortened form of his title by which the ballet-world knew him, the Marquis de Cuevas – was born in Santiago, Chile, in 1885. He married Margaret Strong Rockefeller, grand-daughter and considerable heiress of John D. Rockefeller, became an American citizen albeit he was essentially Parisian, and it was his wife's fortune which enabled de Cuevas to launch himself on the world of ballet in New York in 1944. (He had earlier sponsored the Masterpieces of Art exhibition at the New York World's Fair in 1939). In the early 1940s there were already two large ballet troupes there – Lucia Chase's Ballet Theatre and Serge Denham's Ballet Russe de Monte Carlo (which had decamped to the New World at the outbreak of the 1939-45 war) – who might well claim to have a lien upon audiences (not so numerous as nowadays) and their affections, and upon the most gifted dancers and dance-makers, and on those New York theatres capable of housing

'An Appreciation'
The Journal of the Society
for Dance Research
Vol. 23, No. 1

large-scale ballet, as well as the necessary touring schedules that framed their major seasons in New York and Chicago. The Marquis, nonetheless, conceived the idea of a ballet company which would form part of a larger enterprise, The Ballet Institute, founded in November 1943 and capitalised at $150,000, an educational and non-profit-making organisation of which he was artistic director and sponsor, concerned with 'the advancement of the art of the ballet and its allied arts, for the education and instruction of students in these arts, and for the furtherance of public appreciation of ballet'. It was for these noble if windy ends that the Marquis leased the Park Theatre on Columbus Circle in June 1944, renaming it the International Theatre as a home for his putative school and troupe. The teaching academy was, in fact, the established school run by Anatol Vilzak and his wife Lyudmila Schollar, both graduates of St Petersburg's Imperial Ballet School and Mariinsky company. (Both had later danced for Diaghilev's Ballet Russe with great distinction). Vilzak was also to be the ballet-master of the new de Cuevas troupe, Ballet International.

All did not go well. The International Theatre, though handsome, was inadequate for its new purposes: too limited in space for rehearsal studios and classrooms, its stage too small for ballet performance. What had seemed promising, and well-found financially, was revealed as impractical. Yet work progressed in making ballets and forming and polishing a ballet ensemble during a period of six months. A dozen works were created or revived by ten choreographers – Nijinska, Fokine (staged by his widow, Vera), Massine, Boris Romanoff, Petipa (staged by Vilzak), William Dollar, Simon Semenoff, Antonia Cobos, Edward Caton, and Andre Eglevsky – for a season at the International Theatre which ran from 30 October until 28 December 1944. This gives some indication of the Marquis's ambitions and capabilities, of his undeniable aesthetic sensibility, and also, since the season lost some $800,000, something of his financial resources. The company was headed by such notable artists as Marie-Jeanne, Viola Essen, Andre Eglevsky and William Dollar. It did not survive this season. In the following summer, with peace declared in Europe – and France in the throes of the Liberation, with all that implied of political in-fighting and wild accusations of collaboration with the German occupying forces – Prince Louis II of Monaco invited the impresario Eugene Gruenberg to succeed Rene Blum (who, a French Jew, had been imprisoned by the Germans in Auschwitz, and died there in April 1942) as director of ballet at the Monte Carlo Opera House.

Gruenberg soon assembled a company, recruiting an exceptional group of dancers from Paris schools and from the Paris Opéra. These artists were headed by Renee Jeanmaire, Janine Charrat, Vladimir Skouratoff, Youly Algaroff, Rene Bon, Alexandre Kaliouzhny – young artists of grand gifts – and soon ...

...a skeletal
Japanese danseuse who looked rather like an antler.

Benois de la Danse Gala
25th February, 2004

Yvette Chauviré (the Opéra's finest étoile) joined the troupe. In Paris, the injustices brought by the self-appointed and politically suspect *Comites d'épuration* as they sought to purge France of alleged 'collaborators' included the inexcusable banning of Serge Lifar from the Opéra, where he had revived the ballet troupe during the decade of the 1930s, and sustained it as an emblem of French art during the Occupation years. Lifar turned to Monaco, and joined Gruenberg's Nouveau Ballet de Monte Carlo as artistic director. There, with its exciting group of young dancers, he set about creating a repertory containing his own ballets – they included **Chota Roustaveli**, **Dramma per musica**, **Salome**, **Nautéos**, and revivals of established works. Le Nouveau Ballet appeared in Monte Carlo, toured France, and visited London in the summer of 1946. Protests about the

Duel between Lifar (right) and the Marquis de Cuevas in Paris, following a legal dispute, and stopped after Lifar's arm had been wounded

injustice suffered by Lifar had caused the life-long ban on his appearance at the Opéra to be cancelled, and he returned to Paris in 1947, taking with him some of the dancers from the Monte Carlo troupe.

The Marquis de Cuevas now approached Gruenberg with an offer to assume the direction of the Nouveau Ballet de Monte Carlo, and this was accepted by the Principality. Thus, in the spring of 1947, the Marquis found himself at the head of the Nouveau Ballet, and he set about amalgamating into its ranks the repertory and some of the dancers that he had employed for Ballet International.

There emerged the much stronger and more international (and re-named) Grand Ballet de Monte Carlo, notable not least for the presence of some exceptional American dancers – Rosella Hightower, Marjorie Tallchief, and George Skibine – and American choreo-graphies from the Ballet International season (by William Dollar, Edward Caton, and Antonia Cobos). An added distinction was the presence of Bronislava Nijinska as choreo-grapher and artistic counsellor. The considerable success of the company's first Paris season in November at the Theatre de l'Alhambra was a portent of things to come. Extensive touring, seasons in Paris, London, Monte Carlo, provi-ded a pattern of performance that brought growing acclaim to the troupe over the next years. Vichy, Paris and Brussels were the cities visited in 1947; in 1948 the Grand Ballet de Monte Carlo toured major French cities in January, went to Portugal in February, appeared at the Theatre des Champs Elysees in March, took part in the Spring season at Monte Carlo in April, visited Holland and Belgium in May, spent June and July in Brazil, made a first visit to Covent Garden in August and then toured the British provinces in September and October, returning to Monte Carlo in November, then appearing in Tunis in December.

In January 1949 the company moved on to Cairo, spent February, March and April in Monaco, visited Paris for a week in May and then visited Barcelona, Madrid, Bilbao, and played the Holland Festival in June prior to another Covent Garden season in June and July, before appearing in Deauville in August. I cite this itinerary as an example both of the hard work that the company welcomed, but also as an indication of how greatly the Grand Ballet, its repertory and artists, appealed to the public. And what was it that so engaged public affection? The first Covent Garden seasons were suggestive enough of the real and varied delights that we saw. The repertory was, in the best sense, entertaining and wide-ranging. The leading dancers (Hightower, Tallchief, Golovine, Eglevsky, and Skibine) were brilliant, and brilliantly communicative of the excitements of the danse d'école. Rosella Hightower was a prodigious virtuoso – I recall sitting behind Dame Ninette de Valois when Hightower and Eglevsky sailed in glory through the Black Swan duet during the company's first Covent Garden visit in July 1948. Hightower's *pirouettes à la grande seconde,* Eglevsky's slowly unwinding and interminable pirouettes, caused Dame Ninette (and the rest of us) to gasp in amazement.

The company was still raw – Cyril Beamont was gently critical in reviewing the first London season, noting a weakness in design and in the female corps de ballet – but the variety of the offerings, the appeal of its stars, were undeniable. It is worth insisting that the Grand Ballet de Monte Carlo was very much the creation and the reflection of the Marquis de Cuevas' taste. He loved classical ballet and believed in the undeniable appeal of star dancers, and by the summer of 1949 he was showing Covent Garden audiences such extra attractions as Tatiana Riabouchinska (her husband, David Lichine, had produced the delightful **Le Moulin Enchanté** for the company), Tamara Toumanova, and Leonid Massine (who re-staged his own works) in **Le Beau Danube** and **Les Femmes de Bonne Humeur**. With Hightower and Eglevsky, George Skibine and Marjorie Tallchief, Rene Bon (a sparkling virtuoso) and Ethery Pagava, and a gifted echelon of soloists, the company could – and did – dazzle by its dance-power. •••

The company was not without its faults: design might at times seem more modish than helpful to a ballet's identity, and there was such determination to show the public how astonishing were the dancers' gifts, how easily they could throw off the most astonishing of feats, that choreography seemed at moments sacrificed to display. But, one must add, what display!

In 1951 the Marquis severed the connection with Monaco, and the troupe was rechristened Le Grand Ballet du Marquis de Cuevas. (A title sometimes used in later years was the International Ballet of the Marquis de Cuevas). During the decade of the 1950s the company continued its predictable life of tours and important Paris seasons. Dancers came and went, but Hightower (whom the Marquis hugely admired) remained as leading étoile. Skibine and Marjorie Tallchief left in 1956, and in what might seem a compensatory coup, the wonderfully gifted Nina Vyroubova joined the troupe from the Paris Opéra, and proved a superb complement to Hightower. (Vyroubova's appearance as the somnambulist in Balanchine's **Night Shadow** with Golovine remains one of the defining moments in my own ballet-going. Her beauty, her emotional grace, her ravishing classic style, were perfectly suited to the role, as they were also in the *Cigarette* variation in Lifar's **Noir et blanc**. She was one of the greatest dance-artists of the second half the twentieth century). But it is undeniable that, as the decade continued, the novelties in the repertory seemed less and less attractive and challenging. (In James Starbuck's **Le Mal du siècle** we had the unenviable sight of the cast sporting sunglasses rather than dance-interest). Hightower, Vyroubova, and Golovine remained artists of superlative quality. Guests came and went – most intriguingly, the Marquis asked Harald Lander, former director of the Royal Danish Ballet, to stage Bournonville's **La Sylphide** in Paris in 1953, and invited Alicia Markova to dance the Sylph, a role for which Heaven had surely intended her but which she danced only in this season, partnered by Golovine. The great

Danish ballerina Margrethe Schanne was also to appear in this Paris season, appearing memorably both as the Sylph and as Giselle.

But as the decade of the 1950s advanced, the style of the Grand Ballet and its repertory started to look increasingly self-indulgent and slightly care-worn. The solid achievements of the Royal Ballet, the arrival of New York City Ballet and American Ballet Theatre in Europe, the delights of the Royal Danish Ballet and the furore caused by the Moscow Bolshoi Ballet, took their toll on the credibility of the de Cuevas troupe. We still delighted in the stellar forces, in ballets which took our hearts or prodigiously glittered (not to have seen Hightower, Vyroubova, and Golovine in the *pas de trois* in **Paquita** is not to know theatrical joy), but it would be idle to pretend that the de Cuevas seasons were as richly and sometimes improbably enjoyable as before.

The Marquis, absolute master of these revels, was ageing, his taste, unaltered over the years, seemed to be fighting a rear-guard action. The aristocrat who had made a splendid gesture in 1953 by staging a costume ball by the lake at Chiberta in the Pays Basque, inviting hundreds of guests and entertaining them royally (and appeared in costume as Le Roi Soleil at the ball while his ballet troupe danced Act 2 of **Swan Lake** on the lake), was confronted by inevitable changes of time and fashion. In a last opulent declaration he commissioned a production of **The Sleeping Beauty** for the Paris season of 1960. Nijinska was in charge of mounting the work, and the design was to be by the Marquis's nephew by marriage, Raimundo Larrain. Extravagantly feathered, wildly over the top, the production ran into difficulties when Mme Nijinska decided to quit. Robert Helpmann was brought in to finish the staging, and it opened to considerable publicity. It gained further publicity when Rudolf Nureyev defected during the Kirov Ballet's Paris season in 1961, and found his first refuge in the West by appearing in this staging as Prince Florimund to Vyroubova's beautiful Aurora. But the Marquis was by now ill, and he died in Cannes in 1962. Raimundo Larrain endeavoured to maintain the company with the Marquis' widow, but fate was against this decision. The International Ballet de la Marquise de Cuevas (as the troupe was now and briefly known) danced in Athens in June 1962, and on the last day of the month gave its last performance. A wonderful, idiosyncratic, sometimes unlikely, sometimes prodigious, and always intriguing enterprise was gone. Its legacy was the memories among audiences who had been moved, exhilarated, by superb dancing in performances that made classical ballet thrilling, unpredictable, but always wonderfully alive. They had benefited from the caprices, the taste, the extravagance and the grand passion for ballet of a single man, whose troupe was the mirror of his being: le Marquis de Cuevas. ∎

...a nightmare

of rucked curtaining from the Odeon, Purgatory, which frames a spindly staircase and an apologetic doorway leading to what I take to be a puny loo.

The Lady and the Fool
11th October, 2005

CLEMENT'S CAREER as an observer of dance has been marked by what he terms 'divinities', dancers whose technique, artistry and stagecraft mark them out from the many thousands he has seen in well over half a century of dance-going. In 1994 he set out what he believes constitutes a true ballerina, a much-abused term. "It is rather like calling a private soldier a general. When a dancing girl hits the headlines, the perkier journals invoke the word "ballerina" – as in "Ballerina in Royal love-nest mercy-dash". The facts (to coin a phrase) will reveal that the "ballerina" is no more than young Tiffany Plinth from the corps de ballet" he wrote. "Is the ballerina a doomed species? The box office knows that the public still has the appetite for these stellar figures, and while the old repertory survives – despite the attentions of Frankenstein producers and designers – their place is secure. But the ballerina's world is shrinking, as less and less of today's choreography challenges or justifies her". "She will survive; while ballet survives, she must survive. There is a duty for ballet companies and their schools to make sure she survives. Not to see the ballerina in full and tremendous cry (and step), is not to see ballet". Clement never held the belief that male dancers emerged from the shadows only with Rudolf Nureyev's arrival in the West. From Serge Lifar, the last of Serge Diaghilev's male stars and Niels Kehlet, the near-ideal exponent of his adored Danish School of dancing to Mikhail Baryshnikov, Irek Mukhamedov and Edward Watson are among those he saluted.

The
Stars

Chapter 3

The
Stars

Chapter 3

La Bayadère

Royal Opera House,
Covent Garden

FT

FINANCIAL
TIMES

IT IS THE SPECIAL GENIUS of the Kirov ballerina, Altynai Asylmuratova, that she can show the full implications of the role of Nikiya, the temple-dancer in **La Bayadère**. Making a single guest appearance with the Royal Ballet on Wednesday night, she had established Nikiya's character within a few minutes of appearing on stage. Gravely she descends the temple steps. The High Brahmin removes the veil from her head to reveal the blaze of Asylmuratova's beauty. Her eyes are turned towards the skies, and only when the Brahmin makes his avowal of passion does this Nikiya look towards the world. A central theme of the ballet, the conflict between love sacred – or at least consecrated – and profane, has been stated.

In Asylmuratova's interpretation the drama and the dance live, and how fully and richly are they expounded. From her Kirov training come both the serenity of style and the absolute credibility of her playing – she is heir to the role's long traditions. But it is nature which formed her, as we saw in her earlier appearances this year at Covent Garden, so that pose and gesture seem to flower from the luscious torso, and it is temperament which enables her to give such breadth to the least action.

Asylmuratova constantly astounds by the grand scale of her dancing. Even in a performance, as on Wednesday, when a new partnership (with Jonathan Cope's Solor) was not of the easiest, the momentum of her

movement, and its ever-outward reach to vast horizons of feeling and line, were magnificent. It is dancing of immense generosity, looking at moments, as in a diagonal during the Shades scene, greedy in devouring space.

Asylmuratova's mystery – that unguessable quality which marks the great dancer – lies partly in a contrast between her dazzling, all-conquering femininity, her physical prowess, and the disciplines of academic style: despite the call of Dionysos, she remains a servant of Apollo. In this central balance of her artistry, we can also sense the crisis at the heart of **La Bayadère**, where Nikiya urges Solor to be faithful to a love sanctified over the holy fire. In the Shades scene, she tells him: "Be true! Be true!" And with what grace – and force: she is no pale wisp of air – did Asylmuratova expose these feelings through the amplitude and the intensity of her manner.

For all that there were uncertainties attendant upon a single guest appearance, Asylmuratova gave an interpretation of memorable beauty, and we are grateful. She must return. ∎

**6th October
1989**

Altynai Asylmuratova (Nikiya)
London
(1997)

Alexandra Balashova
National Ballet of Slovenia

La Fille mal gardée

FINANCIAL TIMES

Opera House,
Ljubljana

**25th June
1969**

ALEXANDRA BALASHOVA is a remarkable link with the Imperial Russian Ballet. She graduated from the Imperial School in Moscow in 1905 and entered the Bolshoi company; eight years later she was making a guest appearance during the Lenten ballet season in Kharkov when she received a telegram announcing that she had been nominated as ballerina – a clearly defined official rank usually granted to much senior artists as a reward for their services. Balashova's brilliant technique had earned her this recognition and it confirmed her right to all the principal roles in the repertory. Among her ballets were to be numbered the restagings of Petipa's works that were mounted in Moscow by Alexander Gorsky: *The Sleeping Beauty*, *Swan Lake*, *Pharaoh's Daughter*, *Le Corsaire*, *La Bayadère*, *Don Quixote*, *Coppélia*, and two ballets with which she has been particularly associated: *The Little Humpbacked Horse* and *La Fille mal gardée*. Her beauty and her technical prowess made her the darling of the Moscow public and because of this Telyakovsky, Director of the Imperial Theatres, nicknamed her ponuchka (Little Pony).

She appeared in London in 1911, replacing the senior Moscow ballerina, Ekaterina Geltzer. In *A Dance Dream*, a spectacular farrago by Gorsky that was put on at the Alhambra as part of the Coronation celebrations. During the war and the immediate post-revolutionary period she continued to dance in Moscow, but in 1921 a warning that her husband was to be arrested drove her into exile with him

in Paris. She was given two days grace to leave her Moscow home, and it is ironic that in November of that year Isadora Duncan was installed there on her arrival in Russia – and proceeded to burn the superb Empire furniture and cut up the tapestries. (Duncan's irruption into these luxurious surroundings is excellently detailed in Ilya Ilyich Schneider's recent and fascinating book: *Isadora Duncan – The Russian Years*).

This brief history is by way of an introduction to a performance I have just seen in Ljubljana's pretty Opera House in which Mme Balashova danced again, in *Fille*. At the age of 82, with remarkable skill and spirit she has revived this greatest of her successes, and not content with that, mimes the role of Widow Simone with an artistry that is utterly compelling. On leaving Russia, Mme Balashova managed to rescue her rehearsal score of *Fille*. With it she staged and danced the ballet at the Paris Opéra in 1923, and since the war she has made partial reconstructions for a French concert troupe, and for the de Cuevas ballet. Five years ago she mounted the entire ballet in Strasbourg (and Andrew Porter reviewed that performance); now she has been invited by the Slovene National Ballet to revive the work yet again, and the performance that I saw offered many points of interest to eyes accustomed to the Ashton version. Balashova's presentation, which includes some of the Petipa choreography, is altogether simpler and more direct in manner than one might have supposed. Sincerity seems the key-note;

Alexandra Balashova (Simone) and Noelle Christian (Lise) rehearsing in Ljubljana

there is far less of the humour that Ashton provides, the story is told in more innocent – almost naif – terms, and the characterisations are less complex. The action is largely similar to that we know, though the cornfield scene here becomes Act 3 and serves as a final celebration to round off an intrigue that finishes at the end of Act 2 when Simone accepts the fact of Lise's marriage to Colas.

The Slovene company dance with enthusiasm – one would be wrong to expect the Royal Ballet's classical finesse in their performance – and there is real interest in seeing the role of Lise as Mme Balashova

danced it, given on this occasion with a bright technical ease and charm by Noelle Christian. Mlle Christian and Mme. Balashova work together with entire harmony; and Mme. Balashova's own performance – strong, stylish, acted with a total naturalness that conceals great art – is an object lesson for anyone fortunate to see it. ∎

Mikhail Baryshnikov
The Royal Ballet

Romeo and Juliet

FINANCIAL
TIMES

Royal Opera House,
Covent Garden

**24th October
1975**

MIKHAIL BARYSHNIKOV'S reputation is as a prodigious technician, a dancer who outsoars the common run of men, the new genius of the classic dance. Such he was when we saw him first during the Kirov's 1970 season at the Festival Hall, a youth still, but a marvel in the grab-bag of *pas de deux* and solos which were all he was given to dance.

When he opted for the West in Toronto last summer, he was making an artistic decision for greater opportunities, greater challenges, and with American Ballet Theatre and in his wide-ranging travels since then, he has made the world gasp at his technical brilliance.

Thus the Covent Garden audience on Wednesday night, come to see his debut with the Royal Ballet, might reasonably have expected to be dazzled by virtuosity and all the external show of physical prowess and beautiful schooling. What we saw, though, in **Romeo and Juliet**, was a great actor who is also a great dancer. And an actor first on this occasion. Of course the dancing had its breath-taking moments – speed and vivacity in movement rare and wondrous to see, *double assemblée en tournant* in which he spun high in the air at something like 60 degrees to the ground.

But what caught the mind and the heart was the depth and intensity of this first account of a very complex role. Baryshnikov's Romeo is the youngest I have seen, little more than a boy in the opening scene as he roars through

the feuding streets of Verona. On the verge of manhood he seems still to be caught in dreams of adolescence: despite his amused by-play with the harlots, he is innocent for all the fire and arrogance he can assume. The development of the character from the meeting with Juliet is a study in growing-up; the ardour with which he pursues her, the intensity of passion he reveals in the balcony duet, are the signs of a personality just waking to maturity. No Romeo before has suggested so clearly the initial force of his obsession for her. After his first soaring circuit of the stage in the *pas de deux* – Baryshnikov takes to the air, his body borne up in ecstatic leaps – he kneels, and as Juliet passes by him, he turns eagerly to watch her every step. It is this quality of freshness, of movement and emotion caught on the wing, that made Baryshnikov so compelling throughout the evening.

In Act 2 his vitality, the force of his reactions to every incident, were magnificently right. He enters caught up in dreams of love. Baryshnikov has a unique ability to suggest the contemplative inner life of a character; as I reported of his Copenhagen appearance in **La Sylphide** last winter, his James was a man haunted by an inner vision. His Romeo returns to the brawling streets emotionally still with Juliet, and after the marriage, his joy and sense of bemused happiness is almost tangible. His attempt to stop the duel between Mercutio and Tybalt is full of despair at the futility of the squabble, but Mercutio

dead, he takes up his, sword with a huge ferocity as he turns on Tybalt. Here we can appreciate Baryshnikov's gestural power: action is contemplated, and then bursts out with wonderful clarity. In this it resembles his dancing; movement is fast, the outline quickly drawn, then the body has time to fill it out – accelerated take off, in effect, followed by a *ritardando* in which we can savour the dynamics at full stretch.

With the last act his physical involvement is entirely admirable: the youth, drunk with passion, who leaves Juliet's bedroom, is seen at the last as a figure broken by grief. • • •

Merle Park (Juliet)
Mikhail Baryshnikov (Romeo)
(1975)

At every moment we believe and suffer with him. And, on purely technical terms, we can but salute a phenomenally accomplished dancer. We knew something of this already, albeit we were not perhaps prepared for the maturity of style. The leaps are high, the turns innumerable and easy; preparations for the most difficult steps seem not to exist, as he takes off on flights that suggest a new breed of male classical dancer. And intriguingly, there is the feeling of something still in reserve, both dramatically and physically. If ever a dancer needed roles to stretch him yet further, to open new vistas of artistic and physical achievement, it is Baryshnikov. It would be a happy event if he were to find some of them with the Royal Ballet. ∎

There is a child

in a story by Dorothy Parker whose only conversational gambit is the phrase "Doomed from the womb". She could have been talking about Swan Lake.

Swan Lake
30th July, 2000

Three Preludes
Pergolesi

Sadler's Wells

THE SADDEST WORDS in ballet are "But you should have seen him (or her) when. When the muscles were resilient, the style uncorrupted, the dance fresh". On Saturday night Mikhail Baryshnikov danced at Sadler's Wells with his White Oak project on the second evening of a two-day visit, and ah! you should have seen him then. At an age – he is in his 46th year – when most male dancers have retired, or should have retired, Baryshnikov is dancing with sublimest grace, artistry, physical resource. He has, for several years, eschewed the classic repertory which he illuminated permanently for us with his physical genius. Instead, he has found and inspired roles – notably from Twyla Tharp and Mark Morris – which examine his still dazzling prowess. And he remains what he was when we first saw him in the Kirov season of 1970, a uniquely gifted and uniquely satisfying dancer.

A distinguishing quality of Baryshnikov's dancing has ever been its clarity. The classicist's ideal of movement pure, sharply-drawn and impeccably shaped, is always realised in his art. This was what Leningrad training brought to a God-given physical instrument. And this is still a glorious constant of his art, allied to that other, and intensely personal, gift of seamless, huge-spanned phrasing. We see the dance as an essence, unalloyed and potent, set in long lines of beautiful and subtly-conceived activity. Baryshnikov now is, miraculously, Baryshnikov then.

Mikhail Baryshnikov
White Oak Project

FT
FINANCIAL
TIMES

**8th June
1993**

In **Three Preludes** (in black trousers and top; white socks, vest, gloves) Mark Morris sets him exploring Gershwin's relaxed and jazzy writing. Baryshnikov is insouciantly brilliant, deep inside the syncopations, playing with rhythm, phenomenally exact in line and accent. He takes on the shape of the music – and of its historical period. In **Pergolesi**, Twyla Tharp offers a culmination of her long association with Baryshnikov's dancing, which dates back to **Push Comes to Shove** in 1976, and encompasses such varied pieces as **The Little Ballet** and **Sinatra Songs**.

Baryshnikov, in white, dances tirelessly in a sequence of numbers that show him, as always in Tharp choreography, riding on waves of energy and rhythm, cutting classic steps into fresh and off-beat shapes, whipping into a movement and suddenly holding it in suspension. Mercurial in its physical aspects, light in touch as in execution, the piece is by turns mocking – Baryshnikov sends up with sharpest wit his own repertory, Giselle's wilis, Nijinsky's roles – and shot with intense feeling.

It is about Baryshnikov in several ways – as virtuoso, as repository of a great tradition, as balletic icon. It is a magnificent study, sublimely danced by an artist whose greatness we recognised when we saw him dance Jacobson's **Vestris** solo in 1970 – and in an odd way **Pergolesi** recalls that earlier exercise, too – and whose greatness is undiminished, and even more rewarding, today. ∎

Mikhail Baryshnikov
Pergolesi
(1993)

Natalia Makarova / Mikhail Baryshnikov
Royal Danish Ballet

FINANCIAL
TIMES

**13th December
1974**

**Natalia Makarova (Sylphide)
Mikhail Baryshnikov (James)
(1974)**

THE CURTAIN RISES on the opening pose of *La Sylphide* and there sleeping in the chair, is Mikhail Baryshnikov as James, with Natalia Makarova as the Sylphide kneeling at his side. On Saturday night the Royal Danish Ballet brought off a theatrical coup by presenting these illustrious artists in their first European performance together. The omens were right for the occasion: it was St Andrew's day – the ballet is set in Scotland – and also the anniversary of the death of Bournonville, who I hope was somewhere viewing the perform-ance with as much delight as I felt.

La Sylphide has an almost Racinian intensity of structure. We join the drama just as its tensions are at breaking point: under the sweet paraphernalia of a Romantic ballet there exists that struggle between the real world and the illusory delights of fantasy which was the crux of Romanticism itself, and with Makarova and Baryshnikov the tale is given most touching and urgent expression.

The Sylphide dominates the action. Her passion for James is its motive force, she so obsesses him that he cannot but follow her; the resolution of the tragedy brings her death and James's isolation from both the real world and the supernatural realm into which the Sylphide lured him.

The immediate problem for artists formed in the noble Kirov style is one of adjustment to the domestic scale of the Bournonville manner and of the Danish staging itself. Happily, Saturday night's stars have had experience of their roles in other productions, Makarova with Ballet Theatre, Baryshnikov with the Canadian National Ballet. Makarova possesses every gift needed for the Sylphide. Her incomparable lightness makes the character more truly a being of the air than any other interpreter I have seen, the Bournonville virtue of *ballon* finding what seems a marvell-ous technical extension in Makarova's apparent reluctance to touch the ground, so feathery is her statement of the dances.

Enhancing this physical delicacy is her tender way with the Sylphide's emotions: none of the big dramatic effects that bring her Giselle to life, but a wilful grace, a capriciousness, that are the essential justification for the Sylphide. She is selfish; childlike, she adores James and wants him for her own, and every trick of ethereal charm, every winning pose and delicately sketched attitude of grief has an irresistible allure for him. Yet nothing overtly physical is in this attraction – Makarova's

112

La Sylphide

Royal Theatre, Copenhagen

femininity is spirtualised, and beautifully in period. How prettily she takes the attitudes and bending entreaties of the sylph.

The second act finds Makarova as radiant as I have ever seen her when she fetches water or strawberries to the enraptured James, but she reserves her loveliest effects for the death scene. The poisoned scarf touches her shoulders, the body freezes, then bends in pain; the pathos of her stance, back to the audience, as the Sylphide's wings fall to the ground, is heartrending, and as she turns to James for the last time and gives him back his wedding ring Makarova's face becomes drained of every emotion: the hands flutter lightly over her features, and she dies. Bournonville, who sought dramatic truth in all his work, would surely hail this supremely poetic, truthful moment.

If Makarova is an ideal Sylphide, she is matched at every point by Baryshnikov's James. We first saw him in London four years ago when the Kirov was slumming on the Festival Hall stage. Just 22 years old, he dazzled us then with a bravura, and a classic perfection of style that seemed uncanny in one so young. A series of *pas de deux* spoke of a flawless technique, and a couple of performances in dance sketches inspired by Auguste Vestris, specially written for him by Jacobsen, made us realise that he had a dramatic power no less outstanding than his physical skill. Since his decision to remain in the West during a concert tour of Canada this

summer, he has danced in North America to vast acclaim, and this Copenhagen performance reveals that he has attained an extraordinary artistic maturity.

The role of James calls for more acting than dancing – a brief solo in Act I, a couple of diagonals and some show-off leaps in Act II – but Baryshnikov gives such passion, such vitality to the role that one is held spellbound. As James his face is pale, dreaming, somehow haunted when he wakes to find the Sylphide beside him; then suddenly the concentration of emotion in the body bursts forth. Gesture is vivid, electric in speed, thrilling in pulse and clarity. He turns on Madge, the witch, with a ferocity that goes to the very heart of the drama; the interpolated solo in the group festivities startles by its intensity, so exuberant is it, so faultless in finish, and withal, still in character.

In Act II there is a gaiety of spirit that is matched by the buoyant exposition of the dances. Of course Baryshnikov can jump and beat to dazzle an audience; what is so important is the sense of emotional fantasy that colours each perfect step. The part stretches him not at all technically, and both he and Makarova can be seen to be in need of more space, and more spacious orchestral tempi, but with both there is the sense of great artistry uncompromisingly concentrated upon their roles. It is this totality in interpretation, that made **La Sylphide** so uniquely satisfying to watch. ∎

Natalia Makarova
Kirov Ballet

Onegin

FT
FINANCIAL
TIMES

Kirov Theatre, Leningrad

7th February 1989

THE EXQUISITE INTERIOR of the Kirov Theatre – its decoration of blue, cream and gold as harmonious and aristocratic as its proportions – could not have held another spectator on Wednesday night. Buzzing with excitement, the house seemed poised on the edge of cheers as on the edge of its seats, to welcome back a much-loved daughter. The Leningrad public had been aware for some weeks that Natalia Makarova was coming home. Outside the theatre, members of the Kirov Ballet were stopped and questioned about when and how she was returning, and what she would be dancing. And as a guest of the Leningrad Documentary Film Festival, Makarova last week returned to her native city.

After her 19 years in the West, this was an extraordinary example of *glasnost*, and recognition of her importance as a Russian artist. But there was also the need for her to be seen in the proper frame for her art, the theatre and company in which she had been reared and to which she brought such renown both before and after her decision to stay in the West. Her reunion with the Kirov Ballet in London last summer, in the second act adagio from **Swan Lake**, testified to affectionate mutual understanding. Her return to the Kirov stage itself was the final and logical step in this act of reconciliation.

After the interval the theatre became pitch dark: there were no orchestra lights, since the divertissements were all performed to tape. The curtains parted, and there was Makarova

seated at Tatyana's little table, penning her letter to Onegin. Cheers, of course, but the wrapt, girlish figure held the house utterly, and as Alexander Sombart (who accompanied Makarova to Leningrad as her partner) stepped through the mirror and the duet went its impassioned way, Makarova spoke Pushkin's lyrics to an audience who loved them as much as she did, and a great dancer came home. Not in one sense, that she had ever been away, for as we know in the West, her art has been a constant advocate of Leningrad training, a witness to its integrity of style and beauty when we could not see Leningrad's ballet.

The *pas de deux* ended; the storm broke in cheers and shouts and curtain-calls and flowers, with Makarova moved to tears. But these she had to save for the second duet – Tatyana's parting from Onegin. In Tatyana's farewell to Onegin, Makarova's performance was magical. Her body cleaving the air in Sombart's arms – his partnering and dramatic sensibility both superb – she caught at the ballet's heart and at the heart of her audience. Not, said the cognoscenti, since Anna Pavlova made her last visit to St Petersburg in the summer of 1914, had the public so welcomed back a ballerina. On that occasion Alexander Plescheyev, doyen of Russian critics, had written of "the fusion of her talent and the spectators, which subjugates and totally enthralls them. Such is her power. She speaks to us all; everyone feels for her". These words describe exactly Makarova's effect on her audience on Wednesday, as, surely, in every

performance of her career, and they explain
the seemingly endless applause that greeted
her at the duet's end, the congratulatory
speeches from the stage, and Makarova's own
words of joy at being back in the cradle of
her art. ∎

Natalia Makarova (Tatyana)
Alexander Sombart (Onegin)

Irek Mukhamedov
The Royal Ballet

FINANCIAL
TIMES

Royal Opera House, Covent Garden

**5th March
1996**

**Irek Mukhamedov
(c. 1996)**

GISELLE, RETURNED on Thursday to the Royal Ballet repertory, might be re-titled Albrecht on those nights on which Irek Mukhamedov appears. So powerful is his interpretation, so shot through with the storms and fevers of Romanticism, that the ballet's interest shifts from Giselle's tragedy to Albrecht's journey from unthinking youth to redeemed hero.

It has ever been the mark of Mukhamedov's genius to convey feeling with extraordinary clarity. At the Bolshoi, his repertory tended towards the archetypal heroics required of the Soviet danseur, though his Spartacus and Ivan the Terrible were compelling studies of character in crisis. It is the MacMillan repertory which he gained when he joined the Royal Ballet that has shown us the full extent of his dramatic gifts. Tremendous scale in statement; subtlest effects in expression; absolute conviction in every least action. In *Giselle*, we see these qualities revivify an old and somewhat careworn text.

His Albrecht with the Bolshoi was ardent. In Peter Wright's scrupulous staging at Covent Garden – almost too detailed in such incidents as the Courland hunting party, some of whose members are plainly on day-release from Broadmoor – Mukhamedov has an ideal frame for his portrait.

This Albrecht is no princely cad. His passion for *Giselle* is real, but we sense the social distance that separates them: Mukhamedov

amused by peasant legend; courtly attitudes glimpsed behind the simple manner. The characterisation is so "understood", so sensitive in detail, that we trace his emotions at every instance. The crisis when the hunt appears; his despair as Giselle's reason fails, are done with a High Romantic ardour. It is no small indication of Mukhamedov's talent that he marries an expressive naturalism with the proper conventions of performance-style for *Giselle*.

For the Albrecht of the second act – haunted; remorseful – every praise. Mukhamedov is here the Romantic hero imagined by Berlioz or Géricault. His final pose, one arm raised to hold the last flower Giselle has given him, is profoundly true, a central image of the ballet as we understand it. Ironically, in the original *Giselle* of 1841, Albrecht was led out of the forest and back to the real world by his fiancée at curtain fall. We know better now.

With Mukhamedov we see, in sum, a uniquely grand interpretation. My own memories of the great Albrechts of the past 50 years, back to Dolin and Lifar, cannot summon up a more commanding or more intensely expressed reading. The portrait is superb: dance-drama at its finest. ∎

L'Après-midi d'un faune
The Prodigal Son

Rudolf Nureyev
The Royal Ballet

Royal Opera House,
Covent Garden

WE MAY ASSOCIATE Rudolf Nureyev with all the paraphernalia of the "star", with temperament and sweeping cloaks, technical razzamatazz and companies like the Australian Ballet ensuring an audience by showing him in his own stagings of the classics, but he is also – and I suspect that this is sometimes overlooked – an artist of deep perceptions, and an integrity that no amount of adulation and fan-worship has corrupted. Against all odds, even against his own legend, he will give performances that owe nothing to his star persona and everything to his artistry.

Just so last night, when he appeared as Robbins' **Faun** and Balanchine's **Prodigal**, and was remarkable in both. His Faun is a very individual interpretation which, because of his physical allure, somehow narrows the gap that exists between the Nijinsky creation and Robbins' purification of it. He suggests the eroticism (and something of the poses) that we associate with the original – and how fascinating it would be to see him in it – yet he maintains the modernity of Robbins' conception. The afternoon air in the studio is more charged than is usual; the meeting with the girl (Jennifer Penney, beautifully dulcet in mood) is less cool in emotional temperature; but the spell is not broken, and the imagery is very potent.

Even more powerful is his reading of **The Prodigal Son**, and more richly detailed. The youthful ardour, straining to escape his father's domination, is sharply portrayed;

his passion for the Siren is compounded of inexperience and fascination – seated on the table with her he barely brushes her hand with his, and draws away as if her flesh burnt him – and the last laboured return home is infinitely pathetic. It is, on any terms, an exceptional, totally convincing performance. ∎

31st October 1973

Rudolph Nureyev
(Prodigal Son)
(1973)

Evgenia Obraztsova
Mariinsky Ballet

The Sleeping Beauty

FT
FINANCIAL
TIMES

Royal Opera House,
Covent Garden

**18th August
2009**

Evgenia Obraztsova
(Aurora)

THE MARIINSKY BALLET has brought us a new Aurora, enchanting in manner, brilliant in means, to illuminate Petipa's sleeping princess and the company's handsomely traditional staging which tells her story. Evgenia Obraztsova is youthful, lovely and, by today's standards, might be thought petite.

She has a beautiful physique, an exquisitely placed head on a long neck, and she came on stage on Friday night, when **The Sleeping Beauty** completed the Mariinsky repertory for this all-too-short season, armed with dazzling skills. Her feet sparkle in small steps, and she charms the choreography – as she charms us – with that stylistic clarity, that inevitability of phrasing and pose, which are the product of St Petersburg's long and golden traditions. She made her entrance for Aurora's birthday, and won the audience by the sweetness and grace of her temperament and the freshness of dancing unclouded by mannerism, natural (in these most unnatural of circumstances) as a bird throwing off impossible roulades of notes. Thereafter the role, which can freeze a ballerina's nerves, so absolute are its demands upon security of technique, was Obraztsova's.

The Aurora of the first act was radiant in feeling as in step, though (to carp for one critical micro-second) I wish she had looked at her suitors as she took those death-trap balances. Aurora's Vision in the hunting scene (which was filleted of any sense through concerns about its length, I hazard, and became a miserable travesty of what the Mariinsky knows it should be) was danced with delicately subdued emotion.

The Aurora of the wedding was all assurance and grace, Obraztsova admirably conveying the necessary grandeur of the occasion, and both the artist's acceptance of the need for the very best kind of fireworks for her public and the exigencies of St Petersburg style at this moment. Here was a most beguiling reading of the greatest challenge a ballerina can know. ∎

Don Quixote

Royal Opera House, Covent Garden

FT

FINANCIAL
TIMES

**13th August
2007**

LET US NOT EXAGGERATE, but six stars seem to be in order. I have not known so euphoric an evening at the ballet for a long time: the audience agog; bursts of applause and gasps of amazement during solos; a delight in the dancing matched by a buoyant response from the stage; cheers, yet more cheers.

The occasion? The Bolshoi Ballet's sunny production (by Alexey Fadeyechev) of that unlikely corner of old Spain, **Don Quixote,** with Natalia Osipova as Kitri – we rejoiced in her debut last year – and the 18-year-old wonderboy Ivan Vasiliev as her Basilio. And Pavel Sorokin taking the score at a spanking pace: no time for dither, but a spring to every step, the ensemble fired with joy.

No wonder we bayed for more, and gasped as Vasiliev did impossible things high in the air. Osipova spun and flashed over the stage, and raised the stakes with lighter and yet lighter and prettier leaps. That divinity Yuliana Malkhasyants tore into every known passion (and some I'd never heard of) in her Gypsy dance in Act 2.

To details: Osipova has breathtaking *ballon*, elevation and speed. The dance takes to the skies, races over the stage, its shape enhanced by the youthful freshness of her skills, its effects made vivid by her evident delight in bravura. Character is lovingly shown with a generosity of feeling, a delicious warmth of emotion. Not since Plisetskaya and Maximova have we seen so adorable a Kitri, and never

one so divinely destined to claim the role as her own. This Kitri can do no wrong.

Vasiliev is young, of medium height, already phenomenal in elevation. ("Come down!" as his teachers said to the soaring Nijinsky). He can pirouette for as long as he wishes. His line is clear; academic forms of dance are respected. He is ardent, eager, already an actor to charm us (and Kitri) and generous, in manner, in use of his skill. He faces the danger of turning into a "trick" dancer, of exhausting his gifts before they are matured. His salvation is that the Bolshoi has shown him how tricks may be turned into balletic and dramatic art. His Basilio is a happy, warm-hearted reading.

It was a glorious evening in every respect, and we owe profound thanks to everyone on stage. The Bolshoi owes it to posterity to film this cast in live performance.
* * * * * (and an extra * for the blessed pair). ∎

**Natalia Osipova (Kitri)
Ivan Vasiliev (Basil)
(2007)**

Lyudmila Semenyaka
Kirov Ballet

Raymonda

FINANCIAL
TIMES

Royal Opera House, Covent Garden

**4th August
1986**

LYUDMILA SEMENYAKA, in Friday night's performance of *Raymonda*, had the advantage of Alexey Fadeyechev as her partner. Fadeyechev, a strong dancer, a clear stage personality and an excellent partner, gave the Crusader hero a sense of manly dignity – every Bolshoi danseur seems able to make a single bold arm gesture and command our respect, as he does that of the characters he addresses on stage – and provided the secure and responsive support needed by Semenyaka's lustrous dancing.

In Semenyaka's performance we see a culminating statement about the Russian classic dance. There is, first of all, a ravishing physique. The head is ideally placed on the long neck, a pure line running through her body so that, in the simplest position, with one leg extended behind her, we trace the exquisite rightness of academic rule in the harmonious continuity of an ideal shape, fruit of the Vaganova schooling in which she was educated.

We see, too, a use of arms more generous, more responsive to richness of *contraposto* than is usual even with Russian dancers; at every moment Semenyaka's arms crown her movement, whether by the purity of their form or, as in Raymonda's last act variation, by playing with phrasing, teasing us with the idea of the danseuse as Hungarian heroine, and showing with a lovely daring the charm with which this solo may be presented by a ballerina wholly mistress of her art.

There is, above all, an inevitability and a grandeur about her account of this role – not famous for its dramatic nuance – which speak of Russian dedication to the art of classical dancing, and a loving comprehension of what 19th century repertory and language must mean today. (This is the quality which distinguishes Yury Grigorovich's version of *Raymonda*, making it superior to any other I have seen).

Semenyaka's interpretation, which lives sublimely through her account of the dances rather than through any spurious emoting, can be seen as the summation of the role's history in Russia since the ballet's creation in 1898. From Pierina Legnani, the first Raymonda, by way of such *ballerine* as Marina Semyonova and Natalya Dudinskaya, the process of purification and enriching through experience has resulted in the style as well as the fact of Semenyaka's performance.

Thus the adagio in the Vision Scene on Friday night was to be hailed as an amazing statement about classic ballet itself: profoundly moving as a display of great schooling, it was flawless in utterance, the dance marvellous in its breadth of scale as in its refinement of means. Anyone fortunate enough to have witnessed this adagio was seeing the classic dance plain.

And everywhere the severest laws of the academic style were made to seem proper, liberating of expression, even happy, through Semenyaka's radiant control of technical effect.

She was light, adorable in the variation with the scarf that Jean has given her: she touched movement with the airiest grace in the pretty solo in Act 2, making it seem like the most fluent coloratura; she revealed a blaze of physical power, seeming borne of long phrases of energy, in the coda to the second act's quintet, covering the stage with a fleetness sprung from the music. Her acute musical sense was also part of the marvel of her last act variation which toyed in enchanting fashion with the steps, the score, and the concept of a Hungarian solo of the tautest rhythms and bewitching charm. The temperament which guided this memorable performance is at once serious and gracious, noble and sincere. The proscenium arch is a huge magnifying glass for character as well as for physical gifts. Through its close-ups, Semenyaka is seen as a great artist who speaks ballet's truth with beauty and the surest understanding. ∎

**Lyudmila Semenyaka
(Raymonda)
(1984)**

Sergei Polunin
The Royal Ballet

Rhapsody

FINANCIAL
TIMES

Royal Opera House,
Covent Garden

**29th March
2011**

THERE IS A PARTICULAR exhilaration in watching a young dancer claim a role with an assurance that says: "This is mine!" There is neither arrogance nor hubris in the matter, simply an identification, an awareness of a proper inheritance and a divine right – not of kings, but of talent that cannot help but assert itself. So with Sergey Polunin in his first appearance in Ashton's **Rhapsody**.

Ashton made **Rhapsody**, which is set to Rachmaninov's Paganini Variations, to celebrate the gifts of Mikhail Baryshnikov, and it is a work of the most skilled construction, subtle musicality, felicitous imagination.

Baryshnikov, all Kirov nobility and youthful power, was a marvel in it. And so, by any standards, is Polunin. About his princely manner, his clear and boldly scaled classic style, his unassailably beautiful dancing, there can be no doubts. The machinery is impeccable, and the central simplicity with which he presents dance is unerring: aristocracy may be a naughty word in our telly-prole age but Polunin dances with an elegant clarity that proclaims the virtues of classic dance as a noble activity for humanity. ∎

Diamonds
Jewels

Bolshoi Theatre, Moscow

25th September 2012

IT WAS THE AMERICAN ballerina Merrill Ashley who told me about Olga Smirnova. A superb Balanchine dancer, Ashley had been in Moscow with the Bolshoi Ballet in June, setting *Diamonds*, the final part of **Jewels**, Balanchine's trilogy exploring the ideas of cities, styles, women dancing. "You must see my ballerina in *Diamonds*. She's prodigious – 19 years old, just graduated from the Vaganova School in Petersburg, and just recruited for the Bolshoi. She has the most exquisite upper-body, and a magical presence".

Rarest praise. So to Moscow last weekend to see **Jewels**, which the Bolshoi is playing at the start of its season, to find Ashley coaching, to be knocked sideways by two performances, and to fall under the spell of Smirnova. The young ballerina makes her entrance in the second movement. The score is Tchaikovsky's third symphony, shorn of its first movement. We are to watch Balanchine's homage to the 19th-century balletic spectacles, those grand Mariinsky machines that brought the ballerina in glory to her partner, the incarnation of brilliant femininity as identified by the classic academic dance. The male dancer enters – last weekend it was the assured and powerful young Semyon Chudin. Then Smirnova far upstage, and the immediate, transfixing effect of a physical talent unique in my by-no-means brief experience. I expected something fascinating, but instead was dazzled by a presence and a manner uniquely lovely and obviously entirely natural. No flummery or conscious craft – just an exquisite physique, ideally schooled, and an indefinable authority.

In ballet, *épaulement* denotes the dancer's ability to turn, bend and shape the placing of the trunk, shoulders, arms, neck and head to produce the subtlest contrasts and oppositions. In Italian art it is *contraposto*, and this is what gives life, veracity and power to a drawn or sculpted position. In classical ballet it turns the academic pose into the beautiful, the fascinating Smirnova, with unaffected grace, offers something that is entirely natural: the simplest position or the grandest action seems marvellously to flower as she states it. And her stage manner is simple, authoritative, gracious and allied to a technique that finds no unease with Balanchine's tremendous dances, but rather brings them to a fascinating life. I saw superb performances by Suzannne Farrell, for whom a fascinated Balanchine made *Diamonds*. Smirnova's radiance, the unaffected nobility of her manner and the charm of her means make the role hers. She creates something magical and it touches the spirit. Not since the earliest performances by Altynai Asylmuratova have I seen so luminous a debut. We have much to hope for. ∎

Olga Smirnova, Semyon Chudin

Jean Babilée
Ballet National De Marseille

FINANCIAL
TIMES

Théâtre du Châtelet, Paris

**23rd May
1983**

Jean Babilée
(Le Jeune Homme)
(1984)

I HAVE SEEN VERY FEW dancers touched by the special afflatus of genius, but among them Jean Babilée holds a place apart. He was a member of that exceptional generation of young talents which came out of France at the war's end, led by Roland Petit, who so exhilarated audiences in performances ablaze with verve, decorative brilliance, elegant sophistication. Babilée's roles encompassed a flawless Bluebird as well as those dramatic characterisations, made for him by Petit and others, which fixed a new and modern image for the male dancer. In **Le Rendezvous, Jeu de Carte, Till Eulenspiegel**, as Nijinsky's **Faun**, in his own **L'amour et son amour**, and supremely in **Le Jeune Homme et la Mort**, Babilée gave uniquely beautiful and thrilling interpretations. Now, four decades on, and at the age of 61, he returned to **Le Jeune Homme** during the current Châtelet season by Roland Petit's Ballet National de Marseille.

I awaited Babilée's appearance on Saturday night prey to inevitable doubts, and with memories still fresh from 1946 of his astounding physical allure, his controlled despair and ferocity as the young man driven to suicide.

There, at curtain rise, was Wakhevich's gloriously dingy set of a Paris garret, the light from the neon signs outside flashing on the window above the bed at stage right. There, reclining on the bed; smoking, looking at his wrist-watch (and with apparently the same black watch-strap) was Babilée. As he got to his feet the body in the dungaree overall was that of a young man, and beneath the shock of hair only slightly silvered was the unchanged predator's profile. As the dance began the magic continued. Of course the years have brought certain technical accommodations – the elasticity and largeness of leaps is diminished, replaced by an iconic clarity – but there remains the same boldness of physical outline, an undimmed power of projection, and what seems an even greater profundity of understanding.

Mitou Manderon, in the yellow dress and black gloves of the girl who is also death, looks slightly tall for Babilée, and she lacks the vicious inevitability that was Nathalie Philippart's. She managed very well, however, in the second scene when death appears in ball-gown and mask to lead the young suicide over the roofs of Paris (the Citroën sign still glowing in the night). But the ballet is of course about Babilée, about his brooding, explosive energy as he falls when the girl kicks at him, his rigid body pivoting on his shoulder. It is, supremely, about his astounding ability to communicate the dance from its imaginative centre. Babilée is Le Jeune Homme still, and still a dancer of untarnished grandeur. ∎

The Prince of the Pagodas

Royal Opera House, Covent Garden

THE PRESENCE OF SYLVIE GUILLEM as a Principal Guest Artist with the Royal Ballet poses problems both for her and for the company. The accommodation of a 'star' to a national troupe essentially reliant upon its own style and resources; the use of an artist from a very different background in technique and manner – these are matters which, after more than a year, still remain to be solved. Integration is not in question, but Sylvie Guillem still looks, for much of the time, an outsider rather than a part of an enterprise, even part of the common fact of an inter-pretation during an evening.

Extraordinary fame came to her very early. She has been the recipient of prizes, adulation, and in her dancing has established an image of an artist able to display the most extreme (and sometimes gymnastic) skills with a nonchalant ease. The vibrant figure poised on one beautifully arched point, with a leg stretched in exaggerated *développé* past her ear, seems a trademark of her dancing worldwide. And like any trademark, it is a quick means of identification rather than a truth. It is Mlle Guillem's misfortune that she should be thought of only in those terms of physical prowess and physical excess: audiences having seen her at her most self-caricaturing, suppose that they have seen Sylvie Guillem. I think that the case is different, and that a far more rewarding artist can be discerned in roles other than the whizz-bang virtuosities of the *Grand Pas Classique* that has become a convenient vehicle for her

(and which she dances, incidentally, with none of the finesse shown by Yvette Chauviré for whom it was made).

Maurice Béjart captured the young Sylvie Guillem with rare skill (as he did the young Eric Vu An) in **Mouvement**, **Rhythme**, **Etude** at the Paris Opéra. Here the flashing potential of her body was made pungently theatrical, and the relative coolness of her dramatic presence did not matter. In the traditional classics, though, her understated emotions have not been replaced by any great stylistic rewards: roles have looked wilful, the dramatic argument ● ● ●

2nd April 1990

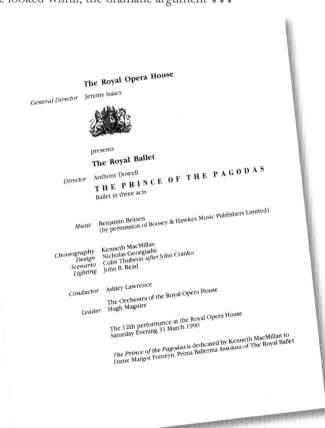

distanced from the body by inexpressive prowess. It was as Ashton's **Cinderella** that Mlle Guillem's talent looked sincere – the disciplines of the text everywhere respected, the role touchingly alive. And, as MacMillan's heroine in **Pagodas** on Friday night, her reading was equally true in feeling. She played the part shyly, with gentle charm, but also with an air of distinction – she was everywhere a princess – and she found the resources of compassion needed to console both her father and the Salamander Prince (Jonathan Cope, on best form). This was not the radiant innocent proposed by Darcey Busell, but a valid portrayal of an introspective, almost secretive girl who blossomed at last in the final duet. During the scene accompanied by the solo violin in Act 2, Mlle Guillem was exquisite in dance and delicately sincere in emotion. Physically the role suits her – though she does not yet have the measure of all its technical nuances – and it is important in asserting her artistry rather than bravura mannerisms that can cloud a rare talent. It was a challenge well met. ∎

...aural effects that sound as if someone is taking to pig-sticking in quite the wrong way.

Far
19th November, 2010

Las Hermanas

Deutsche Oper, Berlin

IT IS THE CURIOUS distinction of the German ballet scene to possess the two ballerinas who, for me, are the most gifted and exciting dancers I have seen in any Western company: Lynn Seymour in Berlin and Marcia Haydée in Stuttgart. Seymour is too well known in London to need any further bouquets here, but Haydée (a contemporary of Seymour and Antoinette Sibley at the Royal Ballet School) has been working for the past seven years with Cranko's company in Stuttgart. Our only proper view of her in London was as the unforgettably beautiful Woman in **Song of the Earth**, but her Stuttgart repertory encompasses all the major classic roles as well as many important creations in Cranko's ballets. During the current Berlin Ballettwoche she is to be seen in two roles that MacMillan has made for her: as the Eldest Sister in **Las Hermanas** and as **The Sphinx** (written for her this year). She also appeared as Anastasia (a part originally created for Seymour) and Aurora in **The Sleeping Beauty**.

I wrote enthusiastically about her in **Las Hermanas** when the Stuttgart Ballet visited the Edinburgh Festival six years ago, but her performance last Saturday in Berlin was, understandably, far superior to that earlier reading. Haydée's technique and dramatic artistry must surely place her at the head of any list of contemporary dancers; she has purity of style, a smooth and effortless classic manner that is totally aristocratic, and her dancing is imbued with a radiant poetic presence. In **Las Hermanas** the role of the

Marcia Haydée
Ballet of the Deutsche Oper, Berlin

8th November 1968

Eldest Sister is a study in frustration, in youth freezing into barren, embittered middle-age. In a sexuality terrified of itself and its expression, brought into conflict with the sweaty animalism of the fiancé chosen for her.

The ballet is also a picture of emotional claustrophobia, with a house of women riven with jealousies between the tragic eldest girl, the envious third sister, and the luscious youngest sister who is eager for the brutal sensuality of the prospective fiancé. Haydée's performance is superlatively good: she can suggest all the repressions of the sad creature declining into despairing spinsterhood, the struggle between her desire for sexual fulfil-ment and her shocked disgust at the fiancé's demands, and finally and most movingly, her agony when she discovers that her young sister has accepted the man's advances.

It is a role of considerable complexity, set in dancing that makes unusual technical demands on its interpreter, but Haydée brings to it so complete a rightness, so touching and fierce a realisation, that it marks her as a great dramatic artist as well as a great dancer. Her body, at first rigid with frustration, achieves a curious blossoming, still tense but more frenzied, as she is faced with her fiancé; then, with the destruction of all her hopes, she conveys the turning inward at all her feelings that now become a furious anger. She makes one last desperate run to the window that symbolises her lost chance of happiness, and then isolation and total despair freeze her body.

It is a heart-rending interpretation, couched in dancing that has amazing neurotic force in its sharp angles in which the beautiful lyricism of her technique is entirely transformed.

It is a cardinal rule of criticism that only an actual performance may be reviewed – a rule that I am happy to break, since I was privileged to see Haydée rehearsing both Aurora and as Anastasia. Even in the bare surroundings of a working rehearsal, Haydée thrilled me more as Aurora than any dancer since Fonteyn. The effortless grace of her dancing, the clarity and eloquence of her statement of Petipa's inventions, the excellently reasoned development of her interpretation were magnificent, illuminating the choreo-graphy with a poetic freshness that yet remained classically pure. She must be seen in this role in London. ∎

Marcia Haydée, Birgit Kiel and Ilse Weidmann (1966)

Zizi Jeanmaire

FINANCIAL
TIMES

The Sporting Club, Monte Carlo

**31st July
1978**

I DON'T KNOW WHEN or how Renée Jeanmaire became finally transformed in "Zizi", but the lightning flash of the name suits her wonderfully well. The double nature of her art – dancer and goddess of the Music Hall – is entirely reconciled in her show which I saw last week at the Monte Carlo Sporting Club. Only a dancer, because dancers are the most adaptable of theatre people, could encompass what Jeanmaire does, from songs delivered with a fine emotional flourish to a final apotheosis amid a cascade of ostrich plumes – pink ones, of course.

London remembers and loves Jeanmaire first and foremost as a dancer, supremely as Carmen in her husband Roland Petit's ballet, and she has remained true to something very like the boyishly bobbed hair that Carmen first wore. Jeanmaire the chanteuse, the divinity of the stage spectacular, with all the trappings of fur and feather and frenzied chorus limbs, we have seen only once when her "show" came to London a decade ago. It is Paris and Broadway and Hollywood which best know Jeanmaire as the incarnation of all we think of as Parisian chic, wit, verve.

These are still the qualities of the essential Zizi: in the Monte Carlo show, devised by Roland Petit, and with the backing of a group of boys from Petit's Ballet de Marseille, she is singer, dancer, star – and quite irresistible. The first appearance is in a cloak of feathers – Saint Laurent dresses her throughout in black and silver – which is thrown off to reveal a

little pailletted tunic, the vivid, magnificent smile, and impeccable, witty legs.

There follow the songs – of love frustrated, adoring – which Zizi sends out into the world with all the proper semblances of despair and joy, but given an extra edge of intensity because gesture is so apt and controlled, and because the dancer's body

The Courland Hunt

was tricked out in barmy costuming and became the Sodom Amateur Dramatic Society in Merrie England.

Giselle
1st June, 2000

number with Luigi Bonino (a fine soloist from the Marseille Ballet) in which a dinner date turns into an adagio dance; and as a final explosion comes her celebrated **Mon truc en plumes**. This is Zizi *in excelsis*, with ten boys, each armed with an enveloping pink ostrich-feather fan, to surround her with a foam of plumage from which, like a Venus of the Music Halls, she seems to be born.

Her exuberance in this, a kind of whooping, urchin glee at moments, the voice ringing out as the boys dash after her, or hide her, or suddenly fall away to reveal their incandescent star, is a magical combination of huge fun and vast stylishness. London could not provide the rockets bursting over the sea from Monte Carlo harbour which preceded Zizi's appearance, but when she comes to London, as come she must, Zizi will bring her own fireworks. ∎

Zizi Jeanmaire,
(*Mon truc en plumes*)
(1995)

doesn't waste a single effort: the way in which she "choreographs" these songs is exemplary. The dance numbers are electric. In white tie and tails she offers **Just a Gigolo** with all the style in the world, and in English: in another St Laurent outfit she joins what I am sure are known as "ses boys" in **Peanuts**, and seems somehow to get herself involved as a passer-by in **I left my hat in Tahiti**. She has a

Niels Kehlet
Royal Danish Ballet

La Sylphide

FT
FINANCIAL
TIMES

Royal Theatre, Copenhagen

**8th April
1974**

Sorella Englund (Sylphide)
Niels Kehlet (James)
(1974)

LONDON FIRST SAW Niels Kehlet as James in *La Sylphide* two years ago, when he was a guest with the Canadian National Ballet, but inexplicably it was not until Saturday afternoon that he danced the role with his parent company. His performance is of quite exceptional merit. Celebrated as a technician in whom we may appreciate all the finest qualities of Bournonville training – a big jump, flawless beats, easy *ballon* – Kehlet also boasts that other quality of the Danish school, strong dramatic projection. In roles as diverse as Gennaro in **Napoli** and the mad teacher of **The Lesson**, or Tetley's moon-struck *Pierrot*, his identification with the part seems total, and totally convincing. When Oehlenschläger first saw Bournonville dance he said, "Surely he is speaking", and in Saturday's *La Sylphide* Kehlet's intensity of expression, his clarity of presentation, deserved the same comment.

James is a complex character; as with Siegfried in **Swan Lake**, we see the birth of an obsessive passion that is ultimately to lead to tragedy, but the structural simplicity of the earlier ballet and Bournonville's concern for the male dancer's identity mean that the role is both better written and more rewarding. And it is Kehlet's distinction that he can show us every detail of the Romantic conflict between the real world and the Sylphide's fantastic realm that is the whole matter of James's personality. He finds in the character ardour, shadows and currents of regret, innocent joy: in his second meeting with the Sylphide Kehlet's James greets her appearance at the window with arms upraised, then dashed to kneel submissively as she drifts down into the room. When she tries to lure him away, Kehlet marvellously suggests James' reluctance gradually ebbing away as he is caught up in her enchantment, but – suddenly aware of the betrothal ring on his finger – he hesitates, and a noise from within the house and Gurn's return break the spell. Kehlet plays this scene superlatively well; the true Romantic manner is warmed by compelling emotional truth.

Both steps and gesture have this same vividness, and I can best explain it by noting how, in dance and mime, Kehlet establishes

130

Élisabeth Platel
Paris Opéra
Ballet

Palais Garnier,
Paris

FT

FINANCIAL
TIMES

an individual time-scale within a phrase, a form of rubato, that follows a brilliantly fast take-off for a jump or a sequence of leaps with a moment when a position is held longer than can most other dancers. (It is a quality that distinguished Markova's art, where little ritardandos within a phrase brought a beautiful variety of physical impulse). With Kehlet, this produces a vigorous upsweep of movement which catches the eye and then allows it time to savour the central, essential shape of the dance; in mime it means that he is swift to find and hold a pose, an attitude, which speaks clearly of the emotion that has impelled it. The effects thus created are intense, inevitable, but they are set within a larger phrasing so that there is no sense of inanition or unevenness; Kehlet dances in superb spans of activity, and his musicality informs every least action. He is, in sum, a great dancer, and there is ultimately a kind of moral force and integrity to his art that is profoundly moving: it shows, in the truest sense, what Bournonville himself felt about the dancer's calling and expressed in both his ballets and his writing. ∎

WERE WE IN ROME, there would have been white smoke appearing from an Opera House chimney on Friday night, and the cry *"habemus Auroram"*. Élisabeth Platel, making her debut with the Royal Ballet in **The Sleeping Beauty**, gave an interpretation lustrous, beautiful. Three years ago I reported from Paris on her Aurora, when she shone like the best of deeds in the naughtiest of worlds which was the Opéra's maniacally flustered staging. Now, in a production which largely respects Petipa's original, the jewel of her dancing finds a worthy setting.

Watching Miss Platel we see, first of all, ideal schooling. The basis of her art is secure, elegant; her use of it is brilliant in effects and subtle in means. She offers that rare combination of physical exhilaration allied to classic sensibility, so that the life of the role, and of the dance itself, illuminate the formal proportions of her style. Hers is a slender yet expansive physique. Legs flash into highest extensions but also find delicacy for the smallest steps. Arms open out into generous though academically ordered gesture. Her temperament is vivid but unforced, without factitious bravura.

She shows us choreography as have ever done the greatest French exponents of *mélodie* or opera in the knowledge that words and music are indivisible, equally to be respected. (The recent reissue of the wonderful Joachim / Jansen / Desormière *Pelléas* recording tells everything of this manner). So Miss Platel •••

**11th November
1985**

articulates her words – the steps – with exquisite diction, not a syllable lost, not a phrase fudged, integrating them with the melody of choreography and characterisation. Aurora is brought to stage life with exemplary clarity, refinement, and an alert musicality.

The young princess of the first act is radiant, the stage lit with the brightness implicit in her name. The Rose Adagio is sweetly dignified; the variation has a kind of melodious joyfulness; the spindle scene catches all the feeling so potent in the score. The vision of Aurora in Act 2 shows that classic style may melt a little, with yearning arms and movement sustained on a long-breathed legato Miss Platel favours less brusque tempi than our local performers – each nuance of accent and phrase displayed without losing the onward momentum of the dance.

The last act duet was limpid. Miss Platel's line stretching out and ever onward, the harmony and nobility of the classic: dance always respected. A performance, in sum, worthy of Petipa and Tchaikovsky. ∎

Élisabeth Platel (Aurora) (1985)

Le Corsaire *pas de deux*

Royal Festival Hall, London

THE LATTER PART of this week has brought an exceptional piece of dancing to enhance a somewhat workaday Festival Ballet programme.

On Thursday night at the Festival Hall Peter Schaufuss unleashed several different sorts of lightning in that child's guide to what is wrong with ballet, the **Corsaire** *pas de deux*. It is a piece so foolish, so open to every sort of abuse, and so risible in the Tarzanesque posturings that are required of its interpreters, that ideally it needs to be done by Morecambe and Wise.

Failing either of those geniuses, I will settle for Peter Schaufuss, all the more so because he is absolutely cast against type. Nothing in his training or stage persona suits him for the Ethel M. Dellery of the character (to which Nureyev, on the other hand, brings a glossy sexual allure which is exactly right). But Schaufuss, bending and swooping dutifully through the required poses of passion and the occasional obeisance to the beloved, dances the piece with such finesse, such joyous clarity of technique – pure Bournonville in aesthetic as in style – that the heart and eye and mind rejoice.

Peter Schaufuss
London Festival Ballet

FT

FINANCIAL
TIMES

**9th September
1978**

He pulls off marvels of pirouettes – flashing *doubles á la grande seconde* with arms linked over his head: multitudinous turns with one leg in *retiré* which are so exactly with the music that they might be part of the score. In a rocketing circuit of the stage he manages a split at the height of a jump that seems to take him even higher: there are arrowy leaps that are buoyed up by a strong and consistent surge of energy. It is classical dancing of the most exhilarating kind. Of course, Schaufuss is showing off – but with a technical mastery of this excellence, there is nothing else he can do when obliged to appear in tosh. ∎

**Peter Schaufuss
(Le Corsaire)**

John Curry

John Curry
Theatre of Skating

FINANCIAL TIMES

London Palladium

**11th July
1977**

I DID NOT SEE THE FIRST John Curry Theatre of Skating. I had seen the phenomenal virtuoso sweeping the Olympic board clean on television, and in a tedious "spectacular" on the small screen which plainly did him little service, but I recalled that during the past 30 years various other ice-wizards had been hailed as inventors of skating ballet, or as ballerinas of the blades. After which apologia I can report that watching John Curry for the first time at the Palladium on Saturday night was a most rewarding experience.

The show begins quite dreadfully with something called *Le Valse Glace* (sic). Ricardo Drigo's music for **Le Revell de Flore** is mauled

by a pit band: Nadine Baylis has set the affair in an exhibition of deranged garden furniture; hussars in green and girls in pastel flounces glide past, forcing their bodies into what they may suppose are balletic poses. Enter John Curry in white. He is so far ahead of his companions in style and sheer ability that they look even dimmer, though even he cannot surmount a moment, apparently from Giselle Act 2, in which he kneels on the ice while a stalwart lady in pink homes in on him like a homicidal blancmange. It is fiercely depressing, but it is the only mistake in the programme. Thereafter Curry Rules O.K.

What I had not understood from any account of Curry's work is that he is not just the greatest skater in the world – an incontrovertible fact because of his Olympic success – but an extraordinary artist, in the best sense of that word. He has beautiful physique (part of his excellence lies in magnificent, open *ports de bras* and fluent line) and the imaginative and emotional gift that can subordinate skating to an aesthetic ideal and convince us of that ideal's validity.

In **Icarus**, choreographed by John Butler to a Gordon Crosse score, you forget skates and ice, because Curry becomes the tragic figure soaring towards the sun. The language of movement is new; Curry transforms the demotic of skating to create heroic poetry, highly charged and allusive, as Icarus seems to rise ecstatically higher and higher. On mere technical terms Curry avoids the boring

**John Curry (Icarus)
(1977)**

134

Swan Lake

Royal Opera House, Covent Garden

FT
FINANCIAL TIMES

5th November 1971

"static" quality of skating in which an initial burst of energy is – aptly enough – frozen because of the absence of friction between blade and ice. His companions impel themselves across the ice, and one senses the unexpended and stagnant dynamics in their bodies. Curry, by the richness and variety of his skills, takes energy and uses it. Changes in *épaulement*, rhythmic acuteness, and an emotional control over movement quite as fine as his physical assurance, show that skating can, in the hands of a master, be an art of real expressive force. His abilities are so far in advance of those of his colleagues, his ambitions and interpretive powers so much richer, that his becomes the isolation of the truly innovative artist. With his poet's face, and that detachment from the world which always seems to surround the uncanny gliding and spin-fling figure of the skater, Curry appears a unique and mysterious being, and one absolutely not to miss. ▋

WE TEND RATHER to overlook our balletic princes; in the woman's world of 19th century ballet the man was neatly manoeuvered into the background role of partner and porteur. Yet **Swan Lake** – as an immediate example – is far more prince Siegfried's story than it is Odette's, and with the renaissance of the male dancer in this century, the importance of the man's role has been gradually re-established. Last night's return of **Swan Lake** to the Opera House repertory made this point abundantly clear when Anthony Dowell gave a performance of the very finest calibre as Siegfried. He is, of course, a dancer of marvellous gifts – a classicist both noble, elegant and virile, whose every movement conforms to the severest canons of his art. And dancing apart, if I dare put it thus, he now takes the stage with a princely dignity and a sureness in dramatic effects that tell of complete control of every aspect of his craft. His Siegfried is youthful, sensitive; he conveys the romantic melancholy of the role, but also its aristocracy, and in his dancing can express to the full the introspection of the solo at the end of Act I as well as the exultant joy of the ballroom duet. In brief, it is a superb example of male dancing. ▋

Anthony Dowell (Siegfried) (1971)

Margot Fonteyn
The Royal Ballet

FINANCIAL TIMES

Royal Opera House, Covent Garden

**17th March
1972**

Dame Margot Fonteyn,
Swan Lake **curtain call
(1971)**

IF THERE IS ANY single image which evokes the Royal Ballet it is that of Dame Margot Fonteyn in **The Sleeping Beauty**. It is a key image, a crucial one in its implication of classic excellence, and one which I must be pardoned for saying dates back to 1939. And last night it was still blazingly true, and still marvellous.

Great art in the theatre must ultimately defy description: in ballet we can talk of line, musicality, of classic grace, harmony and authority, in speaking of Fonteyn, and the essence of her greatness will escape us. I could, indeed, state quite succinctly that last

night Fonteyn's Aurora was profoundly moving, and then leave well alone, since no words can adequately convey just why her performance was so heartening. Critical duty – and a desire, I suppose, to express my own sense of gratitude – impels me to note that Dame Margot brought a total conviction to the role, that her dancing was marvellously proportioned (no extravagance, but a simplicity that bespeaks complete understanding of the choreography) and a musicality in phrasing that makes the dance a perfect extension of the score.

A few of her effects were more restrained than heretofore, but the over-all shape of the performance, the supreme art that gives the role its glow of life and truth, was superbly in evidence. My programme for the evening bears hastily scribbled remarks about her artistry in the Rose Adagio, about her delicacy of phrasing in the Vision Scene, and about the stylistic rightness of her line for Petipa; but ultimately I must record that Fonteyn dances Aurora by divine right, and still enhances the role.

Rudolf Nureyev was Florimund, producing a stunning variation in the last act despite a lack of rapport with the conductor, and the company performance was fine. But the evening – and the ballet – belonged, as it always has, to Fonteyn. ∎

Stephen Jefferies
The Sadler's Wells
Royal Ballet

Sadler's Wells

**2nd October
1975**

WATCHING STEPHEN JEFFERIES gives one that rare pleasure, and how rare it is, of seeing a male dancer in whom drama and the play of emotion find totally convincing expression. Thus far this week he has placed his unforgettable mark on two contrasted roles: the comic Captain Belaye in **Pineapple Poll**, and last night, Balanchine's **Prodigal**. In both he makes a bid for recognition as our most gifted dramatic male dancer. His Belaye is effortlessly funny, resourceful in comedy – the aghast glance or the dandified nod of his head as he dons admiral's uniform, marvellously apt and true: his Prodigal, a creature of puppyish, unshaped passion and eagerness achieves great pathos at the ballet's end. Sustaining the characterisations is a strong dance intelligence which moulds and phrases movement to maximum effect – his actions seem guided by a complete appreciation of the dynamic outline of a dance. But the imprint of greatness – which Jefferies certainly has – lies in his ability to make gesture an integral part of the choreography.

In the first scene of **Prodigal Son** Jefferies prepares the key image, in which the youth beats his fist on his thigh, by a frustrated tapping of his hand upon the gate that leads away from his father's house. With the Drinking Companions in the second scene he confronts them as a young puppy might when faced with a new and unfamiliar object. Here, as throughout the ballet, the vivid dramatic response to a situation springs from within the dance: the whole body is involved – eyes, hands, the turn of the head, are part of a uniquely communicative procedure which speaks with tremendous intensity. The closing sequence when the young man returns home is most beautiful in its suggestion of remorse – the figure dragging itself towards John Auld's nobly restrained Father telling everything of the Prodigal's shame. ∎

Akram Khan
Akram Khan Company

FINANCIAL TIMES

Purcell Room, London

16th April 2003

Akram Khan (*Gnosis*)
Svapnagata Festival, London
(2009)

AKRAM KHAN HAS BEEN choreographer in residence on the South Bank for the past two years. He has done splendid things, not least in those creative essays that seek to build a bridge between his Kathak roots and his contemporary dance interest. Now his tenure is ended, but – merited recognition of his gifts – he will become the first dancer to be appointed associate artist of the Royal Festival Hall. Hurrah for him.

And even more cheers for his closing performances over the week's end at the Purcell Room. In these he shows himself as a virtuoso and notably imaginative artist in Kathak dance. Khan's brilliance in this style is beyond question. Lightning speed. Gesture that pours from him with the richest variety of accent and impulse. An acute ear in those fascinating "conversations" that take place between him and the tabla player (the dazzling-fingered Partha Sarathi Mukherjee), where stamping feet and flickering movement respond to (or goad on) the no less bravura drumming. These exchanges seem both improvisatory and structured: the two artists know how their shared caprices and cadenzas can reflect on and elaborate a dynamic idea, rallies in an exquisite match where the volley is all.

Khan appears in three big dances. In the first, his own **Eleven**, he intersperses explanatory commentary between those bursts of movement where his honey-coloured figure flings gesture into the air, hummingbird-fast or sinuously shaped as if poured slowly from his torso. Khan has that rarest of dance gifts, the ability to alter speed and time itself. He can do the same thing with gesture: in variety of speed and impulse, in contrasting savours of dynamic, he enraptures the eye.

In a more sombre piece, **Ronin** by Gauri Sharma Tripathi, he becomes the warrior Arjuna from the *Mahabharata*. It is a dark solo, marked also by Khan's powerful stampings, the anklet-puttee of bells on each leg telling of his rhythmic command. And in a final **Anandam** (by Sri Patap Prawar) we watch something not unlike those closing (and most rewarding) sequences in a flamenco show, when the god descends, the dance seizes the dancer, and the intoxication of movement (and of bravura skill) burns through the body. So with Khan. He is charming, responsive to his musicians (who are very fine) and then – whether spinning like a dervish, possessed by a rhythm, or drawing prodigious shapes in the air – we see an artist of rare gifts, transcendent, wonderful. ∎

Checkmate

Royal Opera House, Covent Garden

An Appreciation

TALENT-SPOTTING is a perennial occupation for ballet-goers; among the crowd of swans, sylphides, fairies, and friends of the heroine, there is always a dancer who will stand out by reason of technique or a special quality of movement. In the past few years we have watched the emergence of Monica Mason to soloist roles with constant pleasure. She has special gifts that are unusual in Royal Ballet dancers, gifts which were only fully to be appreciated when Kenneth MacMillan cast her as the Chosen Virgin in **Rite of Spring** last year. Chief among them is an extraordinary weight of movement, a quality of muscular intensity and strength which was amazingly effective for the superhuman nature of the role; but Mason is also a very musical dancer, and one with a dramatic power which creates consistently meaningful images.

When these qualities are brought, as they were last night, to the part of the Black Queen in **Checkmate** the result is most rewarding. This Queen was a figure of hypnotic force, menacing, inhuman, a creature of tremendous power. The femininity of the character was not stressed overtly, the Red Knight seemed always the victim of a superior personality rather than of his own feelings for a woman, evidently a deliberate conception of the part, since we know from Miss Mason's performance as a gipsy in **Two Pigeons** that she can be lusciously feminine.

The interpretation, for me, was the most satisfying that I have seen, with new life brought to the part: the duel with the Knight had a greater inevitability than ever before, and the Red King's death took on the appearance of a sacrifice to a goddess. ∎

7th March 1963

Monica Mason (Black Queen) (1971)

Steven McRae
The Royal Ballet

La Fille mal gardée

FT
FINANCIAL
TIMES

Royal Opera House, Covent Garden

**30th October
2010**

STEVEN MCRAE APPEARED on Saturday night as Colas, the ardent young farmer who loves Lise, the wayward heroine of Ashton's pastoral masterpiece *La Fille mal gardée*. I do not recall a more dazzling account of the role in many years – not, perhaps, since its creation by David Blair 50 years ago.

What distinguishes McRae's performances, and his artistic personality, is the academic clarity, the vivid energies and – rarissime – the sense of an entire command of the forces that form his dancing. Outstanding dance talent is proclaimed in the way that temperament as well as schooling can sign a role, even a step, and give it an enduring theatrical value. McRae has a clear-cut, sharply defined identity on stage, an energy both physical and psychic that burns his presence on choreography, gives it tight focus, a powerful shape. In this he resembles, as no other dancer I have seen since, the great dancer-choreographer of the Ballets Russes era, Léonide Massine. Massine was no classical virtuoso, but he made roles for himself in which he blazed with dramatic and dynamic force: you may catch a glimpse of his presence in *The Red Shoes*, where he lights up the film.

Like Massine, McRae inhabits a role with exhilarating physical skill, and the choreography shines with fresh, even startling brilliancy. (The Royal Ballet might revive Massine's enchanting *La Boutique Fantasque*: Massine's own role as the Cancan dancer is ideal for him).

McRae's Colas is a charmer, adoring his Lise (Roberta Marquez, giving the happiest interpretation I have known from her) and cutting the shapes of the choreography with unfailing muscular verve: the dance seems alive with a new urgency, an exhilarating appreciation of its possibilities. Here is a prodigious reading, but one that never oversteps the bounds of Ashton's pastoral vision.

Other performances are no less enjoyable: I think Ludovic Ondiviela a fine and touching (and merry) Alain, and Philip Mosley a Simone who is splendidly true in understanding the rules as well as the delights of a travesty role, and in the clog-dance offering that virtuosity which Stanley Holden, its great original, showed. And Daniel Capps conducts the score with love, good sense, wit. A performance to treasure. ∎

Steven McRae (Colas)
La Fille mal gardée
(2015)

Edward Watson
The Royal Ballet

FT
FINANCIAL
TIMES

Royal Opera House,
Covent Garden

**8th February
2008**

**Edward Watson (Woyzeck)
(2008)**

EDWARD WATSON is a male dancer without precedent in the history of the Royal Ballet. In my long experience of the company, we have never before been shown a danseur of such penetrating and subtle power, one who can so grandly capture and convey the inner life of a role, its choreographic and dramatic reason.

These are bold words, and I do not forget the performances of such superb artists as David Wall and Stephen Jefferies, of Mukhamedov, of those men who were the backbone of the company in its early years. But Watson, intensely musical, intense in the shapes he makes, in the response he gives to a ballet's emotional world, brings a purity of means, almost an effacement of self, rare in male dancers who must sustain a major role. He is not for those old and honoured princely assignments where the man is the discreet support for the ballerina. But in

ballets where feeling must drive and define a portrait (as with his searing Rudolf in **Mayerling** or his mad dancing master in **The Lesson**) and in plotless choreography (such as Balanchine's **Four Temperaments**) where the lines of the dance must be made intelligible to us. Watson displays phenomenal gifts to superlative effect.

On Saturday afternoon (at a godless 12.30pm, and in a triple bill of **Chroma**, MacMillan's **Different Drummer** and **Rite of Spring**, indigestible enough to give an ostrich heartburn). Watson was prodigiously good. Wayne McGregor's **Chroma** offers a sequence of dance ideograms where movement turns in on itself, then escapes with a wiry determination. In Watson's performance, we saw how energy coursed through his body, touching every muscle, contorting his frame. What might in other performers have seemed either contrived or tiresome acquired a fascination and purpose through his ability to savour its every convolution.

The revival of MacMillan's **Different Drummer**, an exploration of Büchner's Woyzeck, brings back one of choreography's most adventurous studies in human distress. Very strongly cast (Leanne Benjamin as Marie, Martin Harvey as the Drum Major, Thiago Soares as the Captain, Bennet Gartside as Andres), it was dominated by Watson's soul-tearing portrayal of Woyzeck as victim of life, of peasant faith and super-stition and military brutality, and ultimately of his own self. Watson shows us every

anguish, every defeat, every deceived hope and eventual fury, that MacMillan identifies in the character and shows them with vast imaginative resource. (I think only in the late, last **Judas Tree**, which came a decade after **Drummer**, did MacMillan so probe and drive dance to such extreme expressive means).

Watson's Woyzeck, pale, vulnerable, accepting brutality as his daily bread, denied hope, cut off from happiness, Christ-like in the ritual necessity of his sufferings (and MacMillan shows us Woyzeck's thorn-crowned double), must finally rebel. Watson takes us on this terrible journey, seizing on every image MacMillan has given him and extracting their every least suggestion of dramatic illumination: seeking to erase his own footprints, watching Marie with their child and seeing her betray him, and finally slashing ferociously at her body before his own suicide. His performance, embedded in choreography and score, tremendous in the imaginative power of its physical outlines (like something from Goya's "Disasters of War"), is shattering. It is one of greatest I have ever seen from a Royal Ballet artist, not least in its command of line and dynamics. It demands to be filmed. ∎

Serge Lifar

Icare: Remembering Serge Lifar

The Journal of the Society for Dance Research
Vol. 20, No. 2

Winter 2002

ON 15 DECEMBER 2000 THE 'CARNET DU JOUR' IN *LE FIGARO*, WHICH FEATURES OBITUARY NOTICES, CARRIED THE FOLLOWING TEXT:

Pour le quatorzieme anniversaire du rappel a Dieu de notre tres cher et inoubliable / SERGE LIFAR / le grand artiste toujours present dans nos memoires / ce vendredi 15 decembre 2000, une pieuse pensee est demandee aux admirateurs et amis fideles.

It was signed *'Lillan Ahlefeld'*. The Countess Ahlefeld-Laurvig was the companion of Lifar's later years, and the notice prompted memories of a man whom I admired as dancer, choreographer, director of a magnificent troupe, writer, theoretician about dancing, collector. The dominant fact in Lifar's life was his passion for ballet. This had its origins in his own history – as emigre youth, fleeing Kiev in the early days of Soviet rule; as immature dancer whose enthusiasm and beauty won Diaghilev's attention; then as avidly receptive pupil, whose willingness to work and learn won Diaghilev's patronage. It was Lifar, quite as much as Nijinsky, who can be accounted the icon of male dancing in Diaghilev's aesthetic. As Lifar's powers were shaped by Cecchetti's teaching, so were they exploited in the late creations of the Ballets Russes. He was the perfect Art Deco hero amid the gleaming talc of La Chatte's settings, borne triumphant on the shoulders of a male ensemble, Balanchine's choreography allying him with the sublime Olga Spessivtseva. In the same year (1926) he had been cast

opposite Tamara Karsavina in Nijinska's **Romeo et Juliette**. The significance of this modish work lay in Diaghilev's decision to pair the 21-year-old Lifar with Karsavina, who was twice his age: the new male star linked with the adored ballerina of the earliest seasons of the Ballets Russes had an implicit reference to Lifar as successor to Nijinsky. When **La Chatte** was staged, Diaghilev told *Le Figaro*:

My joy is all the greater in that, having begun twenty years ago with Pavlova and Nijinsky, I have now reached Spessivtseva and Lifar. The former have become myths. The latter, very different from their predecessors, stand before us and are waiting to pass into legend. That too flattering legend of the Ballets Russes.

Lifar's apotheosis came in the final seasons of the Ballet Russes, as Balanchine used Lifar's physical lustre in **Apollo** and his dramatic urgency in **Prodigal Son**. With these ballets his image was to be imprinted upon public taste as a symbol of gifted and beautiful youth. This was the young man – aged 24 – who faced the crises attendant on Diaghilev's death in 1929. He was armed with his Diaghilev education, his intellectual curiosity, his renown. He had already made one ballet. He had strength of character, but little occasion to test himself in the bleak milieu of ballet after Diaghilev. Like Markova at this same time, he might have felt that the world had ended. Lifar's resilience, his intelligence, an undeniable pride, were to stand him in good stead. What followed was the re-birth of ballet in France. At the invitation of Jacques Rouche, the Paris Opéra's director, Lifar became first-dancer, then ballet-master. His task was to revitalise the company, to overcome entrenched attitudes and, quite as obdurate, such dubious privileges of the *abonnés* as their right to enter the Foyer de la Danse, whose fiefdom it had become. Lifar's energy and dedication, a growing reputation as an iconoclast, enabled him to institute reform, to open windows on to a more generous dance-style, notably in his *cours d'adage* for the leading dancers. He came to the Opéra a creative novice; the passage of the 1930s saw him acquire assurance and recognition. He was independent-minded as a creator, and his ideal was to restore to the choreographer's art a primacy and an unquestioned significance which is more to the taste of our times than it was of the 1930s. His confession *fidei* was *Le manifeste du choregraphe* of 1935, in which he proposed laws about the independence of choreography. These may now seem vehement, but in the light of the Diaghilev repertory in which Lifar came of age, his attitudes are explained. Among his propositions:

We cannot, should not, dance everything. Ballet must remain closely linked to dance itself: ballet cannot be the illustration of any other art. Ballet should not borrow its rhythmic shape from music. Ballet can freely exist without musical accompaniment. When a ballet is closely linked to its score, the rhythmic base must be dictated by the choreographer and not the composer. The choreographer must not be the slave of the painter/designer. A free and independent choreographic theatre must be created.

Brave words. In 1935 they were ardent, provocative, wholly characteristic of Lifar – John Martin astutely described him as 'ambitious, hard-working, and tenacious'. And by the end of the 1930s, Lifar's hard work and tenacity had succeeded. The Opéra ballet was transformed, its tight Franco-Italian dance style refreshed by Lifar's insistence upon the more ample neo-classic manner that he propounded in his choreographies. The demands of the old Mariinsky repertoire were also accepted: Lifar revived **Giselle**, and introduced excerpts for **Swan Lake** and **Sleeping Beauty** hitherto unknown to the Opéra's dancers. Within a decade, Lifar had renewed French ballet, lent it his own brilliancy as performer, made it popular for a new and eager audience. And thanks to him, regular ballet evenings had become part of the theatre's schedule.

I first saw Lifar in the immediate post-war years, in Paris and London. He was then in his forties. The bloom of his youthful presence, almost tangible in photographs of his Diaghilev roles – Le beau Serge – was faded. There was instead a figure of hieratic grandeur. A pose from Lifar could seem an essence of a role. This was clear in his finest interpretations – as Albrecht in **Giselle,** as the Faun, as Icarus in his seminal **Icare**. These he invested with extraordinary power. Bravura technique was gone, but as with certain •••

**Serge Lifar
rehearsing *Phèdre*
(1977)**

other great artists, he was so saturated with
the idea of a character that, whatever the
depredations of time, he performed by a kind
of divine right. This was the key to his fervent
Albrecht. Most danseurs of the era – those I
saw in Britain and Europe, and from America
and Russia – were dutifully partners, attentive
of their ballerina, lit by her effulgence but
hardly firing the imagination. Anton Dolin
was the exemplar of this manner, and marvellously so: his vivid artistry was controlled so
that nothing might come between Markova's
reading (exquisite in emotion and technique)
and her audience. It was the 'Nureyev effect'
from 1962 onwards that would start a
reassessment of such roles. Male dancers,
liberated by Nureyev's example – far more
widely seen than Lifar's – were to claim rights
in the old repertory. They insisted, sometimes
too forcibly in production terms, that **Giselle**
and **Swan Lake** were 'about' them as hero.
(There was a flaw to this argument, if the
danseur cared to examine the genesis and
purpose of the old ballet – but ego was more
important than history).

Lifar and Nureyev provide an intriguing
parallel. Both were late starters in ballet. Both
had to make efforts, daring and chancing
their fates, in order to achieve training.
Both fled Russia in quest of opportunity. Both
had an irresistible drive towards fame. Both

were early hailed for their physical and emotional force on stage. Both sought to redress
an imbalance between male and female
dancing, and both were to make choreographies
that insisted upon the male dancer's rights in
performance. And both were to direct the
Ballet of the Paris Opéra, with massive and
beneficial impact upon a moribund institution.

In everything, I saw Lifar command the stage,
the audience. Character and choreography
were understood on those stellar terms, as
they had been in such earlier works as **David
Triomphant**, **Le Chevalier et la Damoiselle** and **Joan
de Sarissa**. Albrecht was grand in calligraphy
of pose and gesture. Most impressive was his
entry in Act 2. The trailing cloak, an extension
of his own grief, may have been copied by
many another artist: few could so convey the
character's remorse through the lilies, held as
if pouring towards the ground from his hands.
(His insistence upon fresh lilies in a pre-war
performance with Markova in New York led
to a stage covered in green slime and a certain
tension between the performers). Lifar's hands
were superbly expressive: there is a drawing
by Tchelichev of Lifar in **Giselle** Act 2, soaring
in a leap as Albrecht fights for survival and,
truthful as is the shape of his body arched in
the air, it is the hands which also tell about
interpretation. Years later, Lifar showed me
fragments from some of his roles. The curve
of the hands holding Albrecht's lilies seemed
an essence of sorrow. Apollo, striking his lyre,
gave gesture a grand sweep. **The Prodigal**,
mimed as he stood against the pillar, arms
and hands held low in despair, was stripped
of his identity as well of his possessions. And
suddenly, during a dinner, the Shopkeeper's
assistant in **Boutique fantasque** came alive as I
had never seen it in performance. Bright-
eyed, merry, Lifar was transformed into the
youth whose early Diaghilev role this had
been. Alicia Markova has told me of Lifar's
irresistible naughtiness in the part, teasing
her as she (the American couple's daughter)
sat, wearing a very proper hat which had
attached to it the child's plaits. Invitation, of
course, for Lifar to try and remove hat and
plaits. This humour surfaced again in a late

146

role – Lifar's portrait of Charlie Chaplin in his **Cinéma** of 1953 at the Opéra. As the Faun (a role in which he first shone with Diaghilev), Lifar's reading had become egocentric, for the nymphs were gone. Instead we saw a creature who moved with sensuous ease, late – debased – Hellenistic in style. It was, though **Icare** of 1935 that seems to me the summation of Lifar's theatrical character. In it he affirmed his beliefs about the primacy of choreography, about the independence of dance from its score, about the possibilities of a developing neo-classic vocabulary, about the significance of male dancing, and about himself as a dancer. Thus, here, dance's dynamics preceded and dictated musical accompaniment: Lifar notated the rhythms of Icare's choreography, entrusted them to his friend, Arthur Honneger, and they were realised by J-E. Szyfer for percussion. The ballet is still compelling, a rite surrounding the sculptural identity of its protagonist. With Lifar as Icarus, belief was total – so intense the feeling he brought to the role.

Lifar sought to renew dance, not least the sacrosanct five positions of the feet. He believed that these denied mobility to the danseuse, and his invented sixth and seventh positions (the feet placed in parallel) were studied in his own creations. As seen in one of his finest works, **Suite en blanc**, they give a fascinating savour to the choreography. The ballet was made during the war – its first performance, often mis-dated, took place at the Palais Garnier on 23 July 1943 – and it is a sequence of dazzling studies in Lifarian technique. In the dark days of the German occupation, it was also a declaration of the Opéra Ballet's national significance. Its choreography stands, even in today's less than stylish performances, as an affirmation of the force of Lifar's neo-classical manner. Lalo's music for **Namouna** (one of the finest nineteenth century ballet-scores) sustains a bravura display of plotless dance, brilliant in outline, with Lifar's signature of curved arms and legs in parallel, and strong dynamic pulse. It is choreography which illuminates and enhances its interpreters: the two

ballerina variations – **La Flute** and **La Cigarette** (titles taken from the score) – are jewels gloriously worn by such illustrious artists as Yvette Chauviré and Nina Vyrubova. For all his insistence upon male dancing, Lifar wrote admirably well for women.

Like Icarus, Lifar aspired, sought to fly. I lately saw a revival of **Icare** in Bordeaux, with Yann Saiz from the Paris Opéra in the title role. The ballet was fascinating still in its combination of austere language and ritualistic manner. It is no accident that Lifar's posthumously published memoirs should be entitled Les Mémoires d'Icare (*Editions Sauret*, 1993). And Icarus provided a poignant image of Lifar when, in 1958, he quit the Paris Opéra, whose ballet he had directed and inspired for three decades. In his ballets, in his dancing and directorship, Lifar had soared – and gloriously. (It is worth noting that French army parachutists called their uniform coveralls 'des Sergelifars'). When the fall to earth came, with misunderstandings from the administration, Lifar resigned. There is a photograph of his leaving the Palais Garnier, looking sombre, vulnerable, and clasping the mica wings which the stage-Icarus dons in order to fly. For those, like myself, who felt so great a debt of gratitude and such affection for the Lifar, the incarnation of French ballet, the image tore at the heart.

There has been an almost wilful misunderstanding among Anglo-American commentators of Lifar as creator, as dancer, as guardian of a national ballet. This was perhaps a matter of ignorance but there was also a blinkered view which saw the classic dance through eyes conditioned by Balanchine's and Ashton's work. Taste, fashion, are fly-by-nights, and choreographers, once hailed as masters, come to be ignored. Few of Massine's ballets are shown today; some are ill-served in revival: **Symphonie Fantastique** looked a ghost of its former self when mounted by the Paris Opéra. Yet restoration of his **Le Sacre du printemps** in Nice a decade ago proved it a masterly realisation of the score. **Choreartium** and **Les Présages**, as restaged by Tatiana Leskova, have shown •••

that Massine's ballets are still to be appreciated, and, were there dancers stylish enough, **La Boutique fantasque** and **Mam'zelle Angot** would delight audiences yet again.

Lifar has fallen victim to similar disinterest and neglect. His **Phèdre**, **Les Mirages**, **Nautéos**, **Suite en blanc**, **Dramma per musica** (his own favourite, he told me, among his ballets) and **Aubade**, spoke of his distinctive command of movement to me, as to the devoted public in France. A recent revival of **Le Chevalier et la Damoiselle** by the Opéra school showed how apt was his dance manner. And Lifar remained ever faithful to his education with Diaghilev: decor for his ballets was sought from distinguished French artists; scores were commissioned from French composers. Design might come from Picasso, Cassandre, Cocteau, Touchagues; music from Jolivet, Samuel Rousseau, Milhaud, Leleu.

Dogging Lifar's reputation in later years was the question of his war-time directorship of the Opéra Ballet. The four years that followed the fall of France in 1940 were, and have remained, a hot-bed of political in-fighting and misrepresentation. As Robert Gildea shows in his detailed study of Occupied France (Marianne in Chains: *MacMillan, 2002*), resistance was not a way of life, despite the glamorising of facts in film – and memory:

Most French people followed Pétain for most of the Occupation, then de Gaulle. To abandon one for the other too soon was dangerous, to do it too late was imprudent. Lifar, like many people holding important posts in occupied Paris, accepted a fait-accompli: the Germans were there. A national theatre was also there, for whose ballet troupe Lifar had responsibility. Dancers must work. Dancers must eat. Ballet must survive, and serve as an immediate representation of French art. Lifar owed it to his artists and to his adopted nation to maintain dance activity. He was at the height of his powers. He was, ironically, admired by the authorities – Goebbels recalled watching him from the Gods of various German theatres in his Diaghilev days. The Palais Garnier was a tourist attraction for the occupying forces. (A French friend remembers the stalls as a mass of *feldgrau* during performances). By continuing to direct and create, Lifar could give his dancers work, which meant food and lodging for them, and could protect those who might be in danger. Jewish dancers were helped. The Italian-born ètoile Serge Peretti was saved from the threat of deportation to one of Mussolini's labour camps. Then, in the vengeful weeks which followed Liberation, Lifar – like many another was the victim of calumny and ignorance. He had consorted with the German administration – inevitably if unwisely so in certain matters. But his work and his intentions were those of a man who sought to protect his artists, his theatre and his art in the most difficult of times. In the hysteria and political finagling that followed the Liberation of Paris, when rumour was fact, a *comité d'epuration* sought to ban him from the Opéra for life.

Significant comment came from Sol Hurok in *Sol Hurok presents the World of Ballet* (1955). He retracted strictures about Lifar made in an earlier volume, and stated facts that people chose to ignore when Lifar brought the Opéra Ballet to New York in September 1948 as part of the city's Golden Jubilee celebrations.

Lifar may not have been a hero; very possibly, and quite probably, he may have been indiscreet; but it is now obvious to any fair-minded person that there has been a good deal of malicious gossip spread about him.

The Opéra Ballet's appearance in the cramped conditions of the New York City Center Theatre brought enthusiastic audiences, full houses, great admiration for the dancers, and a scant picket-line (so a correspondent wrote to Richard Buckle in the November 1948 issue of *Ballet*) made up of 'an aggressive little group of people calling themselves the Dancers Anti-Fascist Protest Committee' armed with vehement placards. 'They are mostly dancers stemming from New Dance

Groups and I know each and every picket on that line. They are distinguished by the fact that few of them can dance'.

Lifar's return to the Opéra ballet after two years, and the admiration of General de Gaulle, are the most fitting comment on this matter. In October 1963, de Gaulle wrote to Lifar:

Cher Maître, At this moment, when you are leaving the Paris Opéra to which you have devoted all your artistic efforts over so many years for the greater glory of our National Ballet, I must re-iterate my admiration for your great talent, and express to you my thanks for your personal contribution to the expansion of French culture abroad. Please accept, cher Maître, my best wishes.

Lifar was a servant of the dance which filled every moment of his life. He wrote books, treatises, lectured, initiated a university course at the Sorbonne. He had, like Apollo, chosen Terpsichore, and he used his every gift of imagination, determination in her service. Nothing mattered save dance, as he loved it, shaped it. It was a mark of his own greatness that he had made his Opéra troupe great, that his dancing could touch a huge audience, that his ballets delighted Paris for decades. Obsessive, he subsumed himself into his art, soaring in Icarus-like dedication to the flight of the dance.

The last time I saw Lifar on the Opéra stage was in 1977, when the ballet troupe devoted an evening to his choreographies. The spectacle began, properly enough, with a Grand Défilé of the entire company and school. The stage was opened to the depths of the Foyer de la Danse – a perspective of 90 metres. The distant chandeliers shone, and breasting the slope from the foyer emerged, first of all, the children from the Opéra school. Then, each rank led by an *étoile,* there arrived the splendid legions of the company – they, like the children, white clad. Serried ranks of dancers, cheered to the echo as the March from *Les Troyens* rang out, were massed on the stage in a ceremony which Lifar had adapted and extended. Then, finally, a still youthful and handsome figure in dinner-jacket: Lifar, adored, revered, back in his house, his home, surrounded by generations of dancers and students whose careers he had made possible. It is an image as heart-touching and splendid as any I have of him in earlier years. He was Le beau Serge still. ∎

Serge Lifar (Icare)
(1936)

THE CHOREOGRAPHER GIVES THE DANCER the framework in which to display his or her artistry, and while it is possible to see great dancers excel in trite movement, a great choreographic work will allow them to explore themselves in myriad ways. Clement Crisp and Kenneth MacMillan were inextricably linked, the critic chronicling the choreographer's entire career, from his very first essays in movement to his untimely death. Clement's writings on MacMillan's ballets stand as a remarkable record of an extraordinary talent from beginning to end. He has also long held an admiration for Paul Taylor's creative output and has championed the American choreographer throughout, delighting in his distinctive style. I have included appreciations of others – both good and bad – from which emerges a picture of his wide-ranging tastes, from Ashton to Petit, Lifar to Morris. In these writings, Clement's succinct prose identifies precisely what it is that makes good and bad choreography; it is hard to imagine it bettered.

The Choreographers

Chapter 4

The
Choreographers

Chapter 4

**Been Here and Gone
Of Root of the Blues
Variations
Revelations**

Alvin Ailey
American Dance Theater

Sadler's Wells

FT

FINANCIAL
TIMES

THE MODERN DANCE INVASION continues: after the visits of Martha Graham and Merce Cunningham the news has evidently crossed the Atlantic that the London audience is at last in receptive mood. Whatever the choreographic merits of much of this dancing that we have seen, it cannot be denied that it has a considerable vitality and variety, and the Alvin Ailey troupe, which opened last night, presents a very different style from its predecessors. The Ailey company is predominantly Negro, and it aims at using the traditions of Negro folk expression and folk song as a basis for free dance studies. In effect it is a programme concentrating largely upon Spirituals and the Blues, seeking to externalise their fervent emotionalism into dancing.

The result, in the first part of the evening, was a treatment of popular Songs and Blues that fell uneasily between cabaret and serious theatre dance. The programme note for the opening **Been Here and Gone** refers to the "trembling and desperate beauty" of the folk songs, but neither the dances nor the brash musical accompaniment gave much evidence of this. Much more successful was a brief solo by Dudley Williams to a piano fragment by Duke Ellington; the dance language was fluent, and Mr Williams is plainly the possessor of a warm quality of movement that he uses with some sensitivity.

Of Root of the Blues, which formed the major part of the first half, there is little that needs be said, save that it will doubtless appeal to

aficionados of this type of song, and that the presentation is inevitably conceived in terms of popular dancing. There is a great deal of well-amplified singing, the cast dance with vast energy, the girls wear brightly coloured dresses and flounce, the men are masters of the loose-limbed eccentric style of movement, and the coarse immediacy of the music is well caught.

The second half of the programme takes us to more serious dance matters: Joyce Trisler's solo **Variations** is a straight-forward Modern Dance study, which reveals that she is a fascinating lyrical performer. The score is hardly worthy of the dancer, but Miss Trisler transcends both this and the rather fragmentary inspiration of the piece to show beautiful line and an effortless muscular control.

The final **Revelations** proves the most rewarding work of the evening: in it Mr Ailey has devised some moving and simple choreography to accompany a group of religious songs. The staging is clean and eloquent: a white clothed procession moves across rippling blue chiffon that is the waters of the Jordan; sinners flee, but cannot escape: Miss Trisler, admirably partnered by James Truitte, seeks the Lord in an ecstatic duet. Here Mr Ailey has really got to grips with his material and made something touching and expressive out of a people's simple faith. ∎

**6th October
1964**

**Alvin Ailey, Myrna White
and Ella Thompson Moore**
Revelations
(1961)

George Balanchine

'An Appreciation'

FT

FINANCIAL
TIMES

**27th September
2003**

GEORGE BALANCHINE was born in St Petersburg on January 22 1904. In the forthcoming season, starting this autumn, ballet companies around the world – and in particular New York City Ballet, Balanchine's troupe – will mark the centenary of the birth of the dominant and greatest choreographer of the 20th century.

Dominant? Greatest? Yes, for reasons many and glorious. Balanchine, in his every work, proclaimed the seeming infinite possibilities of classic ballet: to delight the eye, ennoble the performer, illuminate the music and assert the rule of clarity over murk.

Maurice Béjart, manufacturer of pious, pompous dance spectacles about Mankind, Peace and a variety of Celebrated Figures – flag days, in effect, and not notable for their dance interest – may have called his French ensemble "The Ballet of the 20th Century". But it was Balanchine who truly produced the ballet of the 20th century – without bombast or *fanfaronade*.

Without him, dance in the last century would have been so vastly the poorer that it does not bear contemplating. Think of the century's music without Stravinsky, Balanchine's friend and frequent collaborator: its painting without Picasso. And we might note that Stravinsky, Picasso – and Balanchine, who is their peer in attainment and influence – were all émigrés, men whose art was transplanted from a native soil to flourish in a new setting.

With Balanchine this is one of the keys – the other is music – to understanding his creativity, his significance, his genius. Balanchine's family was Georgian, their name Balanchivadze. His father was a composer, as his brother Andrey was to become, and, in 1913, Georgi entered the Imperial School in St Petersburg at the age of nine. War and revolution would terribly alter the world in which he was growing up but, by 1920, the student Balanchine had made a first piece of choreography. He was also to enrol himself in the Petrograd Conservatoire to study music. This musical training, albeit incomplete, is a guide to Balanchine's later identity as a maker of dances. For him, music was the only justification for movement and its physical identity. Unique among the century's chief choreographers, he could read a score and play the piano well.

Life in the early years of the Bolshevik revolution was fraught. In 1924 Balanchine and three other dancers (the wonderfully gifted Alexandra Danilova, Tamara Gevergeva – the first of his four wives and Nicholas Efimov) left Petrograd to make a small tour of German theatres with dances mostly produced by Balanchine. They were not to return to Russia – the tour limped through German cities, and finally to Paris where their lack of funds assumed an alarming proportion.

At which moment a summons from Diaghilev – eager for new and well-trained dancers for his Ballets Russes – rescued them.

The four dancers were engaged and, more significantly, Balanchine was asked if he could make ballets for operatic stagings.

Diaghilev had entered into a lifesaving contract with the Monte Carlo Opera House: his troupe provided the dance interludes in the operas that were part of the Monaco lyric season. Diaghilev's question "Can you make opera ballets?" to the wholly inexperienced 20-year-old Balanchine brought the immediate answer: "Yes"."And quickly?" "Yes".

Diaghilev's cult for the young and new was never so bold, nor – as it proved – so rewarding. Suddenly, Balanchine's future was shaped. Within weeks he was the titular choreographer to the Ballets Russes – successor to Fokine, Nijinsky, Massine and Bronislava Nijinska.

Thus George Balanchine, at the age of 21, became choreographer to the internationally celebrated Ballets Russes, and also a dancer. (He was a fine and imaginative performer. In **Petrushka**, his characterisation of the old Grandfather of the Fair-bearded and befuddled – invariably made Diaghilev roar). He was, as a creator, learning his craft. Ninette de Valois, a member of the Ballets Russes at the time, told me: "George came in to the rehearsal room one morning and made a dance for three of us in an opera without any fuss. When he'd finished, I knew that he was a genius".

For five years, until Diaghilev's death and the immediate dissolution of the Ballets Russes,

Balanchine provided choreography, tailoring movement to every demand. Then in 1928, he experienced what seemed to be a Pauline conversion, and this – significantly – with a Stravinsky score. **Apollo**, already staged in Washington, was an inevitable choice for Diaghilev, and for Balanchine as ballet master. He later declared that he looked upon this ballet as a turning point in his life. "In its discipline and restraint, in its sustained oneness of tone and feeling, the score was a revelation. It seemed to tell me that I could, for the first time, dare not to use all my ideas… reducing what seemed myriad possibilities to the one possibility that was inevitable." Music, as always in his ballet making, was the guide. "See the music; hear the dance," he said. Yet it was to take another two decades before the full realisation of this ideal came about.

Diaghilev died in 1929, and with him passed away the justification for the Ballets Russes: its quest for new music, new painting, new choreography, new dancers, new ideas. Over the succeeding decades "revived" Ballets Russes troupes would rise and fail, and a national ballet would emerge in Britain, thanks to Ninette de Valois and Marie Rambert. And Balanchine would, after four lean and wandering years, go to America to make American ballet.

Diaghilev had revealed to Balanchine his choreographic identity. It was Lincoln Kirstein who would provide Balanchine with the ● ● ●

means to prove the greatness of that identity. Kirstein was the son of a merchant family – his father was a partner in the Boston department store, Filene's. Dazzlingly intelligent, Kirstein had shown, as a Harvard undergraduate, rare abilities and artistic boldness: he founded *Hound and Horn*, a distinguished literary quarterly, and was a co-founder of the Harvard Society for Contemporary Art (a seed-bed for the New York Museum of Contemporary Art). He was wealthy, energetic, discerning – and loved ballet. And he was determined to make classic academic dance an American art.

He had first seen the Diaghilev troupe in 1924, at the age of 17. In Europe in the summer of 1933, he witnessed the dying days of a small company that Balanchine had formed. It had been partly funded by the eccentric millionaire Edward James as a showcase for his wife, Tilly Losch, and the backing was now gone. Where should Balanchine go? He had thought of the US: a new society, fresh and untutored bodies to work on, a land of opportunities

George Balanchine,
Union Jack **curtain call**
London
(1979)

where his ideals about dance might be realised. Europe had no appeal for him anymore.

Kirstein knew that in Balanchine he had a creator who bore within himself the grandest traditions of academic dance – those of St.Petersburg's Imperial Ballet – to implant in the soil of the New World. Kirstein also believed Balanchine to be a genius who had already shown (supremely in **Apollo**) how the classic style might develop and flourish. "I knew," said Kirstein, "that's what Balanchine made meant ballet to me, because ballet was about dancing to music, not about painting to pantomime". On American bodies. Balanchine's style would find new impetus, new form, new energy.

The journey towards the realisation of Kirstein's plan was to be a long one. A school ("but first a school", famously declared Balanchine and the School of American Ballet – significant title – opened in 1934 as a prelude to everything that was to come); varied incarnations of an ensemble: work on Broadway, in Hollywood; work also for the fading glories of the Ballets Russes in America; and war, all supervened.

Yet Balanchine as a fashioner of brilliant work as carpenter, as cook (he called himself both of these) went on making whatever he was invited to create, and made it sublimely well. It was in 1948 that Balanchine and Kirstein could at last find a home in New York (at the City Center) and thus establish the New York City Ballet. There ensued a golden age, three glorious decades in which the realisation of Kirstein's dream of American classical ballet, and Balanchine's supremacy as a creator, was clear for the world to see. "Welcome to Moscow, home of the classic ballet", said a radio interviewer when Balanchine took his company to Russia in 1962. "Excuse me", said Balanchine, "Russia is the home of romantic ballet. America is now the home of classic ballet".

In this comment is encapsulated everything that he and Kirstein had succeeded in achieving. Here was classic ballet fashioned by a genius as the vivid realisation of its music, performed by dancers whose clarity and speed of execution, whose command of sophisticated rhythm, whose aerodynamic efficiency in dancing had no precedent, no equal. This was, *pace* Maurice Béjart, the Ballet of the 20th Century. "I only wish to prove the dance by dancing", Balanchine said when he returned to Russia in 1972.

His ballets were for him, as for his artists and for his public, no less and no more than that. On the floor of the music, he set his dancers dancing, exploring the possibilities of motion born of – and borne on – the music. What we see in his choreography is the triumph of academic dance, of the classroom language of ballet training, and the triumph also of an artist who extended the possibilities of that language, made it faster, more free, more potent in its dynamics, entirely responsive to its new situation both geographic and temporal. The seed, transplanted from St Petersburg, had grown and flourished in a new land, on the alert bodies of a different race.

To achieve this, Balanchine was perforce a teacher. The classes he gave to the members of his company – if they chose to attend – demanded a body already prepared to work hard (not for Mister B, as they called him, the slow freeing of muscles and tendons that are the alphabet of a traditional class). "Maybe I shall be remembered as a teacher", he once observed. His classes were a laboratory in which ideas were put to the test. The ideal was of speedy and energetic movement. (Typical was his condemnation of a lazy or leisurely dancer: "What are you saving yourself for?" Equally typical his comment to dancers puzzled or uncertain about a step: "Dear, just do!").

The great corpus of Balanchine's work **Apollo**, the signpost; **Serenade**, his first work made in America in 1934 and a declaration of intent about how ballet could be American: the catalogue of masterworks made for NYCB (his realisation of Stravinsky's **Agon** in 1957 is still the most modern of ballets) – is an achievement to set against the work of Stravinsky and Picasso as emblematic of what an art attained in the 20th century.

What is so singular about Balanchine's achievement is that – with Kirstein's unceasing and self-denying aid – ballet, which had hitherto been an unconsidered art for the mass of the public, became something as vital as any other creative endeavour in the US.

His ballets are now performed by dozens of companies worldwide, and they serve – as they have always served – as assertions of the immense possibilities of human movement using the academic language of dance. Balanchine explored the nature of classic ballet, showing how it can exhilarate its performers and its audience by daring, by speed, and yet still offer those commanding truths about the academic propriety of formal grace, physical rectitude, even angelic potential. (Kirstein recounted how, early on in their venture, a ballet mother had asked Balanchine "Will my daughter dance?" The reply was in French, and sybilline: "La danse, Madame, c'est une question morale". And, for both men, this was so).

Balanchine's idealism about ballet, and his devotion in practising his craft, to him it was a craft: "God creates. I assemble", told us that balletic movement was an aspect of the divine, of something angelic, and he was a religious man, whose Russian Orthodox faith never left him.

A favourite dancer, Merrill Ashley, said of him: "No one who had even the briefest contact with him was left untouched: those who knew him well were changed forever. Many people, on meeting him for the first time, expected to find a man full of false airs, but his disarming lack of pretension and his natural modesty made them feel more important in his presence… he simply thought he had certain God-given talents and the duty to use them". ∎

Merce Cunningham

FINANCIAL
TIMES

Sadler's Wells

**10th February
1972**

Robert Swinson
Rainforest
(1989)

HOW TO BE COOL calm and collected is not the title of one of Merce Cunningham's dance works, but it is an attitude that underlies much of the very stimulating dancing we saw at the Wells during last week. At this moment I feel in honour bound to make some recantation about Mr Cunningham's work, for on the occasion of his two previous visits I was less than enchanted with what I saw. I make my amends not from any desire to go in for public breast-beating, but because I feel that the important changes that have taken place in the British dance scene since Cunningham's last visit six years ago – notably the sterling achievement of Robin Howard's encouragement of Modern Dance at The Place – have helped many ballet-lovers, myself included, towards a fuller enjoyment of what Cunningham is doing.

Still the most adventurous and uncompromising of creators, Cunningham shows us dancing pure and simple: pure, because he purposely alienates any of those 19th century trappings of decoration and music; simple, because his dances don't say anything, they just are. (We are the ones who see a carrier pigeon and ask "Any messages?" Cunningham just shows us the bird and without any comment lets us look at it and enjoy its flight). Paul Taylor, who worked with Cunningham, provides a note in his own programmes which urges us to see his ballets as "food for the eye"; Cunningham doesn't bother with that, but the rule applies just the same.

With a crowded schedule of dancing last week I had to miss two evenings at Rosebery Avenue – most regretfully the full-length **Canfield** – but on Tuesday, Friday and Saturday, a series of new works made for exciting viewing. Not surprisingly they defy the usual descriptions that a critic can essay through reference to themes or mood; a piece like **Second Hand** exists as a sequence of dances, solos, duets, group activities having a common ground of serenity, a catalogue of "happenings with bodies" that can seem like a journey through an exhibition of sculpture forever on the move. It is a work of delicate surprises, as when Carolyn Brown is suddenly lifted by her companions and becomes in some curious fashion totally isolated from the rest of the cast.

Signals touched me by a quality that I can only describe as prettiness (in its best connotation); and how witty and unexpected the passage in which a girl calmly wriggled and insinuated herself under a male dancer sitting on the stage (while he was damned if he was going to make things any easier for her by moving his leg) and then proceeded to reverse the process with just as much disinterested effort.

Moments like this are the incidental pleasures in dance-works that force us into a closer and more searching awareness of movement. Cunningham's creative approach insists throughout upon economy, on maximum results from the most discreet, stylish and

Mark Morris
Dance Group

Théâtre Royal de la Monnaie, Brussels

FT

FINANCIAL
TIMES

**14th December
1988**

often very classical behaviour. When the dancers move fast their trajectories become dazzlingly effective; other, *molto lento* sections impel in us the sort of concentration that we give to a *Noh* actor whose slightest hand-gesture is crucial in the drama.

Only one piece that I saw, **Borst Park**, struck me as being tedious, and that because of its literalism. It is a comment, I imagine, upon people relaxing in a public park; too disjointed as a narrative, with a frankly tiresome score (*Burdocks* by Christian Wolff). It was jokey in a modest way but diffuse, and Cunningham's dancers seemed unable to put across the incidents – an acrobatic outburst for a girl looked far too chancy technically; fun with an ambulant picnic lacked any punch.

The only other "emotional" piece, **Rainforest**, was a stunner, though. The stage is set with silver helium-filled pillow-cases that eddy gently; the movement is slow, almost static at times, and I found it deeply disturbing in its sense of desolation as the tattered figures of the dancers laboured through this weird habitation. Whether the forest is actual, or simply there because of the title of David Tudor's score (taxing sonorities from resonating wood and metal to evoke the ultimate in post-Wagnerian *Forest Murmurs*) does not matter; the dance was novel, and beautiful. ∎

FOR MORE THAN a quarter of a century, Maurice Béjart and his Ballet of the Twentieth Century were the pride of Brussels. Two years ago, after disagreement with the administration of the Théâtre Royal de la Monnaie, Béjart and his dancers took off for Lausanne, leaving what must have seemed a gaping artistic void for the Belgian public.

It is vastly to the credit of Gerard Mortier, director of the Monnaie, that he should have invited Mark Morris and his troupe to replace Béjart as the opera house's resident company, for there could be no greater contrast with the messages and philosophising that are Béjart's stock in trade than the musical sensibilities and choreographic inventiveness of the young American creator.

Morris, New York's darling, was admired in London during the Dance Umbrella seasons of 1984 and 1985. It was significant that one of his works shown then was **Songs** that tell a story. The title was indicative of creative procedures, as the words of songs – ranging from Vivaldi arias to pop – fired dancing both ingenious and elegant. In his setting of Handel's ode *L'Allegro, Il Penseroso ed Il Moderato*, which has just started his first Brussels season, the images of Milton's verses, their resonances and musical repercussions, are central to the choreography.

An excellent programme note by Roger Downey discusses the score's origins in the idea of Charles Jennens, Handel's •••

A combination
to delight Good King Herod.

**Tales of Beatrix Potter /
Peter and the Wolf**
25th November, 1995

collaborator, to interweave Milton's two pastoral odes as a dialogue, with Jennens' own feeble verses for **Il Moderato** reconciling the poet's joyous and contemplative views. Morris explores both Handel and Milton in an evening-long span of fluent, beautiful dancing that gives us a third layer of meaning to the music and poetry. Sometimes his manner seems simple, as when the phrase "smoothing the rugged brow of night" gains immediate gestural realisation in a duet between a man and woman. Sometimes, as in "Haste thee, nymph, and bring with thee/Jest and youthful Jollity", the dance bubbles with humour: three men sport and fall about and the corps de ballet follows suit at the choral reprise of the words. Sometimes, and here Morris touches greatness, the dance opens up enormous vistas on to the European pastoral tradition: the aria "Mirth, admit me of thy crew/To listen how the hound and horn…" occasions a hunting scene so potent in realisation as the dancers impersonate the hunt and its setting, that eye and mind crowd with allusions. We are aware of images owed to Renaissance festivities, to many centuries of such scenes in painting and literature.

The choreography is everywhere responsive to Milton's mind as to Handel's forms, moving from ring dances to friezes of action, playing with ideas in happiest and most adventurous fashion, showing us the moon sailing through the night sky, or birds in flight, or the slapstick of "the well-trod stage" Morris has, indeed, created a form of dance-drama wherein the play of language and music is mirrored for us in another and no less apt medium.

With dance as pictorially, dynamically rich as this, stage decoration has to be minimal. Adrianne Lobel provides a succession of gauzes, admirably lit by James Ingalls, to create a world for Morris' choreography, and Christine van Loon dresses the dozen couples of the cast with comparable economy and elegance. The evening is unalloyed delight and a triumphant vindication of Morris' right to be in Brussels.

What Morris is doing in **L'Allegro** and certain other works begs comparison with those "music realisations" which are part of his ancestry in the early days of American Modern Dance. Then, with the Denishawn troupe, or even with Isadora, the dance spoke innocently about the music. Morris' response to his scores can seem both the most innocent and the most sophisticated. ∎

L'Allegro, il Penseroso ed il Moderato
London
(2010)

Mark Morris Dance Group

Edinburgh Festival Theatre

FT
FINANCIAL
TIMES

**14th August
1996**

THE MAGIC OF MORRIS. Mark Morris is the Edinburgh Festival's darling, welcomed back year after year. His company's appearances have reminded audiences of the artistic standards they are entitled to expect – and have so often been denied by dance offerings of late. That there have been no ballet performances of first quality since the New York City Ballet and the Royal Ballet brought serious classicism to the festival is still a problem. But we delight, and rejoice at a relationship with the festival which is a credit to both host and guest.

Very properly, the festival marks its golden jubilee with a commissioned piece from Morris. This, seen for the first time on Monday night, is **I don't want to love** – the burden of seven Monteverdi madrigals which are the score. "Non voglio amare" sing the artists of the Concerto Italiano, providing splendid accompaniment, and Morris' seven dancers, white clad, tell us why. The madrigals treat of love rejected and unavailing. I am almost tempted to think that we should have surtitles, so intimate is the link between words and dance. But the dance speaks, and a moment's homework with the text of the poems in the programme is sufficient to lead into what Morris is doing, while the first level of the choreography – its acceptance of the music's form – is clear and persuasive.

Morris treats the subject lightly but with sudden penetrating moments, as when a lover's isolation or a girl's anguish pierce us

(and the dancers) to the heart. Loveliest incident is Morris' realisation of "Zefiro torna", in which the breezes of the title blow the dancers, fluttering and flying and skipping with tiniest steps, over the stage and along the music's lines. It is wholly ravishing, and like the entire work, judged with acutest skill. A lovely anniversary present.

The programme begins with **Ten Suggestions**, of which more anon, but its heart is two contrasting dark pieces. **World Power**, which dates from last year, is puzzling. Lou Harrison's score is made for gamelan with harp and trumpet (well played by the South Bank Gamelan Players). The title is owed to Mark Twain, whose comments upon American military action in the Philippine wars are bitterly satiric, and feature in the score.

Morris shows a group of dancers aping Balinese forms without much credibility, gradually succumbing to death and defeat. The patterns of the dance are intriguing; their effect is blatant, and the piece smacks of a polemicism foreign to Morris' work.

As sombre, but very different, is **Behemoth**. This was made in 1990 in Brussels and is performed in silence. For 35 minutes we watch the cast of 15 moving, posing, crossing the stage in waveforms, all trapped within themselves. Non-communication, a bleak sense of isolation, action without feeling (so odd in dance, every gesture speaks) is the rule. The dancers react with chill •••

unconcern to another's move, occasionally link in duets, and finally sink to earth like husks of themselves. The "message" is not clear, but the effect is fascinating, and the jagged dynamics, the anxious outlines of the dance, are gripping. Form and language are brilliantly wrought, and the piece is grandly done by Morris' artists.

Morris himself, pink-pyjama'd, appeared in **Ten Suggestions**. Each of Tcherepnin's brief piano bagatelles becomes a character study, and in each Morris created a world of emotion. He looks like Isadora Duncan with five o'clock shadow, and, like Isadora, he moves with an innocence, an absolute clarity of intention and feeling, that are marvellous. These are like dance-snapshots of a child playing alone, or of the Earth-mothers of modern dance (Morris can evoke lost-lost styles with a stunning imitative grace). A chair, a ribbon, is a toy. A hoop suddenly awakens images of the 1920s. Baryshnikov has danced **Ten Suggestions** with consummate wit and technical splendour. Morris, unsurprisingly, inhabits them as his world. Every step comes from inside the dance and inside him, and the density of his presence (accentuated in the pauses between each, when character falls away and we see a bulky man mop the sweat from his brow) is extraordinary. **Ten Suggestions** are far more considerable than at first seems, and Morris is a great artist when he dances them: beautiful because speaking so beautifully, so truly to us. ∎

A score
like the mating call of an air-conditioner.

Stoolgame
23rd June, 1990

Moves
N.Y. Export Op. Jazz
Afternoon of a Faun
The Concert

Piccadilly Theatre

IN ONE OF HIS LETTERS Degas wrote: "It is the movement of people and things that consoles us. If the leaves on the trees didn't move, how sad the trees would be, and so should we". Well, here, at last, are Jerome Robbins' Ballets U.S.A. at the Piccadilly Theatre to console us for those dozens of other dance visitors over the past decade who have brought programmes at once pretentious and arid, that we have watched for want of anything better. Now here is a company that is better, better than anything we have seen since the war except for the Bolshoi and New York City Ballet.

The real importance of this troupe is not so much how they dance but what they dance (though the two seem indissolubly linked, so perfectly do the dancers interpret the choreographer's intentions). Jerome Robbins is the most distinguished choreographer that the U.S.A. has produced, and together with Balanchine (whose associate he is in the New York City Ballet) he is concerned with the classic dance, exploring and developing its possibilities; but he is also expert in adapting the forms of popular dancing to theatrical use, even as adjuncts of the academic dance.

DANCED IN SILENCE
This can be seen clearly in two of last night's ballets: **Moves** is danced in silence, an exercise in pure dancing free from all the emotional and structural implications of a musical score.

It shows Robbins' amazing virtuosity in creating movement: the dance figures have a clarity and an ingenuity that force one to see them with a fresh eye. Dancing is refurbished and renewed in its impulses, movement by one dancer will demand complementary movement from others, an action splits up into a variety of other shapes: a gesture or a pose is examined, turned round, slowed up or accelerated to show its beauty and structure. It is a fascinating and heart-warming display of the power and excitement of movement, whether academic or naturalistic: the whole work is so clearly constructed with its effects of counterpoint, its little fugues and its varying densities of action (that at the end one is almost persuaded that one has heard music).

MASTERLY ESSAY
N.Y. Export Op. Jazz is the only truly non-classic work of the evening, and it claims a certain kinship with Robbins' **West Side Story**, but where the musical is specific in its treatment of plot and behaviour, **Opus Jazz** is concerned with the essence, both emotional and technical, of the popular dances of young America. It is a masterly essay, compact of interest and acute observation, brilliantly danced.

Afternoon of a Faun is quite simply the best thing that could happen to the Debussy score: since Nijinsky's initial assault, it has become a sort of grubby solo for any dancer with sufficient vanity to challenge comparison with a legend.

Now Robbins has cleared the whole dreary business up with a lyrical study of two dancers: a young man is in a dance studio, with the audience forming the essential mirror before which he practises. A young girl enters, and half unaware of each other, they embark on a *pas de deux*, conscious only of themselves as figures reflected in the glass. Suddenly he kisses her, the spell is broken, and she leaves him stretched out again on the floor.

This is a short work, filled with the warm enclosed atmosphere of the dance class-room, couched in beautifully lyrical language, and most effectively interpreted by John Jones and Wilma Curley.

Finally comes **The Concert**, easily the funniest ballet seen in London for some years. ∎

15th September 1959

Lynn Seymour
with the Royal Ballet Company
The Concert
(1975)

Paul Taylor Dance Company

Orbs

FT
FINANCIAL
TIMES

Sadler's Wells

**7th July
1970**

THAT FINE PLAY *The Contractor*, as you will see from our Entertainment Guide, boasts a notable critical accolade: "A masterpiece. If you have only one night in London, this is the play you should see". With all humility, may I suggest that these words now also apply to Paul Taylor's ballet **Orbs**, given its first London showing last night.

Taylor has taken as his theme the sun, the planets, and the seasons of man's life and love, and so grand and epic is the scale of the work that he has, quite naturally and beautifully, set it to some of the late Beethoven quartets. This is no foolhardiness, but almost inevitable in its matching of noble music and noble dance. **Orbs** is cast in six episodes; the opening finds Taylor as the Sun with a court of four planets, and four moons who appear throughout as handmaidens and attendants. In succeeding sections we are shown the planets as aspects of man's journey through life and love; Venusian Spring (to the Op. 127 variations) is light, joyous, filled with the tenderness that Taylor expresses with such effortless sincerity, as the Sun instructs the planets in the happiness of love. Next, using the Grosse Fugue, comes the burning heat of Martian summer; the Sun is now Janus-masked, pitiless in showing his planetary creatures the harshness of suffering. The dancing becomes energetic, disquieting in portraying the agonies of human relationships, and finally, in an intensely illuminating moment, the Sun drives his student planets from him.

We return after the interval – the work falls into two parts – to a scene of daring theatricality. Gone are the allegorical figures; this is Terrestrial autumn, and the Sun is now a priest in a grey suit, the planets and moons are the bride, groom, best man, bride's mother and attendants bridesmaids, also in naturalistic dress. The Opus 130 quartet somehow becomes the perfect accompaniment for a passage of touching humanity as a wedding is rehearsed and celebrated and is followed by a harvest thanksgiving. The whole section is lightly sketched, full of humour (the priest gets drunk and makes much of a plucked turkey), and yet it has the underlying strength and seriousness of **Les Noces**. It serves, I imagine, as a scherzo before the darkness of Plutonian winter. The Sun has gone, mankind and the planets know the misery of a world without the divine light, and they fall into a sleep of death. But the Sun returns, life and joy are reborn in a final radiant coda, and as the curtain falls we sit back to marvel at the magnificence of Taylor's vision, its deep humanity and its expressive force.

I will add nothing more than to say that **Orbs** is thrillingly danced, thrilling to watch and the work of a master choreographer. I shall hope to return to the rest of the programme, and to some aspects of Taylor's prodigious work, later in the week. ∎

Orbs – Postscript

Paul Taylor Dance Company

FT
FINANCIAL
TIMES

I COUNT THE EVENINGS I have spent watching Paul Taylor's company among the happiest and richest I have known, comparable with those first revelatory visits to the Kirov. The season, which ended last Saturday, has been a failure in box-office terms, I would imagine, since I have not seen the theatre more than two-thirds full, but in every other respect it has been triumphant. We have been privileged to see the work of a choreographer of genius in the full plenitude of his powers, and one piece in particular – **Orbs** – seems to me to be among the most sublime expressions of the power of dancing to be made in my time as a critic.

Orbs, indeed, sums up a great deal about Taylor's creativity. It shows his wonderful musical understanding – which dares to use late Beethoven and wins – and his feeling for structure, which gives all his work a perceptible and beautiful shape. It encompasses much of his range, from serenity in the first scene – as in **Duet** and **Aureole** – through the fierce energy, discord and martial anger in the second section, that we also see in parts of **Junction**, and in **Churchyard**. It is very funny in the wedding rehearsal and the harvest dance (and Taylor is a master of comic choreography: witness **Three Epitaphs** and **Piece Period**), and it can evoke a terrible desolation that is common to the Plutonian Winter scene and to **Scudorama**. Over and above all this is the grandeur of its conception and expression: to see Taylor as the Sun in the first half of **Orbs** is to be filled

with a very real sense of awe as this God-like figure instructs or chides his creatures: I found it a uniquely moving experience.

Taylor himself has described his ballets as "food for the eyes", and this they certainly are. Each work leaves indelible impressions, memories to which I, for one, return time and again to savour and enjoy. The closing section of **Junction** is a case in point: what I can best identify as a wave-formation of •••

12th July 1970

Paul Taylor
Orbs
(1970)

energy pours in a diagonal across the stage as seven dancers roil, curve, surge with slow but certain impetus, finally leaving Bettie de Jong standing upon Taylor's crouched back. It is amazing, and beautiful and, happily, unforgettable. But this describes the whole season; Taylor's ballets are among the noblest and most thrilling works of our age, life-enhancing and beautiful. To him, and to his fine dancers, grateful thanks. ∎

...it looks like

something that might be the floor show in a particularly accommodating Theban bordello.

Bastet
20th December, 1988

**Company B
In the Beginning
Promethean Fire**

Sadler's Wells

PAUL TAYLOR IS A LIFE-ENHANCER. He and his work have been beacons of joy, casting light on both the happiest and darkest aspects of human behaviour, but always providing illumination. His wit is offbeat, irresistible. His sense of compassion, and sometime sense of despair, is the more potent for its Integrity: no fudging of issues, just dance which is beautiful, exact.

This encomium serves to announce Taylor's company at Sadler's Wells – and subsequently on tour – with two programmes, which are essential viewing. The first triple bill, on Tuesday, began with **Company B**, with its Andrews Sisters' songs evoking wartime dances, wartime flirtation, and shadows cast by casualty figures. For all its lightness, it touches nerves of grief. Taylor's newest piece, **In the Beginning**, was made for the Houston Ballet. It is what its title might suggest: a quick survey of the Book of Genesis (rather like the 40-minute dash round the Louvre) set to wind-band arrangements of Carl Orff. Wonderfully merry or anguished dances. Taylor cocking snooks, but worried about the outcome. Jehovah at last relenting, so a rainbow and reconciliation. The piece is sly, ambiguous, riven with what I suppose is Taylor's own agnosticism, and terrific. He must have attended a really wonky Sunday school.

And to close, a masterpiece from last year. **Promethean Fire** features 16 dancers. Impelled by the music – and Taylor's mastery of an ensemble has never seemed more grand –

Paul Taylor Dance Company

FT
FINANCIAL
TIMES

the cast is blown over the stage, piled like dead leaves. Out of this, a superb duet for Patrick Corbin and Lisa Viola, in which anguish drives them apart but yet keeps them together. At last, acceptance, hope, bravery, cry out from the dancers' bodies. Some commentators have seen this as a response to September 11. 1 don't think Taylor is as obvious as that – he never has been before.

Dear Paul Taylor, as always, huge gratitude, vast admiration. More, please! Tremendous performances by the dancers. Not to be missed. ∎

**1st May
2003**

Paul Taylor Dance Company
Company B
(2003)

Twyla Tharp
Twyla Tharp! Dance

Heroes
Sweet Fields
66

FINANCIAL
TIMES

The Playhouse,
Edinburgh

**15th August
1997**

Dance from the West

PLUS ÇA CHANGE, plus c'est le méme at the
Edinburgh Festival, with its trudging hordes
of merry-makers on Princes Street; and its
day-mist giving way to penetrating evening
drizzle. And, for dance-lovers, the gloomy
barrack of The Playhouse, that fun-factory
designed by the Ceausescus.

The Playhouse is host to the first dance event
of the festival. *Tharp!* says the poster – avec
exclamation mark – as one might say *Duck!*
or *Welcome!* The latter is the proper response,
albeit the former is my advice for some of the
later dance items, and Monday night's
performance revealed three recent (late 1996)
works by Twyla Tharp for her new (5f; 6m)
and accomplished troupe.

The evening is, in an odd way, a retrospective:
not of Tharp's work but of her American
identity. One piece, **Sweet Fields**, looks at the
simple religious faith of early settlers,
observed through the hymns of the Boston-
born William Billings (1746-1800) and
traditional Shaker songs. ("Shake, shake out
of me/All that is carnal,/I'll take nimble
steps…" and Tharp's dancers do just that).
66 is about the great Route 66 that ran from
Chicago to the Pacific at Santa Monica, leading
many Americans (including Tharp's family)
westward to new hopes and new horizons.

Heroes, the first work on the bill, is harder to
categorise. It proposes heroic attitudes, some

mythic, some looking rather more like sci-fi,
and even glances at feminism, when a woman
flings herself, unavailing but determined,
against a wall of male resistance. (I do not
think this autobiography: Twyla Tharp is
braver, more combative and more successful
than most male choreographers. Tough is as
tough does, and Tharp's grand achievements
are there to prove it).

The dance is fierce, bold, hinting also at the
uncertainties and defeats that are central to
heroism and the desire and need to achieve.
The score is by Philip Glass, the Minkus of
minimalism, and is very loud and perfectly
tiresome. The dancers work like demons.

Their better reward is the succeeding **Sweet
Fields** in which Tharp's vision of a white-clad
community, held by an innocent Godliness,
ardent in spiritual feeling, is beautifully
caught in dance that is both airy and serious.
(Most serious is a funeral procession for six
men, where each in turn becomes the corpse.
Timor mortis…) The hymns proclaim a direct
and unwavering belief. Tharp (from a Quaker
background) knows in her heart how to
show this and, touchingly, does so in lively,
sincere dance. The piece is a delight.

66, closing the evening, is a romp on a
serious theme. The choreography feeds, as
Tharp has often done, on social dance and
the manners of the 1930s and '40s, with a
junk-music accompaniment. ("Bachelor pad
music" says the programme).

A pair of lovers – the splendid Andrew Robinson and Julie Stahl – disagree and agree (what else is new in dance?), and the virtuoso Shawn Mahoney is an old man embarked on the long road West. He gets his chance in a merry solo. Part cartoon, part parade of bright steps, **66** is a soufflé, but cooked by a master chef.

The three works may have subliminal links, and they share certain leitmotifs of movement – walking backwards is one, and it suggests Tharp's own backward look at an American past – but the only obvious common ground is their creator's skill, and the excellence of the dancing. They make a fine evening in a visit sponsored by Scottish Power.

As my seasonal note about festival programme books, I report that the Playhouse programme for *Tharp!* is dreary in aspect, not immune from mistakes, and a rotten buy at £2. It is about time the festival decided on theatre programmes worthy of the shows they cover. And why not, given advertising revenue, make them free? To hell with the extra bawbees: let us have something worthy to remember the evening by. ∎

Roger C. Jeffrey
Matt Rivera
Andrew Robinson
Heroes

Pina Bausch
Tanztheater Wuppertal

FT
FINANCIAL TIMES

Sadler's Wells

16th September 1982

Javelin

has the grinding (musical) repetitions of echt-minimalism and hints that the refrigerator is on the blink again.

Amores
2nd May, 1987

WHAT HAS TO BE SAID straight away about the Tanztheater Wuppertal, Pina Bausch's ensemble which opened with **1980** on Tuesday night for a first London season, is that you will have to look very carefully to find the *tanz*. At one moment, far against the back wall of the stage, a girl – masked by the rest of the cast – sketches a few steps, and repeats this later on, and there is a lyric interlude when a girl in a white dress dances under the jet from a garden sprinkler which is freshening the turf that covers the stage. Apart from these fragments, the evening is *theater*, and no less than four hours of it.

It is theatre of the currently fashionable kind; disjointed, allusive, illogical, sometimes outrageous, frequently harshly funny. "What are you afraid of?", demands a voice of the cast. "Madness", answers Mechthild Grossman. "What else?" "Death". "Is that all?" Isn't that enough? George Moore was accused of conducting his education in public. Pina Bausch, heroine of the avant-garde dance in Germany and a potent influence through her theatrical comments upon German bourgeois society, seems to be conducting her own psychoanalysis in public, and involving her troupe of 18 actor-dancers in group therapy in the process.

Earlier theatre pieces – she has been working in Wuppertal for a decade – were more obviously danced creations, concerned with social observation rather than judgment, cataloguing the incomprehensions and

brutalities of life. **1980** rejects dance entirely, though the fact that the cast are all dance-trained accounts for their muscular alertness and the physical clarity and often beauty of their acting.

Earlier this year Michael Coveney reported with great enthusiasm from the Adelaide and Holland Festivals on **1980** and on two other Bausch pieces (including the **Kontakthof** which will be shown at the Wells next week). I join him in saluting the Bausch way in which, as he so acutely noted "Death and separation can only be faced by pouring the experience back into our lives, rationalising the pain, as Proust did, in a construction of art".

The starting point for **1980** is the appearance of Janusz Subicz (a Baryshnikov double) as a little boy, eating from a bowl with one spoonful for Papa, one spoonful for Maman. The work's progress – and there is progress, and an ultimate reconciliation of past with present through cyclic form – is decked out with many of the hallowed procedures of theatrical shock. There is the irruption of the cast into the stalls (where they serve tea to the audience); video recording; nudity, as a royal personage graciously waves at us from the arm of a bare, though paper-crowned, consort; outbursts of frenzy contrasted with surreal calm; a chap apparently defecating in a corner of the stage; a conjuror and a stuffed deer; round games; singing; an accompanying musical text which ranges from Alfred Deller with Elizabethan madrigals to Judy Garland

and a snatch of a Beethoven cello sonata; music-hall jokes; exposure of various parts of the body in a manic sun-bathing sequence, and of parts of the psyche; acrid comment on the way women manipulate men, and men manipulate women (in a tearingly funny beauty contest which degenerates into a literal leg-show with Meryl Tankard as the spirit of misrule destroying every hen-witted Miss World cutie, for ever).

And underpinning the action are recurrent flash-backs to the world of childhood, and the anger Miss Bausch feels at the deformation and destruction of the child's identity, at the erosions of joy caused by loneliness, isolation, and the roles given us by parents and social convention, and the roles assumed as a refuge from life. The effect is of Hieronymus Bosch redrawn by Georg Grosz. In one of the most piercing scenes the serenely beautiful Anne Marie Benati stands holding a cushion and repeating "I want to go home. I want to go home". The production's bitter answer seems to be: "You have no home".

It is a long evening: four hours with one interval. It is an improbable evening, and not for the dance fanatic. But for anyone caring about the theatre it can offer unusual and eye-opening rewards. It is in no sense difficult to comprehend: too much has been made of the fact that disparate incidents overlap or are played simultaneously. Life, you may have noticed, is played simultaneously, and we somehow cope with that.

I do not have great sympathy with the "letting your hair down" theatre of self-indulgence, and the simplistic, catch-all procedures of **1980** cry out to be edited, sharpened. But never for an instant – well, only for one instant – was I bored, and the sprawling length of the piece brings many insights and excitements. Not least of these is the chance to savour the exceptional gifts of the cast. Lutz Förster as imperturbable master of ceremonies; Meryl Tankard, who is probably the young Edna Everage; Mechthild Grossman, possessor of a stunning whisky baritone and a mocking and irresistible *furia*; the mysterious Kyomi lchida, the lovely Anne Marie Benati, Janus Subicz, by turns pathetic as a child and puckish when teasing the audience, and the sardonic Arthur Rosenfeld, just restraining himself from throwing a jelly into the stalls, are immediately compelling. But the entire cast is very fine, and **1980** – disturbing, hallucinatory, compassionate – really has to be seen. ∎

1980
(1982)

171

Pina Bausch
Tanztheater Wuppertal

Masurca Fogo

**FINANCIAL
TIMES**

Sadler's Wells

**4th February
2002**

Masurca Fogo
London
(2002)

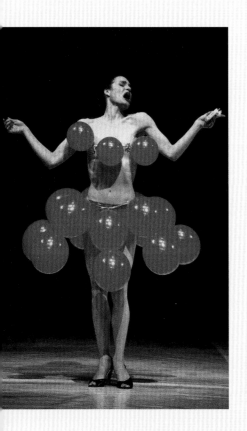

'Disappearing up its own mazurka'

I THINK THE CHICKEN was the star of the show. It played its part – eating pieces of watermelon that had been so kindly splattered over the Sadler's Wells stage – and made no song and dance about it. Nor did it utter a word.

It was once said that dancing was the only type of theatre in which you did not hear a single foolish word at least from the stage. No longer. The forms of physical theatre – "dance" seems altogether too polite a term to describe them – that have afflicted us in recent decades have revealed that their creators have an inability to create movement that is expressive. Hence they resort to chitchat from their casts, who can have serious problems in verbal expression.

Pina Bausch has created fine dance works – her *Sacre du printemps* one of the best I have seen of a dozen and more stagings – but her theatre-pieces are exhausting wastes of babble, posturing, incoherent and disjunct activity, whose ingredients are all too familiar. There are such infantile delights as water-games, mucking around in the audience, eating, building tiny structures, and parrot-like repetition: if it is fatuous first time round, play it again, Sam, and it will miraculously acquire the status of "art".

All of this can serve to introduce the present season at Sadler's Wells of Bausch's *Tanztheater Wuppertal*, heralded with *fanfaronades* of adoring publicity, where **Masurca Fogo** is on view. What this Fiery Mazurka is about I would not even seek to guess – save to note that the old Bausch tricks and a few Bauschian treats are on display for two-and-a-half hours. White-box stage, whose depths are covered with a basalt-ish mound that serves as a beach for various desultory bathing scenes. Portuguese popular music and some dim American songs: film of Brazilian peasantry; water-games (a do-it-yourself water chute: the cast spitting and throwing water at each other; a walrus; a closing sequence in which, brilliantly projected, the sea seems to engulf the stage) and a final paroxysm of sentimentality as we are obliged to watch a lengthy display of time-lapse film of flowers opening and closing, which is projected over the supine bodies of the cast. So restful: so lovely; such a cop-out.

The comic moments are a relief – a couple passing a pair of false-teeth to each other under a table as they dine – and the dance is rough and ready in its physicality (the men busting a gut as they rush over the stage: the women swung around on chairs and emitting orgasmic moans) and extinguishingly the same. **Masurca Fogo** is a fine example of an absurdist collage posing as commentary on the human condition. I find it shapeless, pointless, teutonically portentous, and in danger of disappearing up its own mazurka. The programme book is an offensively clever object: four inches wide, 23 inches long. Useful perhaps as a fly-swat, but about as easy to read as the Rosetta Stone, and both stiflingly pretentious and uninformative. Avoid it. ∎

Pina Bausch
Tanztheater Wuppertal

Sadler's Wells

FT

FINANCIAL
TIMES

THE BAUSCH CIRCUS has arrived in town, proposing two performances each of 10 stagings (inspired by 10 cities) shared between The Barbican and Sadler's Wells. You will doubtless have heard the glad cries that have greeted this news, and the hosannas that halo Pina Bausch's form of Tanztheater.

And among them one or two voices, criers in the wilderness (not least mine), noting that the *Theater* is hobbledehoy, the *Tanz* rudimentary, and the whole business is altogether too neurotic and scattershot to merit so much cheering. That, indeed, the emperor has no new clothes and that these holiday jigsaws (so predictably assembled from the little ideas and observations brought into the elves' workshop by the members of the Bausch troupe as they scoured a town for nuggets of activity to please their leader) made for indifferent drama and arid dance.

It is theatre as grab-bag, and the contents are materials for an ill-focused, rambling staging. The opening event was **Viktor**, which is declared to be "about" Rome. (The Olympic Village, Brazzaville, Gomorrah seem equally probable as locale). During more than three hours of shouting, feeding the audience with buns, offering dogs for auction, swinging on ropes, moving in dullest unison, removing clothes, putting on clothes, sawing wood, serving spaghetti (very funny this, as done by three decrepit waitresses), making tape-loop chatter, shovelling soil from surrounding embankments (the stage is ringed with

earthworks), running into the auditorium, and repeating these activities *ad nauseam*, we have to accept these merry games as evocative of Rome. The city of the Papacy, of Caesars, of fountains, squares, steps, spiffy couture, early artichokes, glorious ruins and churches. Frau Bausch's little helpers found grubbiness, neurosis, fatuities to bring back from their sorties.

This is Tanztheater as it often is: an arena for asphyxiating tedium, dreary predictabilities, incident by rote, performance cast in terms of routine - Bausch events are a safe haven for clichés. **Viktor** drones on, using up – like every major bore – all the air in the world. Breathe freely. Avoid Tanztheater! Two stars, for the three waitresses. ∎

**11th June
2012**

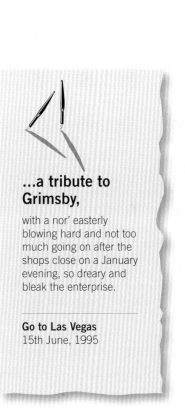

...a tribute to Grimsby,

with a nor' easterly blowing hard and not too much going on after the shops close on a January evening, so dreary and bleak the enterprise.

Go to Las Vegas
15th June, 1995

Mats Ek
Cullberg Ballet

The Sleeping Beauty

FT
FINANCIAL TIMES

The Playhouse, Edinburgh

3rd September 1999

"So *Beauty* is defiled, deconstructed" (2010)

"LET'S BURY DANCING" has been a theme of this year's Festival – implicit if not explicit – and the final nail in the coffin, the first sod to fall on the wooden overcoat, was Tuesday night's showing of **Sleeping Beauty** at the cavernous and 40-watt crepuscular Playhouse. It was like going into a mortuary to take a last look at the Loved One.

This **Beauty** was not, of course, the Tchaikovsky/Petipa staging, which remains the supreme pinnacle of classic dance, but a brutal travesty perpetrated by Mats Ek for the Cullberg Ballet. Ek's mugging of the ballet is carried out in the name of relevance and modernisation because, we must suppose, his audience cannot understand formal order, grace of composition, sublimity of expression, purity of language.

So **Beauty** is defiled, deconstructed. Its score is cut, mindlessly re-ordered, played at extreme speeds, its musical sense denied, and its *disjecta membra* assembled as a basis for an Idiot narrative. Aurora becomes a junkie. Carabosse is her pusher. The fairies are by turns nurses, housemaids, hookers. Much of the prologue is dished up as a protracted scene of childbirth, and is unspeakably vulgar.

The music for Aurora's entrance in the first act finds her parents busily copulating under a blanket. And so – gruesomely, insensitively, mindlessly – on. The recording used is reverberant, lacking something in rhythmic muscle, and it is tormented in many ways by Ek's genius for inapt use of music. I recall that his mother, Birgit Cullberg, made mincemeat of several Beethoven scores in her detestable **Bellman**. Heredity tells.

The Ek dance-style, which is vehement, boisterous, devoid of subtlety – it would suit television advertisements for motor-car airbags – marches across Tchaikovsky like an invading horde. As poor Tchaikovsky (and, inferentially, Petipa) lay trampled underfoot, I thought of other desecrations of works of art, of books burned, of museums pillaged. I thought of the great dancers whom I have known as Aurora – Fonteyn and Markova and Kolpakova and Semenyaka and Nerina and Sibley among many others – who dedicated their artistry and their lives to revealing the beauties of this choreographic miracle, and I listened in despair as the Playhouse audience laughed merrily at Ek's ham-fisted activities and his noxious jokes.

Of course, **Beauty** will survive. But the barbarians are at the gates, and their standards and their corrupting manners have the power to desecrate the past so that we can no longer rejoice in it and learn from it. The Cullberg company banged about the stage, occasionally shouting or screeching to accompany the score. The dancer as guttersnipe. ∎

William Forsythe & John Neumeier

Théâtre du Châtelet,
Palais Garnier,
Paris

FT

FINANCIAL
TIMES

'Paris Woes'

4th July
1997

THEY WERE NOT, as the week began, the happiest couple of days I have spent in Paris. Not because of the steady drizzle of rain, which does nothing for the joy of life on the boulevards, but because of an unrelenting downpour of lumpen choreography owed to William Forsythe and John Neumeier, which does nothing for the joy of dancing.

FRANKFURT BALLET, **SLEEPERS GUTS**

At the Théâtre du Châtelet, Forsythe's Frankfurt Ballet was making its customary summer visit. The season's novelty was *Sleepers Guts*, a corporate effort by Forsythe and seven of his dancers, incomprehensible as to title, and as sulkily uncommunicative as anything I have seen Forsythe make in the past. The ingredients are those we have seen before with the Frankfurt troupe – the piece, indeed, seems a corporately conceived cliché about "what we like to do on stage".

There is an omnipresent feeling of gloom. Four girls gabble. Video projections and tiny slogans are manifest. The sound-track grates on the ear. The setting is a place of desolation. The dancers indulge in those self-contained, self-centred activities that look as if movement has knotted itself irrevocably inside their bodies and can find no way out.

Pretentious, intellectually costive, it is dance as a form of addled theorising about the nature of vision, of space, of time. It is

peculiar and awful, and will – I venture – eventually disappear up its own deconstructed fundamentals. I record that it was greeted by its devoted audience with enthusiasm. The tragedy for me is that Forsythe can make dance of an aggressive and fascinating power. But neither he nor his acolytes have done anything in this new work but strike Frankfurt attitudes – alienated, embattled, dull.

PARIS OPERA BALLET, **SYLVIA**

Rather more serious, far more disappointing, was the new **Sylvia** that the Paris Opéra Ballet commissioned from John Neumeier, which had its premiere on Monday night. In a self-righteous programme note, Neumeier declares that it is "normal to keep a certain distance from the music and rid the work of its 'operetta' elements which have seduced certain choreographers". If only Neumeier had allowed himself to be seduced! And not kept his distance. We would have been spared a score severely cut (but bolstered with inter-polations from Delibes' early **La Source**), and one mistreated to support an addled scenario and choreography both harsh and unyielding.

Delibes' miraculous score (Tchaikovsky, rightly, preferred it to the Ring cycle) is the ultimate "musique dansante", whose effort-less melody, rhythmic vitality, luscious textures, positively invite dance. It is one of the masterpieces of 19th century music. Its original narrative was pretty, very much in the *école pompier* manner, and none the worse for that. (Ashton showed that it •••

could work in one of his greatest ballets). Neumeier has substituted an awkward updating, with Sylvia awakened to passion by Cupid (who is also the villain Orion, who seduces her, and an obliging shepherd) and returning after a passage of years to find her true love Aminta, although he is – apparently – now married to someone else. Pah!

If the narrative is clogged with excess mythic baggage, the dance is so resistant to the score's beauties, so mannered in its modernities, so devoid of feeling or even good old-fashioned sparkle, that it seems downright cussed in its determination to reject Delibes. This is ballet as comic strip.

Visually the piece is also a muddle. The sets by Yannis Kokkos are massively simple. The Garnier stage becomes a green box containing only massive blue trees and a blue rock for Act 1. A white box with a monumental classic male torso is the setting for the first scene of Act 2 – a ball-room of glacial charm – while the second and final scene is the forest in winter. (Neumeier has condensed the action as he has butchered the score). Clothing is modern and largely hideous. Diana and her huntresses are got up like the Lesbos Home Guard. Sylvia returns in the final scene in an ochre New Look outfit that suggests she is someone's concierge. Cupid is very cute in red dungarees and baseball cap.

Faced with this, the Opéra dancers labour with all their prodigious skills. To read the cast-list is to salivate in anticipation. Monique Loudières is Sylvia; Élisabeth Platel is Diana; Manuel Legris is Aminta, who loves Sylvia; Nicolas Le Riche is Cupid, Orion and Thyrsis; Jose Martinez is Endymion, Diana's beloved.

These peerless artists do everything except recite Excelsior is an attempt to make sense of what they have been given. Loudières suffers beautifully. Platel, once rid of an Amy Johnson helmet, is commandingly beautiful and dominating, and looks stunning in white tie and tails, as she does in black velvet (please don't ask why). Legris agonises, and is a

marvel. Le Riche, that phenomenal talent, has a different walk, even a different physique, for each role. Martinez begins the ballet asleep by the blue rock, and must play the somnambulist throughout, save when trapped in a duet in which he has to partner Platel while both lie on the floor. It amounts to persecution. The corps de ballet are elegant, high-stepping, and get the best choreography of the evening. Finally, the curtain falls – like a guillotine-blade on Delibes' beautiful ballet.

Re-doing the old classics (and *Sylvia* has an honourable identity at the Opéra) is a dangerous game. It is one totally lost in this new staging. Let us have back the charming version that Lycette Darsonval danced and then re-mounted at the Opéra. It honoured one of the masterpieces of French music. It honoured French ballet. ▮

Ohad Naharin...
dresses 19 dancers like waiters at Le Pansy Cafe.

Axioma
7th November, 1996

Artifact

William Forsythe
Dutch National Ballet

The Playhouse, Edinburgh

18th August 1999

CRITICS RECEIVE LETTERS. Usually these are serious notes from perceptive correspondents. Occasionally they are not. The oddest was brought on by **Swan Lake**, which my reader identified with biblical events, indulging himself in pages of closely written argument in which illogicality led one into realms of unease and confusion.

I recalled these dread missives on Monday while watching the Dutch National Ballet inaugurate the dance matters of the Festival with William Forsythe's **Artifact**. The piece is quintessential Forsythe, both in its theatrical form – disjunct activity that edges into and away from academic dance; full-eclipse gloom; gabble; pretensions as high as an elephant's eye – and in its ability to persuade the public that they are seeing something significant.

That Forsythe has something to say is beyond doubt. Whether we can understand it, whether it is cast in comprehensible form, is another matter. Criticism of Forsythe's work in Germany and France is ecstatic – when you can dig your way through it – costively intellectual, and in great danger of disappearing up its own fervour. It is, indeed, as glum and portentous as the work it extols.

Forsythe's dance theatre is one of wild flights of disconnected fancy, non-communication, muscular extravagance, sign-language for the use of Papuan tribesmen. That his theatrical sense is intense, and intensely personal, there is no gainsaying. The massed ranks of dancers involved with small nuggets of academic dance; the light that conceals more than it reveals; the inward-turned, self-obsessed and self-abusing manner in which the audience is cast as voyeur rather than participant in a theatrical experience – all this is the alienating and aggressive choreographic style we watch, movement justified by disconnection rather than connection. This is the world of **Artifact**. A collage rather than a choreographic text, made of four parts – music by Bach, Eva Crossman-Hecht (for piano, and sounding like rancid Hindemith, but grandly played by Margot Kazimirska), and with din recorded by Forsythe himself – it purports to have a dramatic scheme and comes fully accoutred with chat. Kathleen Fitzgerald, dressed like a baroque opera heroine, recites nonsense, repetitious nonsense, throughout the evening, and is brilliant. (Her best line, you must forgive me noting, is "Shut the fuck up!") Nicholas Champion also talks, but is largely inaudible – as if that mattered. In the third part, the curtain crashed down six times on some brutish duets, sounding like a guillotine, and were there justice in the world it would have acted like one.

The Dutch dancers slaved away, gesturing, stepping, drawing themselves up in formation, keeping expression at bay. Even so they looked fine. The last section is a choreographic shout in which the entire troupe is involved. And what were they shouting? I suspect it was a message to the audience: "Abandon hope all ye who enter here". ∎

Claire Philippart
Enrichetta Cavalotti
Artifact

Roland Petit
Ballets de Paris

Carmen
(21 February 1949)

Prince's Theatre, London

21st July 2011

Memories of Carmen

It was a first night unlike any other I have known

A BALLETOMANE from the age of… I have been hugely fortunate to be in theatres when audiences have been rocked joyously back on their heels – the Bolshoi Ballet's first appearance in London; earliest sightings of such artists as Plisetskaya, Makarova, Baryshnikov, Nureyev. No ballet, I suspect, has so generated an almost explosive reaction during the performance itself as Roland Petit's **Carmen** at the Prince's Theatre, London, on 21 February 1949. Names can change with the years: Zizi Jeanmaire – a flame at the ballet's heart as

Carmen – was still known as Renée, and the Prince's Theatre is now the Shaftsbury but Petit's **Carmen** is still Carmen after thousands of performances around the world, and Antoni Clavé's designs for the production still rank among the most prodigious stage decoration of the past sixty years. We gain our first impression of a ballet from the images we see as the curtain rises – and oh, the heart-sinking moments we know from so much dreary design today. But Clavé's decors and costumes gave us the first dazzling idea of what was to come on that evening, a firework display of vivid colours, of dramatic shapes, of Spain – Mérimée's Spain, Bizet's Spain – vitally gloriously there for us.

What we saw, as the choreography took irresistible hold, was – to the audience's eager, almost hypnotised gaze – of unprecedented dramatic verve, incandescent with emotion, with what, after the first night, that great critic Richard Buckle called "the stinking, noisy, wonderful life of café, street and public holiday. Carmen has eyes for which cardinals would renounce their scarlet, but her breath smells of garlic and there are bugs in her bed".

Petit had wanted Carmen to seem an almost androgynous figure, and to this end Jeanmaire had her hair cut in that cropped style that has since then been part of her image. The audience responded immediately to the performances; to Petit's elegance, his Don José an impassioned and doomed figure; and to

Zizi, then Renée, Jeanmaire (Carmen) Roland Petit (Don José) (1949)

178

Sadler's Wells

Jeanmaire's fierce emotions, her wit and sizzling energies in dancing, and her utter identification with the role of Carmen.

I can still hear the applause and the shouts that greeted her after her solo in the second scene, which in every sense, stopped the show, and the intensity with which we followed the erotic frankness of the love duet, sunlight slanting through the shutters of Carmen's bedroom. But it was the final *pas de deux*, that culminating moment of passion, which sealed the evening's triumph. Petit has recorded how, as he and Jeanmaire engaged in this lost and furious encounter she was exhausted and whispered "I can't go on!" His response was to turn his mimed blows at her body into real ones, and the duet raced to its conclusion.

From our seats in the auditorium, this closing scene was incandescent with feeling, and has proved unforgettably part of balletic legend. The curtain fell and had to rise again twenty times, so tremendous the artistry we had seen, so glorious its effects. There were, inevitably, the shocked prune-faces who thought that ballet should still be populated almost exclusively with fairies and dainty emotions, and in France distinguished literary figure inveighed against the use of Bizet's score. But Petit's **Carmen** and, I must add, Jeanmaire's Carmen, remain glorious. They don't, alas, make them like that any more! ∎

Near Life Experience

2nd May 2004

WE HAVE BEEN SACRIFICING at the wrong altars. That hecatomb of oxen, the incense – all in vain, dammit, since the frightful Angelin Preljocaj is back at Sadler's Wells with another tedious piece of what passes *chez lui* as choreography. It is called **Near Life Experience**; its more likely title is **Nowhere Near A Dance Experience**. Here are all those unhallowed signs of costive eurodance – Preljocaj and his troupe are installed at Aix en Provence – including the portentous programme notes, the jaw-cracking lucubrations about theme, posturing, both physical and intellectual, and an absence of that vivid relationship between movement and music esteemed by aficionados on the (shall we say) New York/London axis.

I have sat through these trials by Preljocaj for more than a decade and watched in vain for a spark of choreographic wit. The verbiage in the programme about what **Near Life Experience** means and why Preljocaj made it has to be set against the glue-footed trudgings of a dozen dancers, the balls of red wool, the couple wearing cheap wine glasses stuck to their bodies, the birth of a soap-covered male from a ball of wool and the lack of communication.

Frightfully earnest, of course, and burdened with thoughts about life and exhaustion but denuded of interest unless you care for lethargic performers who occasionally fall into agonised poses. ∎

Bronislava Nijinska
The Royal Ballet

The Wedding

FINANCIAL
TIMES

Royal Opera House,
Covent Garden

**25th March
1966**

WHEN THE HISTORY of Sir Frederick Ashton's directorate of the Royal Ballet comes to be written not the least important feature of it will be the chance he has given us to see Bronislava Nijinska's genius plain. He has always acknowledged his debt to her as a formative influence for his own creativity, and by giving us **Les Biches**, and now **The Wedding** (the French title **Les Noces** is hardly justifiable) he has reasserted her major importance in twentieth century ballet.

With last night's staging of **The Wedding** one of the most significant of the Diaghilev ballets has been preserved – though this is hardly the word for a work of such thrilling vitality. On any terms **The Wedding** is an amazing achievement, seen in the context of its creation over 40 years ago, its originality and daring are even more magnificent.

Stravinsky conceived the plan of this choreographic cantata at the beginning of 1914 (his last visit to Russia was to go to Kiev to secure folk material for the libretto); and it is not without interest to remark that it was his next ballet after **Rite of Spring**. Both works are concerned with the Russian past, but by 1914 Stravinsky had moved on from the direct musical statement of Rite to a more refined and stylised manner.

Rhythmic, percussive, owing something to liturgical chant, and more to folk-song, **The Wedding** uses a chorus and soloists, four pianos and a large battery of percussion,

both pitched and unpitched. Stravinsky wrote: "This combination of sonorities arose necessarily and solely out of my music to **The Wedding** and did not spring from the desire to imitate the sounds of a popular festivity".

The score was completed in 1917 (Diaghilev wept on hearing the piano version, saying he had never listened to anything that touched him more) but events prevented its staging until six years later, when, following the success of Renard, Diaghilev asked Nijinska to undertake **The Wedding**.

Stravinsky has stated that her realisation of it was at variance with his own intentions for the work as a divertissement of the masquerade type, with musicians and dancers mingled on stage. Be that as it may, the ballet as seen last night is superb, its four scenes show the blessing first of the bride, then of the groom, the bride's departure for the groom's house, and the final wedding celebrations. Visually austere – the Goncharova costumes are simple peasant uniforms in brown and white, the decor of stark simplicity – musically massive in its wonderful rhythms and sonorities, **The Wedding** comes over as a masterly choreographic abstraction of the rituals and attitudes that are the basis of a peasant marriage.

Nijinska has captured the inner spirit of these ceremonies, giving it a clear-cut intensity that matches Stravinsky's score: their sophistication of approach is equal, though entirely different. The revival of **Les Biches** reaffirmed to our audiences that Nijinska is a splendidly original choreographer; now **The Wedding** shows another facet of a magnificent creative talent. It is a work of massive power, couched in a dance language that is purged of all decorative excess, yet entirely revelatory of its theme. The corps de ballet are the heart of the piece, used as a form of human architecture, moving in blocks, piled in – pyramids, linked in chains, turning and wheeling in great arcs of movement. The very anonymity of the costuming throws into relief the corporate nature of the ritual, with the Bride and Groom as central icon figures, the heart and focus of the seemingly liturgical dance activity.

The work has a hieratic air; the poses and grouping of the dancers possess a bold clarity – like the costumes the movement is stripped down to its essential attitudes – yet it is also densely and subtly organised, Nijinska shows an unfailing authority in handling her forces, contrasting the warm femininity of the women with a taut muscled energy for the men. And the movement is unfailingly responsive to the tremendous rhythms of the score; despite the formal limitations imposed by the ritualistic treatment of the theme, despite a fundamental and essential simplicity of manner, the choreography is wonderfully satisfying. In the wedding festivities it has a cumulative force that is amazing; the action seems carved out of a whole race experience, strong, bold, with its frescoes and blocks of bodies, one piled against the other.

As the central figures Beriosova and Robert Mead are noble, expressive, and in the wedding solos Georgina Parkinson and Anthony Dowell respond perfectly to the very different virtuosity of their roles. The performance from both stage and orchestra pit was vital and strong, and the corps de ballet added cubits to their stature by the rhythmic alertness and intensity of their dancing (particular mention to be made of Kenneth Mason, whose strength and superb involvement in the movement was remarkable even in this fine performance). After the model of the 1926 London premiere, when Auric, Rieti, Poulenc and Dukelcky were the pianists, the Royal Ballet offered us Richard Rodney Bennett, John Gardner, Edmund Rubbra and Malcolm Williamson; and John Lanchbery admirably realised the music's worth with an excellent vocal and percussion ensemble. ∎

Frederick Ashton, Bronislava Nijinska and Svetlana Beriosova at a rehearsal for *Les Noces*, London (1966)

Vaslav Nijinsky

L'Après-midi d'un Faune

FT
FINANCIAL
TIMES

**21st January
2006**

THE MYSTERY OF Vaslav Nijinsky's genius is made clear to us in his first choreographic work, *L'Après-midi d'un Faune*, staged for the Diaghilev Ballets Russes in Paris in 1912. This is the only survivor of the four ballets he created before mental illness imprisoned him in 1919 until his death in 1950. That he was a genius as a dancer every witness agreed. That he was a genius as a choreographer is seen in *Faune*, which has been in continuing performance since its creation. *Faune* was the first truly original choreography of the 20th century.

It proposed nothing "balletic", either in step or bodily articulation. Nor was it conventional in response to Debussy's score – though the 24-year-old Nijinsky was reared in the conventions of St Petersburg ballet. The dance offered a flattened image inspired by antique bas reliefs and vase painting, the body held in walking position, trunk turned towards the audience, head aligned with legs, arms in controlled poses. This was the envelope for an intense sensuality.

The movement emerged from a walking step, the Faun indulging in only one leap. Everything was stylised: the track of the dance a line in front of Bakst's luscious, sunlit Attic landscape; the nymphs, whom the Faun lusts after, wearing exquisite draperies, their movement angular, succinct. The choreography was set against Debussy's music, denying its shimmering light, its structure, asking the seven nymphs (who had to forget everything they had previously known to bring the piece to the stage) to walk between and over the bar-lines.

What Nijinsky created was a personal, long-considered language, conceived solely for this brief work, speaking of sexuality as it had never been seen before in ballet. Here was sex as a natural urge that the Faun must, and does, gratify. Nothing in ballet since *Faune* has so broken with its past, so compellingly, so beautifully. ∎

Vaslav Nijinsky
L'Apres-midi d'un Faune
(1912)

182

La Valse
Symphonic Variations
Sylvia *pas de deux*
Birthday Offering *pas de deux*
Daphnis and Chloe

Frederick Ashton
The Royal Ballet

Royal Opera House,
Covent Garden

A Celebration

IN THE WEEKS leading up to Christmas, the Royal Ballet is offering two programmes of ballets by Sir Frederick Ashton, with the added seasonal pleasure of his **Cinderella**. This is a first and over-due celebration of the work of the man whose creations vitally shaped our national style of classic dance.

Ashton was a genius. First Marie Rambert, then Ninette de Valois gave him his earliest chances, and de Valois – prescient as ever – entrusted him with the role of chief choreographer to her company in 1935. From that moment on he made ballets which can be seen as an ascending curve of imaginative brilliance, craft and poetic sensibility.

I have been fortunate enough to see much of his work with its first casts. (Ashton was often indifferent to dancers who took over roles, and could make such devastating comments as "She's not chic" – by which he meant wit in technique and manner). His maturity as a choreographer came after the war. For the next three decades he made ballets whose variety and felicity of means were central to the Royal Ballet's identity.

He took on the mantle of Petipa and gave us **Cinderella**, the delicious and shamefully neglected **Sylvia**, the tragic **Ondine**, the sunburst of **La Fille mal gardée**, and the romance of **The Two Pigeons**. He explored Fonteyn's gifts in role after role. He could evoke Greek myth

in the mysterious **Persephone** and **Daphnis and Chloe**, and extract the essence from a drama to make a work as emotionally succinct as **Month in the Country**. He could be hugely and subtly funny in **A Wedding Bouquet**, and very moving through no less subtle means in **Lament of the Waves**. He could make dance glitter – one of his own favourite works was the sublime theorem of **Scènes de ballet** – and make his dancers opulent, grand, in **Birthday Offering**.

Above all, his creativity fed on music, and on qualities he sensed in his interpreters – hence his lack of much interest in their successors. His ballets remain the truest portrait of his company for much of its existence. So now, somewhat belatedly, the Royal Ballet makes an Ashton homage. A stage shared with opera precludes the celebrations that New York City Ballet gave in last spring's showing of 73 Balanchine works. But I made a tally of some 30 Ashton pieces which should be in the repertory. A national ballet owes this to its dancers and audiences: the Ashton heritage is no less important than, say, the works of Benjamin Britten, and Ashton must be accounted one of our greatest lyric poets.

Thursday night's first programme brought a revival and re-decoration of **Daphnis and Chloé**, the return of **La Valse** and **Symphonic Variations**, and duets from **Sylvia** and **Birthday Offering**, works spanning 12 great Ashtonian years, 1946-58. The evening was the victim of injuries: four principals, among others, were replaced. It is for this reason that I am **•••**

**15th November
1994**

Sir Frederick Ashton
in dress rehearsal
Symphonic Variations
(1967)

Durante and Irek Mukhamedov. Mukhamedov has the power the dance needs, though he makes it seem more Bolshoi-like than heretofore. Durante seemed flustered by intricacies that Fonteyn played with a delicious and understated amusement in what Ashton had set her to do. But the duet whets the appetite: we really must have the whole ballet restored to the stage with its ravishing designs by the Ironside brothers.

Daphnis and Chloé has been long overdue for return. Now it is back, with new design by Martyn Bainbridge replacing John Craxton's original decoration. The initial impression of Bainbridge's work is excellent. His permanent set is of creamy stone walls with a distant landscape shimmering through horizontal lines which mask the backdrop. The costuming is timeless yet suitably archaic, in natural-coloured linen and wool for the villagers, rather more conventionally piratical for Bryaxis and his crew. I think it a miscalculation to use an obviously theatrical moon and tinselly stars for the pirate scene, and to make the last act seem like a dowager's sequinned bosom glittering all-too-brightly in the morning light. These seem trumpery when contrasted with the earlier aptness of the design.

The Chloé of Trinidad Sevillano – a replacement for an injured Sarah Wildor – was deliciously soft in outline and tender in manner, and the character lived. So did Stuart Cassidy's Daphnis, happily combining innocence and passion. Lykanion and Dorkon, who must tempt the young lovers, were given first sketches by Benazir Hussein and Adam Cooper, but the pirate Bryaxis needs a far weightier presence than Matthew Hart's physique can bring – the part cries out for Mukhamedov. This is, nonetheless, a welcome revival. Let it be the precursor of much more Ashton – and MacMillan – restored to the stage: their work is our national ballet's treasure, and identity. ∎

reluctant to say much about **Symphonic Variations**, which looked studied rather than spontaneous. Because this work has been elevated to the status of a sacred text, it is too often danced as if its cast were in church. Bruce Sansom in the leading male role was fine: the rest of the cast looked tentative. They might adopt some of the freedom and sense of giving themselves to the pulse of the music which made the opening **La Valse** look so handsome as Ravel's whirlwind bore its couples along.

The two *pas de deux* made me long for the entire ballets from which they were extracted. **Birthday Offering** was, in 1956, a loving portrait of the company's seven ballerinas in the year of its silver jubilee. (I wish I thought that the present troupe could field seven such varied and fascinating artists). At the heart of it, of course, Margot Fonteyn and her cavalier, Michael Somes. On Thursday, Lesley Collier and Jonathan Cope gave the duet its proper grace. Collier has wit and the proper understanding of Ashtonian nuance, and Cope is a handsome partner: the piece was alive.

The **Sylvia** duet – one of Ashton's most brilliant and demanding creations for Fonteyn and Somes – did not look happy with Viviana

**Samples
Out of doors
Concerto Grosso
Homage**

Mark Baldwin

The Place,
London

FT
FINANCIAL
TIMES

**14th March
1995**

MARK BALDWIN, a fine dancer with the Rambert troupe in its earlier incarnation, has in recent years turned to choreography, to excellent effect. I might add that in earliest Rambert times, Dame Marie would have been goading, squeezing dances out of him just as soon as he showed the least interest in making movement – and perhaps even before that.

Well, the wait has been worthwhile. From his first slight creations a few seasons ago, Baldwin has shown that he is a true choreographer – unlike so many of those graceless optimists who come before us with meagre technique and rampant pretentions, he has craft, imagination, wit, and a sense of formal structure.

Baldwin worked with several serious creators in his Rambert years. What he offers, though, is not earnest reminders of other men's steps, but something happily fresh and personal. And, rarest of joys in today's choreographic world, he feels no need to give us messages about life, despair, disease, or the dreadful plight of the oppressed.

Baldwin, with that fugitive from the Royal Ballet Jonathan Burrows, makes dance whose originality and very artistic existence owes much to a serious theatrical experience, and in this lies the strength of both their visions of what they wish their dance to be. Like Burrows, Baldwin is forging his own language, and like Burrows – whom he in no other way resembles – he knows what he wants to do.

There are two clear characteristics in what he creates, and they shone like the best of deeds in his brief season at The Place last week. He has a dry, sly wit – shown in the structure of his work as in its manner – and he is intensely musical. Not for him a Mickey-Mousing step-for-note obedience. Rather does he find pleasure (and perhaps some amusement) in running counter to a score's surface while yet respecting its essential form and nature.

So, in his **Samples**, which is set to the Ravel *Introduction and Allegro*, the music's opening serenities are confronted by wild activity for four dancers. Yet we soon notice that musical phrasing is matched by dance phrase, that the shape and pulse of the score has conditioned what the dancers do. It is a surprising, and surprisingly happy realisation of the music.

These same qualities were apparent in two other pieces, set to Bartok's *Out of Doors* and a Handel concerto grosso. Baldwin's imagination matches, comments on – even makes jokes about – his music. (He is, in this, like Paul Taylor and Mark Morris, and like them he has musical taste far above the common run of his contemporaries). Movement can be unexpected. Baldwin sets his dancers curling, falling, leaping, following a gesture to unexpected conclusions, riding on and with the score in a symbiotic relationship. Faced with the mysteries of Bartok's night music, he creates a world of nocturnal mystery quite as beautiful as that in the piano-writing. In **Homage**, a cunning piece played in silence and, •••

At times,
the sets suggest
Oklahokum!

**Far from the Madding
Crowd**
26th February, 1996

I'd venture, made as a tribute to Richard Alston, Baldwin creates phrasing as musical and neat as if there were an audible score.

The extra distinction of Baldwin's work is his use of fine dancers – including himself. (He sometimes appears as a quizzical master of ceremonies, not a little entertained by what is going on). In this Place season he presents two extraordinary talents, Lynne Bristow and Paul Old, together with the admirable Deborah Saxon and Shelley Baker. The lovely Miss Bristow moves like an angel. In her Royal Ballet days she was a classicist's treasure by reason of her clarity and purity of style. In modern work – she has danced in most of Jonathan Burrows' pieces – dance pours through her in long, marvellously shaped phrases. Everything she does is fascinating, beautiful.

Paul Old, a superb dancer with Rambert, has similar distinction: his dancing is rich in its variety of pulse, harmonious. In a solo in **Homage**, and in **Concerto Grosso** (a work riven with marvellous quirks and shifts of activity, from mad tremblings to long swirls and swathes of energy), Old moves with splendid authority. But everything in the evening enhances the dancers, shows them at their best – another sign of good choreography.

Baldwin's dances have clear roots in his own performance past – Cunningham and Alston are points of reference – but they are unmistakeably Baldwin's, because sophisticated in means, and unmistakably good. ∎

Paul Old
Concerto Grosso
(1995)

David Bintley
The Sadler's Wells
Royal Ballet

Sadler's Wells

FT

FINANCIAL
TIMES

**4th May
1978**

DAVID BINTLEY WAS the Dr. Coppélius of the Royal Ballet School performance three years ago. He graduated into the Wells Royal Ballet, and there he swiftly gained a reputation for character dancing of exceptional ability: his blind reveller in **Prodigal Son** was a brilliant, daring piece of theatre; the non-existent role of a footman in **The Lady and the Fool** was suddenly made vivid. Bintley also started making choreography for workshop performances, and in these an evident talent was to be appreciated.

Last night his first professional ballet was given its London debut by SWRB, and although I am not going to declare: "Hats off, gentlemen: a genius". It is plain that Bintley is very gifted. Just how gifted the next ballets and the next years – with all their attendant disappointments and uncertainties – will show, but not since the first night of MacMillan's **Danses Concertantes** have I been so persuaded of talent bubbling and fighting to express itself in the Royal Ballet.

Bintley's theme is taken from Albert Camus. His title, **The Outsider**, and something of his manner, are MacMillanesque. His sense of theatre – and the ballet has a harsh, driving energy to it – is all his own. As a first work it has the faults, and more than all the virtues, one might expect: a narrative that does not stay entirely in focus, but which is brought off with a seemingly intuitive understanding of what the theatre can do for dance; characters that are stereotypes – whores, pimps,

faceless "other selves" of the anti-hero – but drawn with sharp choreographic strokes; a theme not completely coherent, but so cleverly presented that one cares not at all about its vaguenesses.

Meursault, the hero of Camus' *L'Etranger*, was uninvolved, unfeeling. Him Bintley borrows, together with incidents from the novel, to create a fantasy in which Meursault, Dariol, a pimp, and Renée, a whore, play out their drama, while Meursault's detachment from life is expressed by a chorus of three other aspects of his own self.

Bintley's score is the *Suita Dramatica* by Josef Bohàc, suitably tense and atmospheric; the setting is urban dismal, a skilled design by Mike Beckett which catches the feeling of those films of the late 1940s in which it always seemed to be raining. With these elements, Bintley concocts an action in which passion, sudden death and brutality are commonplaces. But because he has an essential originality of manner and a gift for stimulating strong, alert performances from his cast, **The Outsider** becomes far more than an intellectualised, but rather coarse-grained anecdote. It is so well danced – by Stephen Wicks as Meursault, by David Morse as Dariol, by Lois Strike as Renée, and by the whole ensemble – and is so pungent in its atmosphere, that it suggests an authentic choreographic voice is to be heard at the Wells. And that is a cause for rejoicing indeed. ∎

Michael Clark

No Fire Escape in Hell

FINANCIAL
TIMES

Sadler's Wells

**18th September
1986**

IN AN AGE OF GRAFFITI there is little very surprising in the sort of angry scrawls that Michael Clark choreographically daubs. That the writing appears low-down on the artistic wall and is largely confined to the more brutish monosyllables is unsurprising. Over the past few years Mr Clark has gained a reputation as a child of his time, an easily recognisable symbol of mocking and disorientated youth. The darling of the colour magazines, the hapless subject of a television documentary of numbing fatuity seen on Channel 4, his identity is now fixed – thanks to media hype – as a "shocking" young performer. Diaghilev's apostrophe to Cocteau – "astonish me" – finds a willing exponent in Michael Clark, and so he astonishes us by the hallowed juvenile means of talking (or dancing) "dirty" and making lot of noise.

His newest piece, **No Fire Escape in Hell** had its first performance at Sadler's Wells last night, and repeats all the usual tricks with which we have in the past been variously amused or bored. As a self-proclaimed advocate of dance as real-life – though whose remains a debatable point – Mr Clark again offers us the smutty jokes (fellatio with police truncheons; an artificial penis; genitals drawn on costumes; padded and squeaking buttocks) and the ill-organised capers which are now his stock in trade, during two tedious acts.

He then plays his "serious" card for the closing section of the work. Laibach, a Yugoslav rock band, perform live on stage,

and the Wells management were astute enough to provide critics with ear-plugs. Whether the unplugged audience escaped at the end without impaired hearing I do not know: even through layers of pink wax, the din was horrific, barbarous. It did not, though, disguise the demure and flimsy choreography which the nine members of the troupe displayed with madcap abandon.

What saves the evening from being merely an exercise in misdirected energy is, as always, Michael Clark's own presence as dancer. Whether seen in a contemplative solo which begins the evening, or being carried across the stage (in drag, not surprisingly) impeccable insteps supported in high-heeled shoes, he remains a continually fascinating performer. If, as I am told, **No Fire Escape in Hell** is about living in fear, the worst we have to fear is the loss of Michael Clark as dancer amid the scribbling of Michael Clark as choreographer. ∎

**...in a short
brown lace
number**

with a head-dress like
a suicidal meringue, all
malignly conceived to
make her look like a
teenage hooker.

**Now Languorous,
Now Wild**
9th February, 1996

Siobhan Davies
Davies Dance Company

Gardner Arts Centre, Brighton

FINANCIAL
TIMES

'Mistress of her dance'

**2nd May
1997**

WHERE HAVE THE YEARS GONE? It seems no more than a moment ago that we saw Siobhan Davies as a tall, elegantly-articulated young performer with London Contemporary Dance Theatre who was just starting to make choreography. But her first piece came in 1972, and within a couple of years she had made works which I remember admiringly to this day: **Pilot**, with its group of dancers stranded by night; **The Calm**, so serene; and the lucid, contemplative **Diary**. Here was a true, fresh and perceptive creator. Here also was a dancer who could reduce a theatre to hysterics as she set about putting up a deck-chair and changing her costume in Robert Cohan's **Waterless Method**. It was the world war organised by Bea Lillie.

Throughout the next decade these columns continued to record Davies' progress. At one moment it seemed as if her talent was becalmed, as if she had sunk too deeply within herself, but the distinction of her means, a feminine sensibility and clarity of form, were constants even of her less successful pieces. Visually her stagings were no less precise in their stylish look, and a decade ago, after a visit to America, it was as if Davies had renewed her talent, gained in physical drive with no loss of her natural refinement of expression. Her **Embarque** of 1988 for Rambert seemed to me a crucial development. The dance had a sweeping, more generous physicality than anything I had seen before.

Since then, Siobhan Davies' work has shown that confidence which comes to a creator secure in her craft as in her view of her art. Her concerns are about form and how that form may tell us about our world. Sometimes the dance's calligraphy is more vivid than the message, but the power of the brush-strokes, the subtleties of ink on paper, are handsomest rewards. And Davies demonstrates a rare virtuosity in handling her material. She dares, and knows how to bring a dare to success. In works as different as **Winnsboro Cotton Mill Blues** (made in 1992 for Rambert) and the stunning **Art of Touch** for her own troupe in 1995, she has a commanding skill in making dances. She is mistress of her art.

And never more so than in her newest piece, which forms part of a double bill of recent work now touring Britain. The Brighton Festival brought the Davies Dance Company to the Gardner Arts Centre last Thursday, where I saw the brand new **Bank** and her revision of **White Man Sleeps** which dates from 1988. **Bank** is a dazzling construction, rooted in Matteo Fargeon's percussive score. If I say that it is intellectually exhilarating, it is because Davies shows how movement may be shaped, developed, knotted, untied, spread over the stage or confined into angry clumps of dynamics. But there is also a perceptible structure of phrase and variation, and – best of all – a kind of intoxication about the nature and quality of movement itself. Her dancers – Gill Clarke, Deborah Saxon, Sarah Warsop, Sean Feldman, Paul Old, David ...

Hughes – are tremendous (and the men more tremendous than the women), and she and they are exactly attuned.

There is a drum-driven energy to the score which colours the dance; changes of dynamics, of pulse, of density, give it emotional as well as physical force. It is typified for me in the dancing of Sean Feldman. A dancer of almost transparent physicality, he accepts the choreography's impulse, and can show how a phrase begins with a sharp accent of the head which then impels body and limbs into a seamless and subtly varied phrase. (Feldman is one of the most distinguished dancers in Britain today, and over the past five years, Davies has explored and extended his mercurial gift to splendid effect).

Bank is Davies at her most Lisztian – creator as virtuoso. The revised *White Man Sleeps* is undeniably fine, albeit its language is softer, its emotional and physical climate more secretive than in **Bank**. Its score by Kevin Volans (in a version for harpsichords, percussion, viola da gamba) is, I suspect, less inviting to dance. The piece is filled with fine lines of action, but I felt slightly under-nourished by it.

Watching **Bank**, which followed, I was held by a magisterial command of stage, of movement, of theatrical effect, though – and Siobhan Davies will laugh at me for saying this – these were hinted at, oh so slightly, in **Pilot,** nearly a quarter of a century ago. She has, across these 25 years, been true to her talent, without compromise. What she has given us is a body of work of integrity, lasting significance, resonant grace. And there is (D.V.) much more to come. Doddering though I may well be by then, I look forward to her Golden Jubilee. Until then, admiration, gratitude, tremendous good wishes. ∎

White Man Sleeps

Lindsay Kemp
The Lindsay Kemp
Dance Mime Company

A FAR FROM ILLUMINATING EVENING, this, and any thoughts of either Blackpool or Rimbaud can be dismissed at once; billed as "an extravagant musical entertainment", I found that the most extravagant thing about the enterprise was that anyone should consider it entertaining.

As performed last night by The Lindsay Kemp Dance Mime Company the programme consisted of four flabby little dramas in movement, in which both dance and mime seemed reduced to their lowest common denominators.

With scores of startling monotony, and designing that looked at best haphazard, a cast of 10 cope with variously intractable choreography and a fine collection of dramatic clichés. Whether involved in a version of the Orpheus myth, an excursion into childhood, or a sea legend, the performers are not powerful enough to deal with unhelpful material: there is no achievement in using dance, mime, singing and a lot of good intentions, and then coming up with works so lacking in shape and pace.

Of ideas there are plenty; some – such as the view of Hell as a tatty bordello into which Orpheus descends down a ladder – are interesting: others – as in the story of the **Fisherman and his Soul** – seem void of theatrical life. There is no pleasure in reporting so unfavourably on what is presumably intended as a serious attempt to extend the range of dance and mime, but the results are hardly of the quality to justify presentation in the harsh world of the London theatre. ∎

11th May 1965

Lindsay Kemp
(The Flowers *Illuminations*)

Kenneth MacMillan
The Royal Ballet

FT
FINANCIAL TIMES

Royal Opera House, Covent Garden

2nd January 1961

KENNETH MACMILLAN'S latest ballet, given its London premier last Friday, is a work of major importance both for the Royal Ballet and as a development of a choreographer's great talent. From the repertory point of view it represents a choreographic manner neglected by the company, for here is a study of emotions, and an exploration of the psychology of interacting characters, revealed through wonderfully inventive dancing – an achievement that recalls the best of Antony Tudor's ballets.

Anne Heaton (the Wife) and Christopher Gable (the Boy) (1960)

DESTRUCTION

The Invitation tells of the destruction of innocence by experience. A boy and a girl, just out of the schoolroom, are shown at that precarious moment when youthful affection is ripening into a more conscious love. An unhappily married couple meet them: the wife, rejected by her husband, shows an awareness of the boy's feelings that the girl still lacks, and seduces him. The husband is drawn to the girl, who is innocently flattered and attracted by his interest. He misinterprets her attitude to him, and brutally rapes her. This cataclysm shatters the girl; when the boy returns to her she is suddenly revolted by his affection and frenziedly rejects both him and, we may understand, any chance of future happiness in love.

From these elements Macmillan creates a ballet of poetic truth and real understanding, unsentimental and without romantic falsification. The setting is a rich bourgeois household in a warm country at the turn of the century, so that period conventions and social conditions clearly "place" the characters. Macmillan has made his quartet completely real; during the ballet's 50 minutes so much is revealed of their motives and their emotional states that it is hard to believe that they cease to exist at curtain fall.

MAGNIFICENT

The Invitation is most carefully constructed, with variations in tension and tempo that allow the implications of the dance behaviour to be clearly seen, and choreographically it is

192

Kenneth MacMillan
The Royal Ballet

Royal Opera House,
Covent Garden

**11th October
1974**

magnificent. Macmillan has always been a masterly creator of movement, and he has now extended his range with dancing that is more lyrical than before, more expressive, with ensembles that sustain or amplify the action. He has made a series of *pas de deux* for his principles (sic) which show a notable fusion of technical beauty with dramatic truth, and they must be accounted at least as fine as anything he has done before.

He is splendidly served by the Company and he has inspired his four soloists to display the best of their interpretive ability; Christopher Gable makes an entirely convincing boy, Anne Heaton shows the passion and the compassion of the wife, and Desmond Doyle gives a powerful portrait of the husband.

OUTSTANDING
In the central role of the girl, Lynn Seymour gives a performance of such beauty and authority that it must rank as one of the outstanding dance interpretations of the decade: it is a further indication of the extent and richness of her talent, both as dancer and actress.

Matyas Seiher's score is entirely attuned to the choreographer's intentions and Nicolas Georgiadis has done a brilliant series of sets and costumes that not only evoke a period but complement the choreography in every situation. ∎

HEAVEN KNOWS we need our spirits raising at the moment, with the weather and the politicians rivalling each other in sheer tiresomeness, and **Elite Syncopations**, Kenneth MacMillan's jolly lollipop given its first showing last night at the opening of the ballet season, is as good a cure for the dumps as any I can think of at the moment. It is a ragtime frivol, crammed with steps and zany humour, a romp for a lot of very good dancers who involve themselves whole-heartedly in the fun; and since this is Scott Joplin Year, the tunes are by Sedalia's favourite son and six of his confrères.

You must imagine the Opera House stage in a state of undress, cleared to its remotest depths with odds and ends of equipment still in place, in front of which a ragtime band is set on a rostrum. No ordinary ragtime band, though, for Ian Spurling has dressed them with characteristic exuberant fantasy. He has also dressed the dancers, who are first seen sitting on chairs (shades of **Danses Concertantes**) in front of the band. For them, Mr Spurling has allowed himself to go too far – much, much too far – and the result is witty, hectic dazzling: a phantasmagoria of fashion at its most absurd, miraculously controlled by being transferred to overall leotards. And because Mr Spurling has a massively clever talent, in both colouring and the most daring caprices of patterning, the result is brilliantly successful. These dancers, a dozen of the company's best with attendant corps de ballet, are unleashed by Mr MacMillan in a sequence of 12 jazzy variations that have •••

other purpose than to make us delight in the expertise and wit and ebullient good humour of the dances and their interpreters.

The pace is fast, the fun is easy, nicely contrasted. At times it looks as if Petipa had been caught larking in a bawdy-house: there is a solo for Monica Mason that is the apotheosis of the cake-walk, a duet for David Wall and Jennifer Penney that mocks sincerity and romantic passion and yet manages to be sincere and romantic. Michael Coleman is given a twisting leaping variation of ferocious difficulty: Merle Park follows a light-hearted solo with a cane by a *pas de deux* with Donald MacLeary that explores a choreographic idea of movement turned in on itself with extraordinary ingenuity, containing a magnificently quizzical moment when Mr MacLeary considers Miss Park's foot that has somehow found itself reposing next to his ear.

The lowest comedy (and the loudest laughs) come in a duet for the frantically mismatched Vergie Derman, who has never looked taller or more elegant, and Wayne Sleep as an adoring mite manfully trying to get to grips with her, and succeeding only in involving her in wildly indelicate poses.

And so **Elite Syncopations** goes merrily on. But if it is light-hearted – which it is – it is not lightly made: structure and invention are sure, and the marriage of ragtime and the academic dance is neatly effective. MacMillan has poured out a cascade of well-made dances, and his cast respond with no less well-considered performances. It is a jape that has come off without a foot or a step put wrong: no mean achievement. ∎

Vergie Derman and Wayne Sleep
Elite Syncopations
(1980)

Gloria

Kenneth MacMillan
The Royal Ballet

Royal Opera House,
Covent Garden

FT

FINANCIAL
TIMES

**14th March
1980**

DEATH AND THE AFTER-LIFE has been an inspiration for Kenneth MacMillan's choreography since the early **Journey** which he made for American Ballet Theatre over 20 years ago. Two major works of his maturity **Das Lied von der Erde** and **Requiem**, have shown how potent is the response which this theme excites in his choreography. Now, in a setting of the Poulenc **Gloria** which received its first performance last night, MacMillan returns to this same subject, to magnificent effect.

The immediate pretext for the work is that lost generation who felt the full brunt of the First World War. As programme note MacMillan quotes a poem by Vera Brittain from *Testament of Youth*. The crucial lines which help fix the mood of Gloria run: "But in that song we heard no warning chime/nor visualised in hours benign and sweet/The threatening woe that our adventurous feet/ Would starkly meet". The fine setting by Andy Klunder, recently graduated from the Slade School – is a skeletal metal frame placed on a rising slope of ground. The cast appear, breasting this slope. They are revenants, the girls ghost-grey, the men in tights that seem rotted, vestigial uniforms, and wearing tin hats.

The ballet's progress is a contemplation of lost hopes, lost joys, lost selves. And as so often with MacMillan, the evocation of the past – **Anastasia, La fin du jour** – is a matter of fixing feeling and attitudes rather than of a superficial naturalism. The choreography uses a large cast, but is centred upon a trio –

Jennifer Penney, Wayne Eagling, Julian Hosking – and a quartet in which Anthony Dowson, Ross MacGibbon and Ashley Page support Wendy Ellis. There is no identification of relationships, though *Testament of Youth* may suggest certain parallels, and the true importance of the ballet lies in the thrillingly inventive, rich and entirely apt movement that theme and score have inspired in MacMillan.

To the soprano solo *Domine Deus* there is a duet for Penney and Hosking of gentle, trusting affection; the succeeding *Domine Fili unigenite*, musically joyous, is no less so in the writing for Wendy Ellis and her companions. The *miserere nobis* finds Penney, Eagling and Hosking caught in poses of heart-stirring sculptural beauty. Everywhere, MacMillan finds dance imagery that matches both the gravity and the happier aspirations of his score, suggesting that his ghosts survey what was, and what might have been, with some dispassion. If there is the bitterness of regret and accusation, it is most clearly felt in the writing for Eagling, to whom falls the final section of the ballet when his companions have returned to their rest – like troops going over the top into action – and he makes a last tearing circuit of the stage before plummeting backwards out of sight.

Performances are magnificent. Penney, Eagling, Hosking; Wendy Ellis and her companions, all are seen at their best. Musically **Gloria** is no less commendable, with Teresa Cahill and a section of the Opera chorus under Ashley Lawrence. ∎

**Jennifer Penney
(1984)**

Kenneth MacMillan
The Royal Ballet

The Prince of the Pagodas

FINANCIAL
TIMES

Royal Opera House,
Covent Garden

**9th December
1989**

THE PRINCE OF THE PAGODAS is, as Donald Mitchell writes in a programme note, Britten's biggest and longest purely orchestral score. It was made for John Cranko's fairy-tale ballet (which combined elements from *Cinderella*, *Beauty and the Beast*, even *King Lear*) in 1956 and, naturally enough, fixed character and situation with absolute exactness.

Hearing the score again in the theatre on Thursday night, when Sir Kenneth MacMillan's new version of *Pagodas* received its first performance, I was struck, far more than in the Cranko staging of 30 years ago, by the intensity of dramatic flavour, the clarity of portraiture that Britten provides. In this has lain the inhibiting factor for anyone seeking to bring the music back to the theatre. Cranko's libretto was conceived as a peg on which to hang dances. The weakness of the action denied any real emotional life to his characters, and fine though Cranko's choreography often was, the absence of coherent or gripping dramatic argument was ultimately to cost his ballet its place in the repertory.

The masterly score remained. Could anyone – though Heaven forbid that anyone should – re-choreography **The Sleeping Beauty**? The question is posed since behind Britten's writing there lies the example of Tchaikovsky's most perfect masterpiece, which served as a point of reference for composer and choreographer in 1956. MacMillan, during a decade in which he has periodically contemplated restaging **Pagodas**, has realised that a radically

altered narrative for this score is unthinkable. Character, incident, are so explicit that change would deny the music utterly. Hence Colin Thubron, as new librettist, and MacMillan have decided on a strengthened but only slightly adapted scenario, while giving the original story an added seriousness of emotional values.

The action still tells of an old Emperor dividing his realm between his daughters, the Princesses Epine and Rose. How Epine casts an evil spell on the kingdom, seizes power from her father, turns Rose's betrothed prince into a salamander, and how at last Epine is defeated and Rose's compassion wins her the prince and restores her father to happiness is essentially Cranko's tale. Colin Thubron and MacMillan have provided a subtext concerning Rose's journey of self-discovery which allows MacMillan to consider elements that have ever concerned his finest choreography. And, be it immediately noted, the choreographer has responded with some of his most radiantly open and classically brilliant writing.

Sleeping Beauty must inevitably be in our minds when watching this new **Pagodas**. Not because there are elements of pastiche in score or dance, but because Tchaikovsky and Petipa have served as example and inspiration. The narrative, the formal structure of the music with its short and marvellously crafted incidents, succinct and sharp in drama, invite and receive choreography of comparable felicity and emotional resonance.

A prologue sets the scene, and the first act shows the kingdom under Epine's curse, a monkey court surrounding a doddering monarch (Anthony Dowell magnificent as a kind of senile baby). Kings from the four corners of the earth come to court Epine (Fiona Chadwick, maliciously dazzling in step), each representing some flawed aspect of manhood. The King of the North (Antony Dowson) is brutish; the King of the East (Bruce Sansom) is narcissistic, in a prodigious variation of slow controlled steps and quick trippings, ever consulting his image in two mirrors; the King of the West (Mark Silver) is a nincompoop; the King of the South (Ashley Page) is of menacing sexuality. Princess Rose (Darcey Bussell, whose freshness and technical grace give the role exquisite life) also rejects the Kings, and it is the ambiguous figure of the Fool (Tetsuya Kumakawa, bounding through the action as if air were his element) who guides Rose into a spiritual journey that takes up the second act. The Fool seems a symbol of the power of innocence, a Zen figure, and leads Rose to self-discovery as she faces the nightmare elements of her world, until she at last finds the Prince (Jonathan Cope: noble, expressive) whom she can see only as a salamander, though when she dances blindfold with him he takes on human form.

In the third act Rose returns to what is now Epine's realm. Her compassion frees the Salamander from enchantment, and he battles with the four Kings, defeating them, so that Epine is vanquished and truth and spiritual health are restored to the Emperor's kingdom.

MacMillan presents this action through a torrent of dancing, classical in manner, ever inventive in revealing character. The choreography is set within the framework of a production that, like Nicholas Georgiadis' grand and stylish design, has the clarity and directness of a child's storybook, but also the psychic reverberations that are the other world of fairy-tales. We are aware of the deeper meanings, but what greets the eye first is a dance spectacle of tireless virtuosity. There will be much more to say after further viewings, and it suffices at the moment to salute the entire Royal Ballet performance, not least the soloists who are so handsomely displayed in the writing for the clouds who feature in Rose's journeyings.

The principal players are magnificent. For Darcey Bussell, so radiant in her gifts, with floating jump and lovely ease when faced with the exciting demands made by MacMillan, every praise. For Jonathan Cope, great admiration for his sensitivity as the salamander and his shining power as the prince. Fiona Chadwick gleams with menace and dances superbly as Epine; Anthony Dowell is both commanding and pathetic in a role which MacMillan has now made crucial to the drama, and the Four Kings, the dazzling Fool of Tetsuya Kumakawa, Leslie Edwards as a Counsellor, and four grotesque doctors, are all marvellously conceived • • •

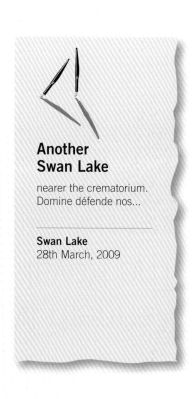

Another Swan Lake

nearer the crematorium.
Domine défende nos...

Swan Lake
28th March, 2009

and interpreted. Ashley Lawrence, happily returned to the Opera House, led a most satisfying account of a score whose riches have been restored to the theatre.

MacMillan shows in **Pagodas** how the language and formulae of the old classic ballet are still true and vital exactly a century after **The Sleeping Beauty** was first performed, not through blind emulation, but through love and understanding and trust. A grand achievement. ∎

Darcey Bussell (Princess Rose)
Prince of the Pagodas
(1996)

The Judas Tree

Royal Opera House, Covent Garden

SIR KENNETH MACMILLAN'S *The Judas Tree* was given its first performance by the Royal Ballet at Covent Garden on Thursday night. On its most immediate level it concerns harsh and all too familiar incidents of urban brutality. Jock McFadyen has made brilliant designs of a building site – ladders, walk-ways, unfinished walls, two derelict motor cars – peopled by a group of workmen under a foreman (Irek Mukhamedov).

A girl, Viviana Durante, is brought in, sexually predatory and flirtatious, who provokes jealousy between the foreman and one of his friends (Michael Nunn). She is eventually subjected to gang-rape by the men, is killed, and the foreman accuses his friend of her death. The friend is murdered. The foreman hangs himself. The girl reappears as a grieving memory and reproach for what has happened. The curtain falls.

Violence is the common-place of life in many cities: last week a report told of appalling gang-rape in the Halles district of Paris. MacMillan's argument – and it is one sustained with extraordinary choreographic imagination – is that beneath the animal crudities of the incident, we may learn about the human condition, and a continuum of human suffering and remorse. This he relates through a series of emotionally resonant images, and through actions mysteriously and subtly revelatory of his larger theme.

Kenneth MacMillan
The Royal Ballet

FINANCIAL TIMES

20th March 1992

Betrayal is explicit in the narrative. In Mukhamedov's staggering performance the role is black in tone, but shot through with the man's need for love and his mistrust of that love – we know both sympathy and despair (but mainly sympathy) for this combination of brute power and vulnerability. With Durante we see a girl whose sexual bravado and street-smart personality are a mere shell which is shattered by her terrible suffering. In her relationship with every man on stage (she is one woman faced with 14 men) we must consider both the battle between the sexes and a battle for sexual equality – or supremacy. When she first appears, she is carried in under a white sheet, and at moments throughout the action she dons this as a symbol of her untouched and, I would suggest, inviolable femininity, which must eventually be recognised as that of a mother. That, at the end of the piece, she acquires yet another identity – the grief-laden figure of the *Stabat Mater* - is the haunting last note of the ballet.

For, at the deepest level of MacMillan's creation, lies the historical Judas. The references are fleeting, but clear. After the girl's death – and it has been mysteriously presaged by Mukhamedov's drawing round her recumbent body with chalk, just as police use to outline the body of a corpse – Mukhamedov betrays and accuses Nunn with a kiss. Nunn's body is placed in one of the ruined cars at the back of the stage a latter-day Christ in his tomb – and Mukhamedov, like Judas, hangs himself. It is then that

Durante, draped in the unstained white of the cloth, stands like the Virgin Mother.

These various levels of interpretation would be mere cleverness were they not shown to us in dance of the most searching – and revealing – imagery, identity, motive, feeling, speak through movement unfailingly expressive. Durante's ambiguous relationship with Mukhamedov and Nunn is made clear to us as Nunn carries her above the recumbent Mukhamedov, her feet treading over his body. (A woman aggressively "walking over men" is a recurrent image). The weak "friend", so well played by Nunn, is given a questioning, ambiguous solo in which his indecisions are exposed. (He finds refuge with Durante under her white sheet, who thereby becomes a mother-figure). The group of workmen indulge in games, races, that speak of suppressed sexual energy, undirected physicality, ill-defined but pungent menace. Mukhamedov is by turns dominant – astonishing in physical prowess – and broodingly dangerous as he "fingers" a character in accusation.

There is much to discover in the dance. With **The Judas Tree** MacMillan has again challenged ballet's perceptions about its own identity: he shows the human condition, in actual and symbolic terms, as the central matter of a dance theatre that he continues to enrich. He has also brought two welcome new talents to the Opera House stage. Jock McFadyen's designs are bold, sure. ● ● ●

Brian Elias' score is powerful as drama atmospheric in sonorities, providing an urgent motor force for the action. The Opera House orchestra under Barry Wordsworth were fine advocates for it, in an evening which also brought distinguished accounts of Stravinsky's **Violin Concerto** and Bizet's **Symphony in C**. Of these, and their bright danced performances, I shall hope to report after a further viewing of this triple bill – which I would urge dance-lovers to see. The interpretations given by Durante, Mukhemedov, Nunn, and their colleagues in **The Judas Tree** are magnificent. ∎

Neil Skidmore and Shi-Ning Liu (workmen)
The Judas Tree
(1992)

Anastasia

Royal Opera House, Covent Garden

ANASTASIA WAS A BALLET close to Kenneth MacMillan's heart – and to his psyche. The 1971 Covent Garden production was his second full-length ballet. His **Romeo** of 1965 was a conventional three-acter, its narrative sustained by Prokofiev's realisation of Shakespeare. With **Anastasia**, MacMillan turned away from convention. Here was ballet inspired not by literature but by history, by the tragedy of a woman still living. Anna Anderson claimed she was the Grand Duchess Anastasia, escaped from the Bolshevik massacre of the Russian Imperial family.

MacMillan's concern to bring emotional actuality into the ballet theatre, to break the Petipa-mould after a century of dance-as-unreality, found its first expression in **Anastasia** and the portrait of the Romanov court in its last days. It presaged his more assured treatment of a similar theme (an extraordinary family in extraordinary circumstances) in **Mayerling** seven years later. In **Anastasia**, as in **Mayerling** and so many others of his ballets, MacMillan looked at a recurrent theme of his creativity: a personality isolated, at odds with the world.

Anastasia's genesis is well-known. Director of the ballet at the Deutsche Oper in West Berlin from 1966 to 1969, MacMillan was in several ways a man cut off from the world around him. Berlin was even a city isolated in an inimical setting. MacMillan had a chosen few colleagues with him, including his favoured ballerina Lynn Seymour, and it was for her

FINANCIAL TIMES

**6th May
1996**

that he made a one act *Anastasia*, which studied the anguish of a woman who finds herself in a Berlin hospital, uncertain of her identity, and gradually – through the terrors of memory – asserting that she is the miraculously survived Anastasia. (In the ballet, the woman's first steps are to tread along the lines of the floorboards in her room: these are her only reality).

This production was a triumph of expressionist dance, a triumph for Seymour. Her portrait of Anna Anderson, fleeing through nightmare, was for me the greatest thing this great artist ever did. Returned to London in 1970 to become director of the Royal Ballet, MacMillan's first major creation for his company (and for Seymour) was the expanded *Anastasia* of 1971. To explain Anna Anderson, to identify the woman whom she thought she was, MacMillan showed the child Grand Duchess with her family in Act 1, surrounded by love, by the fears which attended the little Tsarevich's haemophilia, by her mother's obsession with Rasputin, and by those mysterious signals from a grown-up world which so puzzle a child.

MacMillan made a deliberate contrast between the worlds of Anastasia and Anna Anderson. The two new acts were replete with ravishing, taxing classic dance, and grand ensembles. Anastasia's world – and we must not forget that we see through her eyes – was coloured by Tchaikovskian melody and texture. Anna Anderson's journey was told in anguished dance, using Martinu's *Fantaisies symphoniques*, music that might have been made for the shifting memories that beset the poor derelict surfacing with no identity in a Berlin hospital. The designs, by Barry Kay, were among the finest made for the Royal Ballet in the past three decades. The company performance was magnificent, and throughout, Seymour's genius gave the piece its motor force, its central truth.

The reception of the ballet in 1971 was dismaying, incomprehension, and what Dame Ninette de Valois called "a campaign of slaughter on the part of certain critics" wounded MacMillan deeply, precipitating his own crisis of identity. I record that in these columns, Andrew Porter wrote two long, perceptive notices after the first night which exactly identified the work's significance, speaking of "one of those rare and precious works of art in which a major creator consolidates all that he has done before and on this firm foundation goes on to build something new, larger, stranger and more exciting".

True then, these words remain so now, with the restoration of *Anastasia* to the Royal Ballet repertory after 18 years. MacMillan had long contemplated bringing the piece back, but with the editing which he knew was needed – slight cuts in the Tchaikovsky scores which would avoid those longueurs and repetitions which he was obliged to make for the music's sake. His widow, Deborah MacMillan, and the ballet's director, ...

Anastasia
London
(1996)

Anthony Dowell, knew what was intended. With the collaboration of Monica Parker, MacMillan's notator, and of Lynn Seymour as coach, a revised text was shown to us on Thursday when *Anastasia* returned to the stage.

It is a ballet I loved in its original, and watched constantly. I salute this new version, which differs only in the smallest detail through welcome and skilled musical editing by Barry Wordsworth, as a triumphant restoration of a tremendous ballet. (The one extended cut is of the fugue at the end of the first act: it is wholly beneficial). The staging honours MacMillan's intentions absolutely. It shows off the Royal Ballet as a strong, sensitive ensemble – as did the first production.

The significant change comes with the new design from Bob Crowley (who worked with MacMillan on *Carousel* at the National Theatre). The first act now takes place on the Imperial yacht instead of on the Baltic coast, catching exactly the world we see in the film of the Tsar and his family which features in Anna Anderson's memories. The ballroom setting is placed against a structure suggestive of the Winter Palace. The third act is a grey box with invisible doors, which exists as background throughout the ballet, a foreshadowing of

Anna's mind, and is superbly right. Costuming is admirable: glamorous for the court; beautiful and simple for the women of the Imperial family. An admirer of Barry Kay's work, I find Crowley's work no less convincing.

There will be time to discuss this staging and the fine quality of the ensemble after further viewings. In the first night cast, Viviana Durante was Anastasia/Anna. Her child princess was touching, fragile, and experience will teach her how to dominate – as Seymour dominated by her sense of questioning the society around her – the second act ball. In the third act, Durante was very fine indeed. Utterly unlike Seymour in physique – edgy, quick-accented in dynamics, in movement – she yet conveys the distress, the blind impetus of that headlong flight, actual as well as psychic, which drives Anna towards self-knowledge. Proof of Durante's quality comes in the last moments. As she circles the stage in her bed, we believe her as we believed Seymour and know that this is Anastasia. No further praise is needed. I salute the other performances, notably Adam Cooper as Anna Anderson's husband, and the conducting of Barry Wordsworth, and the orchestral playing. A major work of art is returned to us. ∎

Afterlight

Sadler's Wells

FT
FINANCIAL
TIMES

THE WAY A PERFORMANCE is lit is vital to our understanding of dance in the theatre. Diaghilev took infinite pains to give his Ballets Russes productions the atmosphere that design and dance demanded. In an otherwise awful event last year at Sadler's Wells where choreographies were staged "in the spirit of Diaghilev" but more accurately in the spirit of Attila the Hun, one piece fulfilled the evening's title. Russell Maliphant's solo for Daniel Proietto evoked Nijinsky in dance inspired by the circlings of Nijinsky's drawings, themselves fruit of his disturbed mental state. The piece drew upon Maliphant's fascination with sculpting movement through lighting devised by Michael Hulls, providing a chiaroscuro to define both dancer and dance. The choreography, as in Maliphant's other works, owed much to what Hulls' lighting suggested about the flow of action.

Now Maliphant has extended this Nijinsky study and *Afterlight* is the intriguing result. Running for just an hour, it still stars Proietto, but has acquired two danseuses, Silvina Cortés and Olga Cobos. The score is Satie's piano *Gnossiennes* for Proietto's initial solo, then uses a composition by Andy Cowton that echoes the pentatonic disciplines of oriental music (shades of Nijinsky's **Siamoise**) to feed incidents in which the women dance together and with Proietto, hinting at ideas from Nijinsky's life and choreographies.

Hulls' lighting is vital, the shadowed action awakening our perceptions about the dance

and its theme, it is complemented by animation devised by Jan Urbanowski and James Chorley, so that the stage becomes leafy, or cloudy, haunted by memories and a darkening mental state. *Afterlight* asks us to think of Nijinsky's inner self as seen in his drawings and in slight hints of his choreography, not in those tedious "reconstructions" that are more like three card tricks, but in Baron de Meyer's photographs, which so allusively captured his physical magic.

Maliphant's manner is sinuous, flickering in its fleeting glimpses of Nijinsky, of his inner world, quite as much as of his physical identity. Proietto is superb at every moment, the dance curling or racing through his body, drawing lingering whorls of movement on the retina. He is a fine artist, finely used in Maliphant's fascinating dances. ∎

**1st October
2010**

**Daniel Proietto (Nijinsky)
(2009)**

Norman Morrice
Ballet Rambert

Conflicts
The Travellers

Sadler's Wells

**17th July
1965**

IN THE 1930s the two divergent streams of British choreography were mirrored in the repertories of the Ballet Rambert and the then Sadler's Wells company. The Wells had Ashton, Rambert had Anthony Tudor, and 30 years later it is surely not an entirely false analogy to see the same difference in the second generation of British choreography, with the Royal Ballet's Kenneth MacMillan countered by Rambert's Norman Morrice. MacMillan is in the direct line from Ashton – how else could he have developed so admirably in the classical/academic tradition (in its warmest, fullest sense)? It is, I think, permissible to see a parallel development with Morrice in the Rambert ambiance.

Tudor's ballets still figure large in the Rambert repertory (this is the first year in which we have not had a Tudor evening during the Sadler's Wells fortnight), and Tudor is still the ideal choreographer for the company's dancers – for all their **Don Quixote** and **Giselle** and **La Sylphide** – because his ballets best display their fine qualities of dramatic sensitivity. The dramatic and emotional style of Morrice's works place him most acceptably in the line of succession to Tudor – and he is certainly the best choreographer they have had since the late 1930s.

Morrice has an extraordinary sense for dramatic situation, the list of locales for his ballets – a Mexican church, a desert, Oxford Circus underground station, an Iron Curtain airport – all demonstrate this, and he has

during the past eight years forged a commendably revelatory theatre style. His choreography as such does not linger in my mind as do long, heart-stirring passages from MacMillan, but I don't feel that Morrice works towards this type of memorable enchainment, (I may be doing him the most grievous injustice and demonstrating my own insensitivity to his work at the same time). Is not his ideal a more totally dramatic image, indivisible from its dramatic (as opposed to its structural) situation, each reacting on the other?

It is thus that the cross, the ramp and the sweating labourer straining towards the church form a series of dramatic rather than dynamic images in **Hazana**. Morrice pinpoints emotional states most tellingly in movement: the wife dipping her hands in the water and cooling her husband's brow in **Hazana**, the Cain-brother curled in foetal position in **Two Brothers** (very Tudor, this), the unhappy girl resting her forehead against the man's back in **Conflicts**.

All these thoughts, and many more, are roused by last night's Rambert programme which presented two of Morrice's most assured works, **Conflicts** and **The Travellers**. Curiously, both dealt with ballet companies – but on very different terms. **Conflicts** I find a most satisfying piece, a cunningly constructed exercise in reality, with situations nestling inside other situations like one of those Russian dolls that always contains other dolls. It is concerned with three problems, as I see it. First with the nature of a choreographer's

204

task when faced with a group of dancers awaiting the life that his inspiration is to give them as stage characters, then with the fact of their personal relationships - as human beings, and interacting with this their relationships as personages in the choreographer's work. The conflicts that are implied in all this are sufficient explanation of the title!

There are emotional tensions arising from the unrequited love of a girl understudy for a leading dancer, and a further drama involved in the relationship of the understudy with the ballerina she is covering, since the latter is loved by the principal man. This particular theme is told with extraordinary sensitivity, both dramatically and choreographically, and was admirably expressed last night by Gayrie MacSween, Jennifer Kelly and John Chesworth. Morrice created **Conflicts**, significantly, on his return from a study period in New York where he worked with both Martha Graham and Balanchine; although the actual dynamic range of the dances is deliberately limited, the effects are achieved in a fascinating choreographic language.

The ballet troupe in **The Travellers** is used as a group brought face to face with totalitarianism. We see them arrive at an airport, then give a theatre performance (an over-long sequence), and then the mood darkens as they find themselves trapped in the airport as a civil disturbance breaks out beyond the walls of the building. One member ventures beyond its confines, and returns as a broken figure

after brain-washing by the police; another is shot in an attempt to defy the régime as the curtain falls on the restoration of whatever order existed before the uprising.

It is a fascinating work in its implications, an excellent one in its use of the resources of the theatre, but it suffers from a discursive beginning: with some tightening here it could be even grimmer as a protest against the encroachment on personal liberty of our modern world. It was given a compelling performance last night with Jonathan Taylor outstanding in the leading role. ∎

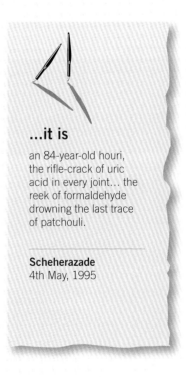

...it is

an 84-year-old houri, the rifle-crack of uric acid in every joint... the reek of formaldehyde drowning the last trace of patchouli.

Scheherazade
4th May, 1995

David Nixon
Northern Ballet Theatre

The Three Musketeers

FT

FINANCIAL
TIMES

New Victoria Theatre,
Woking

6th June
2006

FOR CONNOISSEURS of the improbable, collectors of theatrical clunkers, let me recommend Northern Ballet Theatre's new *The Three Musketeers*, now touring, and a marvel of the historically and balletically unlikely. NBT believes – *et comment!* – in Titles People Have Heard Of. What better, then, than Dumas' flashy, sword-flashing drama, with Louis XIII and Anne of Austria, Cardinal Richelieu, a diamond necklace, illicit passion, and a quartet of heroic fighters? And Milady de Winter as villainess. **And** the Duke of Buckingham. **And** Cinq-Mars. **And** letters lost, stolen and found.

And what worse as a subject for a ballet? Yet David Nixon has done the deed, accompanied by a score of unrelenting perkiness and teeth-grating jovialities culled from the music of Malcolm Arnold, with long wigs and flimsy

Keiko Amemori (Constance)
Patrick Howell (D'Artagnan)
(2007)

frocks, busy scenery that makes the Louvre look like a bordello in Trieste circa 1930, and a cast more vivacious, more busy leaping and feigning sword-play, than in an eternity of Douglas Fairbanks (Senior) movies. It is all furiously, indomitably silly, driven onward by NBT's dancers, who do everything at full pelt (and few pelts have been fuller) in scenes manically hard-driven and merrily incomprehensible.

Determined study of the programme notes will tell you what is supposed to be happening, and why Cardinal Richelieu (in miles of red silk heavily pleated train below his posterior, something, I fancy, that Philippe de Champaigne missed in his portrait) is looking so miffed. Little on stage will give you a clue to narrative, and I incline to the belief that this Queen of France was more aptly named Anne of Australia. Nixon's choreography is, shall we say, eager, and vivacious in its blinkered way.

The redeeming feature on Wednesday night, in the rat-maze of Woking's New Victoria Theatre, was the performance of Patrick Howell as D'Artagnan. He has a happy way with the rumbustious tricks and leaps of his role, and a devil-may-care air that makes real and attractive his love for Constance and his ability to avoid death by sword-thrust – and choreography. Hurrah for him. ∎

Lilac Garden
The Dark Elegies
Judgment of Paris
Gala Performance

Antony Tudor
Ballet Rambert

Sadler's Wells

FT

FINANCIAL
TIMES

TUDOR IS ESSENTIALLY a psychologist: the heart's tragedies, the labyrinths of mental suffering are the subjects that he has chosen to explore in his maturity, dissecting and then recreating them in movement both beautiful and expressive. His four ballets currently in the Rambert season, and shown last night are probably the most important that the company possesses, and they are always presented with the care and skill that maintain their impact.

Lilac Garden shows us the sorrow of a love sacrificed to an Edwardian *mariage de convenance*: on the eve of her wedding a girl part snatches a final frenzied meeting with her lover, while the man she must marry disengages himself from "an episode in his past". Set to Chausson's "Poême" for violin, the ballet is a masterly evocation of the last agonised farewell, inevitably broken into by other guests and by the counter-stresses of the future husband's liaison. The movement is nervous, hurried, with brief moments of stillness as the lovers manage a moment alone in the moonlit garden: it is not so much a representation of actual behaviour, but rather the exposition of the character's emotions.

With **The Dark Elegies** Tudor created a masterpiece that is unique in the English repertoire for its complete expression of deep feeling. On the basis of Mahler's "Songs on the deaths of children", he has set a heart-rending portrayal of a community mourning the loss of its children, with bereavement that at the last manages to give place to

resignation and acceptance of the tragedy. The Rambert dancers, thanks to their expressive training, manage to preserve the full impact of the work: the dancing ceases to be theatrical, but rather do we seem to be present at a rite in which we are all implicated.

Judgment of Paris has no equal as an acrid comedy: into an appalling boîte, served by a scrofulous waiter, stumbles a drunk who is subjected to the attentions of a sleazy trio of goddesses. These three are both horrifying and pathetic in their terrible inadequacy as entertainers. They are all distinctly past their prime, though there is considerable doubt if they ever had a prime: one has a gnawed and dusty boa, the second essays a sluggish Spanish dance that jerks into horrid vitality when it seems possible that the drunk is reacting favourably to her, while the third is a tousled blonde who totters through a repulsive routine involving two pink hoops that all too plainly she will soon be unable to force over her hips. The drunk collapses into incapability, and like vultures these harpies are rifling his pockets, aided by the waiter. The ballet is brief and deadly in its satire: there is no real pity for the drunk or the slatterns, and we can be sure that it will be re-enacted the next night.

The company dance the whole programme magnificently: the ballets reaffirm Tudor's importance, and reveal at the same time how great a talent has been lost to our ballet. ∎

**12th September
1958**

**...the Queen
Mother**

has either been lying madly about her age or has found the world's best plastic surgeon back-stage. She didn't look old enough to vote, let alone rule a kingdom, not even a balletic one.

Swan Lake
12th January, 1996

Matthew Bourne
Adventures in Motion Pictures

Swan Lake

FINANCIAL TIMES

Sadler's Wells

16th November 1995

SWAN LAKE is not only the most popular of ballets, it is the most mauled and misunderstood. From its first staging, in Moscow in 1877, score and narrative were subject to revision, and subsequent history has been of constant tinkering. Five versions in Moscow between 1900 and 1924 is no record: of recent years it seems that every ballet company has had to have a staging, so insatiable is public appetite for swan feathers and lush melody. And every company must have its own individually butchered presentation. So we have had Prince Siegfried as an opium-freak and as Ludwig of Bavaria; von Rothbart as villainous tutor, as alter-ego, even as mother-figure; productions modernised, productions aiming to give "what Tchaikovsky intended", and any other mayhem that the arrogance of a producer can conceive. What has been evident on every occasion is that the recension staged in Petersburg in 1894/5 by Marius Petipa with Lev Ivanov is still unrivalled, because blessed with superb choreography and cogent dramatics.

Now, amid rather too many publicity tantaras about "outraged critics and ballet-lovers in a tizz", we have a modern dance version by Matthew Bourne for his Adventures in Motion Pictures troupe with – on in-drawn breath – Men as Swans! What I saw on Tuesday night at Sadler's Wells is a curious and intriguing mixture of the imaginatively good and the blatantly under-done.

Bourne has modernised the setting while retaining much of the original narrative.

The period – to judge by the hideous clothes – is the 1960s. A prologue shows us the child Prince Siegfried beset by royal duties and dreaming of a swan as symbol of freedom. Grown to manhood, he finds the royal round no pleasure. The relationship with his mother is Hamlet-ish: the shadow of *Mayerling*, which matches Swan Lake's theme of ideal love found only in death, lies dark over the stage. A Private Secretary is von Rothbart (and, in another *Mayerling* gloss, Count Taaffe, with the Prince's "girl-friend" as Mitzi Caspar). After a visit to a seedy club – more *Mayerling* – the Prince (Scott Ambler) visits a lake and contemplates suicide.

Thus far the staging has been typical of AMP's manner in its jokiness and absence of choreographic interest. The action rattles from scene to caricatured scene in Lez Brotherston's clever design, while poor Tchaikovsky is mauled unmercifully. But with the appearance of the swans, the piece becomes musically responsive, mysterious. Bourne is no Ivanov, but his cohort of male swans (chaps naked save for feathery breeches, black v-shapes marking their foreheads) takes to the stage, and we believe.

Swans are large, powerful and sometimes belligerent birds. Bourne has found imagery that conveys this avian nature, and because there is nothing either graceful or emotional about their manner, they appear absolutely swanlike. Far more so than the usual ranks of tutu-ed girls, and never more so than in Adam Cooper's remarkable playing as the swan who incarnates Siegfried's dreams of liberty. Cooper has ever been a dancer of focused presence, and his portrait is untouched by human feeling: it is truly a bird, and all the more potent for that. Nor, be it gratefully noted, is there the least strain of homo-eroticism in the dance. The narrative is what it is, and no "gay" sub-text need bother us in the relationship of the prince with the Swan.

The third act ball reverts, initially, to the coarseness of the first scene: these are an odd lot of royals, with morals as shifty as their manners. (So unexpected). There arrives Cooper in black – leather trousers as blatant as his sexuality – to make advances on every woman there, including the Queen. He is both Eros and Chaos, and the Prince views the entire scene as an orgiastic nightmare in which the symbol of his desire for freedom is destroyed. (In a brilliant touch, Cooper smears cigarette ash on his forehead to evoke the swan-marking: an exact reflection of Odile's mimicry of Odette's swan-like pose). The act ends with the Private Secretary shoot-ing the Prince's girl-friend. This is dramatically odd, but serves to send the Prince into madness. Confined to his bed, he sees visions of the swans. They attack him, then attack and kill their leader (Cooper). The Prince dies, his mother grieving over him, while the apothe-osis shows Cooper and the Prince united at last.

As an up-dating this **Swan Lake** is, against all the odds, a success. Bourne clearly wants the court scenes to be as hallucinatory as the lake-side encounters, but he has not found a choreographic language as effective as his writing for the swans. What he imposes upon Tchaikovsky in the first act is barely forgiveable. But his vision of the swans, of the lake-side tragedy, is powerful and original. I find it pref-erable to many of the lumpen activities offered by companies who foist ineptitudes on the public in the name of tradition. Here, in Bourne's imagery, is something authentically tragic, attuned to Tchaikovsky's mysterious world. And with Adam Cooper, the role of the Swan has commanding power and resonance.

Among the other players, Fiona Chadwick makes much of the Queen, and Emily Piercy has a good deal of fun as the Prince's bimbo girl-friend. The score is well played under David Lloyd-Jones. ▌

Jonathan Ollivier (Swan)
London
(2009)

THOSE WHO THINK THE LIFE of a dance critic is all **Swan Lake** and Tchaikovsky, tutus and *grands jetés* could not be more mistaken. The world of dance is exceptionally broad, stretching from the obscure and experimental to the obvious and extravagant, from the traditions of Noh to the innovations of hip-hop and it is truly international, from Argentinian tango to Japanese kabuki. It is all in a day's work for the dance critic, and Clement has always approached each and every style not only with the same gimlet eye for hokum, but also a genuine desire to discover talent and artistry and a readiness to be pleasantly surprised. Underpinning it all is his core belief in the vital force of dancing which will shine whatever the idiom.

The Diversity of Dance

Chapter 5

The Diversity of Dance

Chapter 5

ANNABEL FARJEON

Lyric Theatre, Hammersmith

IT IS REMARKABLE THAT, in a week crammed with grand dances and grand dancing, the most exciting thing I saw was a group of performers, variously handicapped, making a statement about disability.

Imagine, if you will, the Lyric Hammersmith stage, with a group of musicians playing the Rose Adagio from **The Sleeping Beauty** (sublimest music for dance). A young man, grievously disabled, is helped from his wheelchair, and kneels centre-stage. Four women dance round him, and offer him roses. One of them, a beautiful Japanese girl, is blind. Watching them are other members of the cast – many have Down's Syndrome. Slowly descending from the flies on a strand of white cloth is the splendid dancer and gymnast Lindsey Butcher. She also gives the young man a rose, and holds him in a warm embrace. He kneels – he cannot really do otherwise – and stretches his arms towards us. Cheers from us all, and, frankly, tears from me.

Here is the entire justification for the work of that exceptional teacher and dance-creator, Wolfgang Stange, and his group, Amici. Art has been made from the unlikeliest yet most willing source. Dance-theatre of a truly potent kind has been given to us by people whom society all too often sees as inexpressive, or marginal, or merely pitiable. Not so. Amici affirms life, creativity, and, of course, the power of compassion. But also the finding of beauty in the gifts of men and women whose potential Wolfgang Stange

has devoted his professional life to encouraging and revealing.

This show at the Lyric celebrated 20 years of Stange's work. With a commentary and songs by Julia Pascal, admirably and sardonically performed by Barb Jungr; with music by Billy Cowie; with the New London Orchestra on stage, it proposes a despairing view of how the 20th century coped with disability. So, the war-wounded from the 1914-18 conflict: the Nazi's solution to the "problem" of Jews, homosexuals, and those social undesirables whose appearance was not Aryan; even a Swiss decision to solve a "problem" by electro-convulsive therapy for gypsy children. All this done with Stange's usual vivid theatrical sense.

I have reported, with greatest admiration, on three of his earlier stagings. Once again he marshals his so-willing forces in group movement, in what are almost tableaux-vivants, as "undesirables" are despatched to such camps as Theresienstadt. Once again physical disability gives birth to theatre magic. And once again, Stange – a saint, in my book: he also works to magnificent effect with mutilated soldiers in Sri Lanka – is denied funding.

That this show has had no official or private subvention is incomprehensible. That our own funding authorities do nothing for Stange is a disgrace. (The continued bolstering of 10th-rate dance troupes by annual hand-outs is much more to their •••

**25th July
2000**

taste). So here is the begging bowl. There may be readers of these words who have access to charitable funds, to sponsorship monies. If you believe that in making art we can help to improve the world around us, look at Amici. From these gentle and gently gifted people, there comes a creativity that enhances both their lives and ours. ∎

"Amici affirms life, creativity and the power of compassion" wrote Clement Crisp. Suitable images of '20/20' do not exist but the company's dance-creator, Wolfgang Stange, has continued to create remarkable works giving opportunity to those who otherwise could never have taken to the stage before a ticket-buying public. The company continues to challenge conventional attitudes about disability and the arts as this image from 'Elegy' (2007) shows so well.

Amici Dance Theatre Company
Elegy
(2007)

Dead Dreams of Monochrome Men

ICA, London

HOMOSEXUAL MURDER and necrophilia might not seem the most promising matters for a dance piece, but in **Dead Dreams of Monochrome Men** the ever-alert DV8 troupe has produced a taut and powerful work which explores these terrifying aspects of psychosis.

The starting point is Brian Master's remarkable study of Denis Nilsen, "Killing for Company", but this is not an explicit narrative. DV8 rightly identifies itself as "physical theatre", and **Dead Dreams** has found a movement language that explores and exposes a sequence of emotional states – of loneliness, longing, despair, aggression – that interlock and exist as layers of meaning for us and for the performers about the theme.

Dead Dreams is a collaborative creation of its four-man cast. Lloyd Newson, as artistic director, must take much credit, but his colleagues Nigel Charnock, Douglas Wright, and Russell Maliphant (lately with Sadler's Wells Royal Ballet and Dance Advance), are admirably attuned to the style and implications of the piece, and very gifted. There results an 80-minute journey through a homosexual underworld of desolate encounters that seek some ideal of love and physical beauty, before a giddying descent into the depths of mania.

It is the especial distinction of this production that the links between the "ordinary" of brief sexual encounters, and the "extraordinary" of necrophilia – that ultimate unreason in a relationship – are subtly suggested. A fine but

FT

FINANCIAL
TIMES

uncredited setting of walls that conceal ladders, a Venetian blind, a bath-tub placed against a mirrored wall, excellently lit, become a street, a pub, a house. The four players establish a world of erotic posing, then take us below the surface to sexual fantasies, to unassuaged and unassuageable desires, and to the final acts of violence and the hopeless manipulation of the dead.

What grips the attention is the physical bravado and sensitivity of the performers and of their language. They balance the most delicate expressive effects of gesture against wildest activity. There are ferocious outbursts of slamming – that boots-first foray by skin-heads into dance – and heart-stopping moments when Mr Charnock flings himself from the set on to his companions. There are images of chilling power as a corpse is assaulted, as Mr Charnock climbs like a succ-ubus over the stage, or clings waif-like on Douglas Wright's shoulders. There are passages of frank eroticism, of bleakest loneliness, and an appalling finale pose as Mr Newson sits in uncompromising lighting, while the body of Russell Maliphant hangs upside down from a harness, like a side of meat, and the two other performers lie on the stage. And we have understood.

As creators and interpreters, the cast deserve every praise for the clarity and imaginative force of what they do, for the risks they take, and their funambulist skill in crossing over a gulf into which most dance-theatre blunders.

In an exceptional year for variety of dance, *Dead Dreams* remains an exceptional work of art, powerful, uncomfortable, true. ∎

4th November 1988

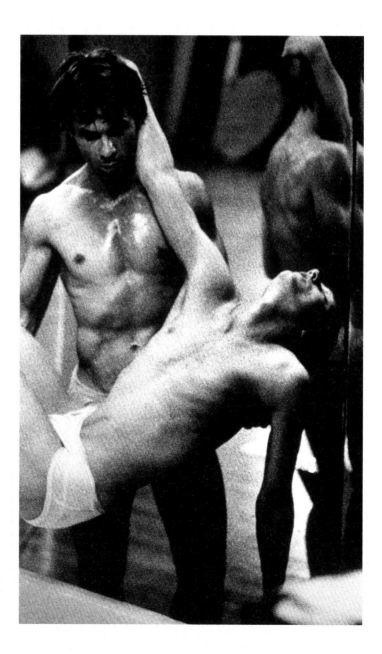

Douglas Wright, Nigel Charnock
Dead Dreams of Monochrome Man
(1989)

Circus Oz

FINANCIAL
TIMES

Queen Elizabeth Hall, London

8th August 2005

I THINK CIRCUS OZ is the best fun. I loathe traditional circuses – tiresome animals doing foolish tricks, and clowns outdoing them in stupidity – but these Australian zanies subvert just about every desperate cliché of the things, except in matters of skill. The troupe is small, peculiarly (in every sense of the word) gifted, and has a distinctly off-beam view of what the game is all about. "Why do I always get the worst dressing room?" demands an upside-down and gloriously disillusioned clown walking blithely across the top of the flies. Things burst into flames. Two female acrobats seem (in the words of the old joke) to be close, even for sisters.

Captain Frodo London (2005)

Most of the cast play musical instruments well, and Suzanne Simpson is a dazzling dominatrix-violinist – which seems a pretty recherché avocation. The tricks are slick, even unto the world's fattest cockatoo as aerialist, and the sudden irruption of a vegetable-slicing Ninja hero is perfectly ordinary in these manic circumstances.

The troupe has lost its antique boy scout who was shot from a gun last year. This time, the victim is the supposed conductor of the band, who is projected into a collapsing grand piano. (Personal listings of maestri whom you would like to suffer the same fate are the obvious reaction to this). There is a blissful and almost *Kath and Kim* sequence in which a dizzy blonde is taken over by hula-hoops. Best of all is Captain Frodo, on whom I now have a schoolboy crush. Norwegian, double-jointed (life really stacks it against some people) Frodo yet again forces his body through the impossible limits of an unstrung tennis raquet – and the raquet is not the only unstrung thing, since we are reduced to hysteria. The Captain does the unlikeliest things – he seems at one moment to be trying to pull his face off, from behind – and also involves a microphone and a small table in the battle. Sardonic comment ("It's great to be back in the community") and teeny handfuls of glitter-dust pulled from exiguous white shorts are also part of the glory. He is unique, as prone to the unexpected as Bea Lillie, convulsingly funny and probably a genius. The show is hugely amusing. ∎

Elissa, Queen of Carthage

Peacock Theatre, London

'Jumbo Pearls from Lebanon'

EVEN IF IT IS APOCRYPHAL, Queen Alexandra's observation after some eager but artless display – "So kind, and all in national costume, too" – seems the best comment about **Elissa, Queen of Carthage**, enthroned at the Peacock Theatre, London WC1 this week.

The enterprise is owed to the Lebanese troupe, Caracalla Dance Theatre. It ill becomes anyone to speak other than with respect for an artistic organisation that has survived the past tragic decades of Lebanon's history. I report merely that the evening is of radiant innocence, and is not best to be savoured – even on terms of wildest kitsch – save by those interested in the renaissance of Lebanese theatre.

The setting is Tyre in the ninth century before Christ. The drama – a triumph of the inconsequential – concerns a throne divided between Elissa (who is also Dido) and her brother Pygmalion. Costuming is richly improbable in Cecil B. de Mille fashion: crowns like over-ambitious tea-pots; tinselled fabric in deep mauve and gold; Assyrian beards, and hats even more Assyrian.

There is a chap with a hurricane lamp, a mermaid, so much dry ice that it recalled the pea-soupers we used to know, hollow laughter, villains taking to drink, the building of Carthage (six bricks and a tea-trolley), grunts from the men, and tremendous enthusiasm from everyone on stage.

The score is cheerful, and makes slight but misguided borrowings from Delibes.

The narrative is explored – with some difficulty – in energetic gesture that would not disgrace Theda Bara or Francis X Bushman, and there is a great deal of running about. Choreography is not quite the word I would first use to describe the style, and why anything happens really does not matter, even if you can make sense of it.

It is the belief of the performers and the lambent naivety of the means that tugs the viewer along. I still don't understand why Elissa should want to swap a casket of unlikely pearls for a cow-hide wrap when she lands in North Africa. (Part of Elissa's problem, I suspect, is that her retinue of women contains some chaps in frocks: perhaps she is aiming to be *Priscilla, Queen of the Desert*).

Towards the end of the evening, the narrative is tossed to one side – Elissa having taken to self-immolation – and we see a merry chunk of folklore showing a Lebanese wedding: the bride (so says the programme) quick to accept the groom when she learns of his wealth – which is Elissa's casket of jumbo pearls coming round for a second time.

It is all very different, and – to quote her late Majesty – all in national costume, too. ∎

14th November 1996

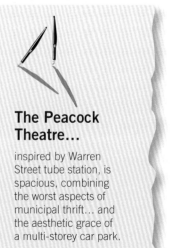

The Peacock Theatre...

inspired by Warren Street tube station, is spacious, combining the worst aspects of municipal thrift... and the aesthetic grace of a multi-storey car park.

7th November, 1996

Breakin' Convention

FT

FINANCIAL
TIMES

Sadler's Wells

**22nd May
2004**

'Hip-hop: I'm hooked'

His friend thought he said "hip op" but, far from needing surgery, the FT's venerable dance critic was revelling in an electric, energetic dance form that absorbs influences with lightning speed.

THERE WAS A SLIGHT misunderstanding when I told a friend I had been to last weekend's celebration of hip-hop dance at Sadler's Wells in London and that it was a Good Thing. She thought I had said I was going for a "hip op". That she seemed to feel that a hip operation was more proper for someone of my age was, I thought, jumping the gun a bit.

I saw hip-hop dance on the streets of Los Angeles and New York 20 years ago, and, contrary to any preconceptions about my taste, I liked it at once, as I like any good dance. The urgency of it, its extraordinary truthfulness as manifestation of a social condition since it was born of the emotions and alienation of young black men, and born also of their music and the newest tricks of scratch-DJs – gave it a vitality and an emotional directness that one rarely finds in classical ballet today.

Hip-hop dance wins our affections because of its honesty. It also wins my admiration because of the virtuosity of its language – the product of a sharp-eyed and eager view of the world. Everything, from acrobatics to rapping, from graffiti (that other street product of the same period) to film and kung-fu, can leave its

trace on the dance. The young see something, like it, determine to make it theirs, and the dance grows.

The dance also reflects the toughness of social and emotional conditions, as young buck challenges young buck and they eyeball each other in movement. So, as the dance exploded over the theatre like a hundred rockets, Sadler's Wells was crammed to the rafters with an audience passionately involved, joyously vocal, alert to every nuance: half the stalls had been removed to enable us to stand near the stage.

What was I doing, bellowing for the Holloway Boyz and Electric Boogaloos? No more than I should, in such surroundings. The dancers were splendid, and we wanted every yelp to drive them on to further spins and wild balances on one shoulder, to more eye-defeating tricks.

This weekend celebration – "Breakin' Convention" directed by Jonzi D, our leading hip-hop artist, and I found it grandly enjoyable.

Of prime significance is the way in which the dance continues to evolve. It is born inalienably of its music, and dancers and audience know the minutiae of breaking and popping, of boogaloo (that marionette-like sloping dance as walk) and locking – as well as the lastest fashion from Los Angeles, krumping.

Influences are absorbed with lightning speed (it is like the technical development of classical

**A bunch of
carrots**

was lowered from the
light-boom at one
moment: very puzzling,
since we had not
ordered vegetables.

J'aimerais tant rester
5th August, 1993

218

ballet speeded up 100 times). As I watched some of the aspirant breakers – the dashing Boy Blue team and the Holloway Boyz – I started to list the elements that had made this electric, eclectic dance-brew. There were acrobatics, moon-walking, ten-pin bowling, fighting, gymnastics, belly-dancing, the adorably grubby "bumps and grinds" of old American burlesque shows, tap, puppetry, scratch-DJ sound (an essential formative influence), and even ballet.

The dancers hone ideas with the sharpest skill. I spoke to one young virtuoso from the Boy Blue group who told me that he used *capoeira* (Brazilian dance duel) as part of his movement vocabulary. And in this lies the power and vitality of hip-hop. On a basis of technical discipline, the dancers add any influence that touches them. And, like their movement, their dress has an effortless chic, from baggy pants and tops to sneakers and baseball caps.

Steps become observation of the world as these youngsters see it, youthfully aspiring, youthfully rebellious. Others may use their dance, commercialise it, corrupt it, but the young go on making it different, making it because they must. ▌

Clement Crisp, suitably attired for "Breakin' Convention"
illus: James Ferguson, The Financial Times

Takarazuka

FINANCIAL
TIMES

London Coliseum

**13th July
1994**

'Japanese cross-dressing'

TAKARAZUKA IS A SHOW that needs
psycho-analysis more than criticism. The
mysteries of cross-dressing on stage – let alone
the mysteries of cross-dressing in the Japanese
theatre are not to be gone into here. Suffice it
to say, as a television programme and a lot of
press coverage have lately made us aware, this
is an all-girl show whose "male" stars are the
darlings of Japanese housewives. The girls'
training, as television helpfully showed us,

**Takarazuka
London
(1994)**

starts them off as housemaids and they end
up as Gary Glitter. Can education aim for more?

Now Takarazuka is at the Coliseum, hideously
loud, brash, slick, inexorably vulgar, and
awash with feathers and sequins, transformations, japonaiserie, cherry-blossom, a stuffed
seagull, baritone ladies singing love-songs –
though not a single scene takes place near
that celebrated beauty-spot The Well of
Loneliness – and relentless smiles. It is the
apotheosis of kitsch, and is wholly uninteresting on any other terms. Yet given the heady
mix of clichés, of second-hand ideas, of feeble
dance routines and witless songs, anything
better would dilute the kitsch-value.

What you must go for is the rampant fatuity,
the glitz, the megawatt seriousness of the
thing, purveying mindlessly unreal fantasy in
giant Dayglo dollops. Not for our audiences,
of course, those inscrutable passions that the
show inspires in the hausfraus of Tokyo, even
unto offers of marriage. (The local drag-queens
are, I am told, also fans of Takarazuka's chaps:
but here we enter a world of treble-bluff
identity which sets the mind reeling). It is
sexually quite peculiar, in a sanitised way, and
should be immediately comprehensible to
British audiences reared on pantomime, where
the principal boy is a girl and her mother a man.
The show lasts three hours (Was that all?)
The first part is the *menu touristique* with
tripping maidens, a samurai serenading a dead
seagull (the programme alleges it is a hawk;
I was surprised it didn't claim it as the Dodo)

220

and cherry trees. Transformations brilliantly done. Colours very bright. Pause to wonder why the Japanese, whose popular art – from Kabuki to wood-block print – is so stylish, so ineffably elegant, so beautiful, can tolerate such tara-diddle. Answer comes there none.

Part two is a scena, based on an O Henry story about a bank vault, in which a little boy (believe in that performance and, like the White Queen, you will believe six impossible things before breakfast) is locked in the vault for 30 years. He is, alas, rescued by a reformed bank thief engaged to the bank owner's daughter. Songs, sober-sided dancing, a multitude of bar-boys, a lot of auburn hair, spoken dialogue obligingly given surtitles ("I thought he was in Africa – or Monaco"). A hero called Ralph – and you may guess how that sounds in Japanese. Ill-controlled hysteria from your critic.

The last section – by which time I was lobotomised by neon, scene changes and the curiously shrill tone of the amplified Japanese female singing voice – is called *A Million Dreams*. (Mine were all of escape). Mira Anju, the star of the show, appears in a succession of numbers, variously resembling Michael Jackson, Makarova *en smoking*, Jack Buchanan, without effacing memories of these.

She is, like Billy Bennett of blessed Music Hall memory, almost a gentleman. A pianist goes three rounds with a Chopin *étude* while a quartet caper. More. Much, much more.

Someone singing *By a sleepy lagoon*. Someone else having a go at *Besame mucho*. The roar of the big-band sound that, even so, cannot make the score sound like music. At the end, down the obligatory staircase come the entire cast in pink: pink tail-suits, pink ostrich feathers, pink Dubarry frockery. Not so much *La vie en rose* as *L'enfer en rose*. Miss Anju, in gold pailletted tails and feathers, looks splendid. I recalled a be-plumed Zizi Jeanmaire, whose **Mon truc en plumes** had more wit in ten seconds than Takarazuka in its three hours.

It is a very odd experience indeed – a collector's piece, I suppose. My companion thanked me "for an unforgettable evening". I am going to try and forget the evening as soon as possible. ▌

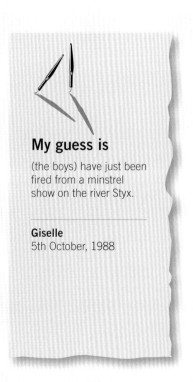

My guess is
(the boys) have just been fired from a minstrel show on the river Styx.

Giselle
5th October, 1988

Batsheva Dance Company

Naharin's Virus

FT

FINANCIAL
TIMES

Barbican Theatre, London

**3rd May
2004**

"THIS IS DANCING you will not see anywhere else", says the Batsheva Dance Company's flyer, quoting an American newspaper. "Promise me, promise me!" is my response, "and I'll eat up all my spinach!" Of course you'll see it all over the place. It is, despite its Israeli creators, just another damn dull example of German *Tanztheater*.

The Batsheva Dance Company from Tel Aviv has returned to Stalag Barbican with this jaw-dropper from its resident choreographer Ohad Naharin who gives it the unlovely title, *Naharin's Virus*. (Would you buy a cologne called "Zouave's Armpit"?) On Wednesday night, there were all the doggedly aggressive ingredients favoured by the *Tantztheater*

crowd. Sullen stares from the stage. A long blackboard on which the cast can make silly chalk marks. (For this alleged comment upon Middle East matters, the letters PASTELINA feature in bold capitals. Someone can't even get an anagram right). The performers ("dancers" seems too flattering a word in this context) shout and, of course, one girl must scream unintelligibly. They indulge in disjunct bursts of activity, wear unisex coveralls in black and white, hang from the blackboard wall, glare at us, go slow or go frantic, scribble, scribble, scribble with chalk on the board, while a man orates from Peter Handke's asphyxiatingly tiresome text *Offending the Audience*. This is something the show achieves through its ineptitudes but not on Handke's terms, even in its final catalogue of mealy-mouthed insults. There are fragments of music from an Arab composer (cue reconciliation!) and some faint quartet music. If this is supposed to be some gloss upon the fearful conflicts, internal and external, in the Middle East and the hopes for peace, then it is as inept a political statement as it is fatuous as theatre. ∎

Batsheva Dance Company
Naharin's Virus
(2007)

222

Tango Fire

Peacock Theatre,
London

FINANCIAL TIMES

"A VERTICAL RAPE", Jorge Luis Borges said of the tango. That was just a whisper exaggerated, I would suggest, but certainly the attitudes of a tango couple is of sexual electricity – although not, perhaps, of very high voltage. For all that the troupe is Argentina's Tango Fire, and that the show is entitled **Flames of Passion**, the erotic charge is more acrobatic than lustful. Indeed, the event indulges in so much Apache-dance manipulation of the women that the plea of a headache is probably welcome.

The evening's components are absolutely basic: five couples, a few tables and chairs, good lighting, gents' natty suitings and brilliantine, somewhat over-the-top frockery for the women (sequinned embroidery is dangerous, no matter where it finds itself – but especially on the lower back) and a superb quartet (bandoneon, piano, double bass, violin) of untiring virtuosity. Et voilà tout! There is also a singer, riven by emotion, pouring his heart out to us more than generously, and wearing the last pair of co-respondent shoes in captivity.

It is all such great fun, because the tango itself is so fascinating, so seemingly adaptable, so encouraging of sinuous or blazing dance and music. There are sublime Piazzolla tangos on offer, sensational in wit and drama and fascinating sonorities, given with no less fascinating artistry by the musicians.

The cast do what they do with most eager abandon and dizzying, slashing legs and feet. The five couples are gifted, seriously adept, and beguilingly able to involve themselves in the arbitrary confrontations, the sexually charged poses and lightning-flash dramas of the tango.

I note that acrobatics seem increasingly to be a part of the language of the troupe, with bodies (female, of course) raised in the air as trophies, tossed and spun on a factitious tide of passion and generally given the heave-ho. I find this – curiously, in view of the tango's history of not-unwitty sexual stereotyping – an act of supererogation. ∎

**1st February
2013**

Flames of Passion
London
(2011)

Les Ballets Trockadero de Monte Carlo

FT
FINANCIAL
TIMES

Peacock Theatre, London

21st September 2008

THEY'RE BACK! Those outraged swans, the toe-shoe terrors of Les Ballets Trockadero de Monte Carlo (who should be the pride of the principality) have returned for a London season and then a long regional tour.

The opening programme on Tuesday night at the Peacock Theatre played all the usual cards. A "classic" given the chop before our very eyes – it was **Swan Lake's** second act that here met the chainsaw – and then a succession of scenes that verge between mockery and a curious seriousness, as if to say, "We are chaps who want to be ballerinas, and by heaven we'll show you why!"

This last aspect of the show poses intriguing questions about gender, about impersonation as homage (since, unlike *onnagata* roles in Kabuki Theatre, there is no artistic purpose to the sex reversal), and about the nature of ballet dancing as cross-dressing.

But audiences rock with laughter and the cast responds with a generosity of temperament and technique that is irresistible. And, of course, awful truths about ballet are exposed for our delectation.

Chief treasure of the troupe remains ballet master Paul Ghiselin, whose version of **The Dying Swan** in performance by Ida Nevasayneva boasts a terrible resonance as well as impeccable comic resource.

There are ballerinas in the outside world who still persist in forcing themselves (and their audiences) through this feathered assault of sentimentality and droopy self-indulgence. Ghiselin, with tormented limbs, and the face of an affronted toucan, kills the bloody fowl for good and all.

He deserved even more applause than the ecstatic reception he gets for laying it to what I trust is its ultimate rest.

The **Swan Lake** is frenzied, and given with massive emotional bravura and flawless comic timing by the divine Lofatkina (Fernando Medina Gallego). The trio of odalisques from **Le Corsaire** dance all (but all) the right Petipa steps with gay abandon, and a recent La Trovatiara quintet turns Verdi ballet music to its own sunny ends: it looks in Peter Anastos's astute choreography rather as if it had also dropped off a production of **Corsaire**.

The final Majismas is (as Degas said of José Maria Sert's paintings) "very Spanish, and in such a quiet street, too", and is played with a certain earnestness as if the chaps would have us believe in their oh-so-Hispanic credentials. Not quite the point, I'd suggest, but as vivacious as you could wish.
All great fun. ∎

The Plague of Egypt

that the Bible forgot to mention.

Nine Sinatra
11th October, 2007

Paul Ghiselin
(Ida Nevasayneva)
The Dying Swan

WHEN IT PREMIERED as *Le Sacre du Printemps* at the Théâtre des Champs-Elysées on 29th May 1913 to choreography by Vaslav Nijinsky, Igor Stravinsky's score for Sergei Diaghilev's Ballets Russes signalled a shift in western classical music, such was its impact. In retrospect, Nijinsky's movement was secondary and it has been the music, massive, elemental, still troubling, which has attracted countless choreographers over subsequent years and decades, persuaded that they cannot only stand up to its onslaught but make something of it. Most take some or all of the underlying narrative of the original concept – the selection of a sacrificial victim – as their point of departure, but the forces used, both musical and dancing, and the movement idiom chosen, vary as much as the talent and artistry of the choreographers themselves.

'The Call of The Rite'

How choreographers have risen
to the challenge of *The Rite of Spring*

Chapter 6

'The Call of The Rite'

How choreographers have risen
to the challenge of *The Rite of Spring*

Chapter 6

A discussion with Marie Rambert

**3rd May
1962**

AT TONIGHT'S COVENT GARDEN GALA the Royal Ballet will give its first performance of Stravinsky's **The Rite of Spring**, with new choreography by Kenneth Macmillan. Here Clement Crisp talks with Dame Marie Rambert about the 1913 premiere of the ballet in Paris.

The riot that greeted the first performance of **Le Sacre du Printemps** in 1913 ranks high in the macabre ratings of "worst first-nights". The audience screamed and laughed, Diaghilev stood up in his box appealing for quiet, fighting broke out not only in the gallery but in the stalls, and one elderly countess stormed out with the cry that never before in all her sixty years had anyone dared make a fool of her.

The public's reaction has somewhat obscured the aims and merits of the ballet, but in a conversation a week ago Dame Marie Rambert brought vividly to life the creation of a work with which she was closely associated, both as Nijinsky's assistant in preparing it and as a member of the cast.

EURYTHMICS

In 1910 Marie Rambert had started a career in Paris as a dance recitalist, and in that year she went to study with Jacques Dalcroze in Geneva where he was teaching his theories of Eurythmics – a system of according music with movement. As Dame Marie says: "I went for a fortnight and stayed three years". The Dalcroze school transferred to Hellerau, near Dresden, and it was there, late in 1912, that

Diaghilev and Nijinsky came one day to watch classes. Three days later Rambert was told that Diaghilev wanted her to join his company to help Nijinsky in preparing **Sacre**, for it was recognised that the score was rhythmically very difficult, and Nijinsky was unable to cope with its complexities.

It was Marie Rambert's first task on joining the Ballet in Budapest to elucidate the score and assist Nijinsky (whose second ballet this was) in explaining his needs to the dancers. With the aid of a stout German rehearsal pianist known as "Kolossal" the score was counted out, divided into convenient sections for work, and Nijinsky would rehearse the passage, while Rambert would count out the movements to the dancers (hence the nick-name given her by the cast: 'Rhythmitchka'). In the piano reduction of the score which she used Dame Marie showed me her complete rehearsal notes; phrases like "The old woman falls into the circle of youths; she falls on her knees with her little feet up;" are pencilled throughout the pages just as Nijinsky said them.

Of Nijinsky, Dame Marie says quite simply: "He was a genius as a dancer and as a choreographer". During their association she was able to appreciate his intellectual stature, but, as she explains, "he had no small talk". A profound thinker, he was unable to express his admirable ideas with any fluency.

His choreographic theories were of great interest: most importantly he believed •••

that every movement of a dancer on stage had
to be composed. Unlike Fokine, for example,
who was prepared to allow improvisation
from his crowds in rehearsal and who would
work with his interpreters in creating a role
by a kind of mutual stimulation, Nijinsky knew
what he wanted down to the most minute
gesture, and dancers had to submit their
temperament and gifts entirely to his creative
imagination. He did not want his interpreters'
reactions, and sought to evolve a dance form
of the utmost precision and severity, demanding a complete subordination of his cast to
the pattern of the dance. With each of his
ballets he found a basic position or pose which
was a foundation for choreographic development: in **Faune** the feet and hands were
parallel to the footlights while the body was
placed facing the audience; in **Sacre** the feet
were turned in and the body was held heavily.

FERTILITY

The idea of **Sacre** was of a prehistoric community beseeching fertility from the sun, and
Nijinsky chose a vocabulary of very simple
steps, stamping and jumping with often only
one position of the arms. The main role of the
Chosen Virgin had an extraordinary quality; the
girl is fated to be the sacrifice and her dance
was a tragic parting from life. When Nijinsky
was rehearsing Maria Pilz in the part, Dame
Marie recalls the epic force of his movements:
he seemed unaware of the power of his
dancing and Pilz's magnificent interpretation
was only a reflection of Nijinsky's intensity.

Nijinsky aimed at reproducing every note of
the score in movement and every beat was
stamped out, but when rehearsals were under
way Stravinsky arrived in Budapest to play
the score. His tempi were different from those
of "Kolossal" and Nijinsky thought it impossible to dance his choreography to them:
eventually the adjustment was made, and
rehearsals continued throughout the company's
tour of Germany, during the Monte Carlo
season and later, when the Ballet moved to
Paris to inaugurate Astruc's new theatre, the
Champs Elysées in a top room of the
unfinished theatre.

BEDLAM

The 1913 season was to see the first performances of two Nijinsky works: **Jeux** (significant
as the first ballet to show modern man on the
stage – the three characters were tennis
players) was unenthusiastically received, and
a fortnight later **Sacre** was given. Within
minutes of the curtain-rise bedlam had
broken out in the auditorium: the reception
was not expected by the dancers, who were
soon unable to hear the music and were
forced to count frenziedly while Nijinsky
stood on a chair in the wings counting and
conducting to help them. (During the relative
calm that heralded the Chosen Virgin's dance,
Pilz had to stand shaking during the intro-
ductory bars, and a voice from the gallery
called "Un Docteur" to which a second voice
added "Un Dentiste" and a third "Deux
dentistes"). After the performance Nijinsky
made a single comment to Marie Rambert:
"This idiot public".

Dame Marie still remembers **Sacre** as an epic
ballet, a work that scaled great heights, and
her final judgment on it is uncompromising:
"It was one of the greatest ballets I have
ever seen". ∎

Théâtre des Champs-Elysées, Paris

FT

FINANCIAL
TIMES

**22nd September
1990**

THE SHOUTS AND CATCALLS echo down the years. It was, I suppose, the century's most notorious first night as the Stravinsky/ Nijinsky *Sacre du printemps* was unveiled to Paris on the stage of the brand new Théâtre des Champs Elysées on 29 May 1913. Amid the din from the auditorium the old Comtesse de Pourtalès declared; "It's the first time in 60 years that anyone has dared make a fool of me", while Florent Schmitt bawled abuse at the "sixteenth arrondissement bitches" and, as Maria Pilz, the Chosen Maiden, began the tremors that started the solo, voices called for "A doctor! – a dentist! – two dentists!"

On Wednesday night the Nijinsky *Sacre* came triumphantly home to the stage on which it had been so rowdily born, when the Joffrey Ballet showed it as part of a Diaghilev triple bill. The fascination for Paris was in seeing a *Sacre* which is the fruit of seven years dedicated research by the dance scholar Millicent Hodson to establish a choreographic text from nothing but hints and fragments of information.

Nijinsky's ballet had just eight performances in 1913 by the Ballets Russes – five in Paris and three, soberly received, in London. It was then abandoned. Dr Hodson's task has been to piece together a ballet from any surviving testimony – most significantly the sketches taken during the first performances by Valentine Gross, Stravinsky's notations on his own score, and another copy of the score on

which Marie Rambert – Nijinsky's assistant on the production – had written her memories of the dance action. (Rambert's notes were lively. Thirty years ago she talked me through part of this score – "Here, you see… they stamp the ground with their little feet – Nijinsky said 'little' feet").

From such evidence, Dr Hodson assembled a dance action. Kenneth Archer, an art historian and specialist on the work of Nikolay Roerich who designed the ballet for Nijinsky, recreated the sets and costumes, and three years ago Nijinsky's *Sacre* was reborn in Los Angeles on the Joffrey dancers. And is the staging like the lost masterpiece whose image has haunted dance-lovers for seventy years?

If such devoted scholarship is enough, then we do see something "like". It is clearly the work of an innovative dance creator in whom an acute feeling for ethnic history (owed to Roerich, who was obsessed with pre-history) united with a no less innovative musical sensibility (which must have been influenced by the eurythmic theories of Jaques-Dalcroze, who was Rambert's teacher). And what I perceived, more surely than in any other staging I know, is the Russian-ness of the music. A relationship between Roerich's vivid designs, the driven groups of dancers, and Stravinsky's melodic and rhythmic forms is very clear.

Here is Ancient Russia as imagined by Russian artists at the beginning of this century, ● ● ●

and if we cannot see the actuality of Nijinsky's choreography, we sense very strongly the urgency and excitement that its creators gave to **Sacre** on stage. The production is a success, for all the differences in weight of movement and sophistication of dance understanding between the Ballets Russes and Joffrey's dancers. This revival must inevitably lack the innocent power that was central to the original. But it tells us why Nijinsky's **Sacre** was important, and why it remains so even today.

The juxtaposition of Nijinsky's **Faune** (which has an honourable line of theatrical perform-ance) with **Sacre** was fascinating. **Faune** is, as we believe the original **Sacre**, a masterpiece by reason of its simple yet profoundly novel language – walking as dance; the frieze as choreographic form. The Joffrey troupe has a good version of the text, scrupulously

costumed for the nymphs, complete with glorious Bakst set. On Wednesday the company proceeded to ruin the piece through atro-cious lighting. Bakst's luminous dream of an Attic hillside was cast in a murk of shadow. The faun and leading nymph were daintily spotlit. Diaghilev prided himself on the lighting of his ballets and this was unworthy. ∎

**Erica Lynette Edwards
(2006)**

Royal Opera House, Covent Garden

FT
FINANCIAL
TIMES

9th May 1962

LAST THURSDAY'S GALA programme has now moved into the general repertory and allows us an opportunity to judge it away from the glitter of a grand occasion.

First and foremost **The Rite of Spring**: fully noticed in this column after the first performance. Another viewing confirms it as marked with Macmillan's signally unflagging invention, his musical understanding and his skill in matching Stravinsky's technical effects, mark it as a notable acquisition.

The Adoration of the Earth strikes one afresh with the magnificence of its floor patterns; the surging groups of dancers, the steady development of the tribal excitement, the movement that so clearly expresses the animal forces waiting to be unleashed, are a masterly achievement.

The Sacrifice, in which our whole attention is centred on the Chosen Maiden, seems even more remarkable. The extraordinary potency of the dance images which MacMillan has devised to show the transformation of the girl into a tribal goddess are amazing, and Monica Mason gives a performance that demands superlatives; she conveys the mounting frenzy of the possessed girl, and the inevitability of the sacrifice, entirely by muscular means. Yet despite the novelty of the dance language and its deliberately un-balletic style, the whole choreography is

clearly marked with MacMillan's signature: it is a notable creation that will repay the closest study. ∎

Monica Mason
(Premiere, 1962)

Tanztheater Wuppertal

FINANCIAL TIMES

Sadler's Wells

15th February 2008

Ruth Amarante (2008)

I OWN TO A MISTRUST of *Tanztheater*, or dance-theatre, or Euro-tedium – call it what you will. There are all the merry appurtenances of pretension: the secret physical language, the chatter, the angst and the cheery assumption that we need to understand about these private anxieties, these ill-behaved and self-obsessed dead-beats. But there is a public that eats it up with a spoon, and their guru is Pina Bausch.

Bausch's *Tanztheater* can move me (**1980** was terrific), but the greater part I find self-regarding, and I remember Randall Jarrell's comment that "there are people who would swallow a porcupine if you dyed its quills and called it Modern Art". Which brings us to the programme of Bausch stagings by the Tanztheater Wuppertal, which opened a 10-day season on Wednesday night.

On offer are two early works: **The Rite of Spring**, from 1975, and **Café Müller** made three years later. **Café Müller** features everything I find most tedious about the genre. A café which is a child-Bausch's memory of her father's establishment. Three men, three women, revenants banging into chairs, memories, tables, walls, each other, grappling in dreariest repetition with their neuroses. Unendurable. Cheers from the thronging faithful.

Then **Rite**, which is a choreographic masterpiece – and has nothing to do with *Tanztheater*. The stage covered in earth. Sixteen men and 16 women, inexorable in a

tribal ritual. Bausch's language elemental, superbly organised. Terror focused upon the scarlet shift which must find its sacrificial wearer among the girls. Dance rooted in the score, excavating terrified gesture from its energies, dancers with every anguished bone in their faces marked with sweat and earth, gasping bodies driven ever onward. At last, Ruth Amarante is the Chosen One, her dancing possessed, inevitable. (Her face, *in extremis*, might be a drawing by Käthe Kollwitz). Her (and Bausch's) power and expressivity are marvellous: this is a superb work of art. Forget the café, this is the real dance theatre. ▐

London Coliseum

FT
FINANCIAL
TIMES

Of THE SEVERAL ACCOUNTS of **The Rite of Spring** that I have sat through, three have, for me, realised Stravinsky's vision of pagan ritual: Kenneth MacMillan, Pina Bausch, Leonid Massine. They were utterly different but unfailing in their response to the music. Let me now add a fourth, as powerful as these, by Michael Keegan-Dolan for his Fabulous Beast troupe.

It forms part of a double bill at the Coliseum with English National Opera's new staging of Bartok's **Duke Bluebeard's Castle**. Be it said at once that Edward Gardner's account of the score with the ENO orchestra could drive a weaker production than Keegan-Dolan's to glory with its rhythmic discipline. Keegan-Dolan shows us an Irish rural community of today: a crowd of men; a Wise Woman (the splendid Olwen Fouere); her boy acolyte, dressed as for his first communion; and three young women. Snow intermittently falls on an open space, with a statue of the Blessed Virgin a haunting presence.

The Wise Woman begins the ceremony, puffing on a cigarette. The men bring cardboard boxes. They dance, their movement rough, rudimentary, urgent. A young man is, briefly, a potential victim for sacrifice. An old man is carried above the crowd on a table. The girls are given a potion (in teacups) and fall into a trance. They put on hare masks, and are held (thrilling image) totemic on men's shoulders. The men's dancing becomes orgiastic and they copulate with the earth. From boxes

they take dog-head masks and become a menacing pack of hounds.

As the rite intensifies, one of the girls becomes the chosen figure. The men strip naked, put on frocks and dance, inspired by the girl's revealed identity. The rite avoids sacrifice, but retains its intensity.

I detail these actions because they suggest the force of Keegan-Dolan's vision. Movement is demotic in its stampings and circlings, yet acquires sacramental dignity. The power of Keegan-Dolan's response lies in this simplicity: in the complexities of Stravinsky's score he has discerned an elemental directness. His artists give thrillingly frank and unassuming performances, their strength that of the music. Here is a **Rite** whose modernity is utterly remote from the prehistory that inspired Stravinsky, yet it knows that there are trace memories within us, potent and cathartic. ∎

10th September 2009

Artists of the Company (2009)

THIS A DARK, BROODING, COMPLEX BALLET for which Clement holds immense admiration. It is by his friend Kenneth MacMillan, whom he had known from the choreographer's very earliest essays in dance, and whose career he followed – in some cases literally, as Clement flew out to Stuttgart and, later, Berlin, to see his work – and supported. He considers this ballet as his greatest achievement in the three-act form, such is its emotional and scenic intelligence and the opportunities it affords true dance-actors.

MacMillan's Mayerling:

The male dancer's
ultimate challenge

Chapter 7

MacMillan's Mayerling:

The male dancer's
ultimate challenge

Chapter 7

Royal Opera House,
Covent Garden

FT

FINANCIAL
TIMES

**17th February
1978**

THE TRAGEDY AT MAYERLING in 1889 is best known to us through the cinema versions, which have cheapened and sentimentalised a mysterious incident that seemed a terrible symptom of the degeneracy of the Austro-Hungarian empire. In his new three-act *Mayerling* for the Royal Ballet, Kenneth MacMillan has made use of the cinema's procedures while resolutely deromanticising its view of events. By inviting the novelist Gillian Freeman to provide him with a scenario he has benefited from her understanding of script-writing for films to create a fluidly cinematic form, making use of the equivalent of the camera's "dissolves" and swift narrative devices. At the same time he has rejected the popular, cinema-bred idea of the Crown Prince Rudolf and Mary Vetsera as a grander, Viennese Romeo and Juliet, to show us something much nearer the historical and psychological truth of the characters.

In *Mayerling* MacMillan returns to a major concern of his large-scale choreography: the reshaping and developing of the form of the three-act ballet, moving away from 19th century structure and its conventional fantasy figures, to forge a manner able to deal with the harsher realism suited to late 20th century taste. (An interesting case can be made out for seeing *Mayerling* as *Swan Lake* 100 years on: love in death, royal duty, emotional instability are common to Prince Siegfried and to Prince Rudolf). *Anastasia* suggested MacMillan's way ahead, as a study of a real woman caught at a moment of

crisis: as in Grigorovich's *Spartacus*, and more especially his *Ivan the Terrible*, the stuff of history nurtures the development of ballet, and substitutes fact for convenient fiction.

The result, in *Mayerling*, is a tense, searing ballet in which a tragic figure is seen in his very special and dramatically fascinating social setting, his motives and his psychology explored in dances of rare power, his destiny explained in terms of political, family and social pressures. The central character of Rudolf is not a new one in MacMillan's ballets. He is the outcast, the victim, whom we know as the girl in *The Invitation*, Anastasia/Anna Anderson, *Rite's* Chosen Virgin, Juliet, the younger brother in *Triad* – all driven to isolation or death by events they cannot or will not control. But Rudolf is the most complex, and most fully extended in analysis, and as a result the ballet provides what I assume to be the lengthiest role yet created for a male dancer – more demanding even than *Spartacus* or *Ivan the Terrible*. And be it said straight away that as Rudolf David Wall is superb: in the role of a lifetime he gives the performance of a lifetime.

The ballet charts the eight years which begin with Rudolf's loveless marriage to Princess Stephanie of Belgium, barely out of the school-room, and which culminate in the double shooting at his Hunting Lodge at Mayerling where he first kills Mary Vetsera (his mistress of but two weeks) and then ends his own life. Mayerling's hero is never •••

heroic, but he wins all our sympathy, and this without distorting historical fact. His every demand upon his parents rejected, he turns to a life of compulsive womanising and to debauchery – the Rudolf who lies dead at the ballet's end is venereally diseased, a morphine addict, a Prince trapped in political and sexual intrigue, a gun-fetishist obsessed with the idea of death, heir to a throne which cannot be his for years to come. And unlikely as it may seem, MacMillan and Wall show him as a man infinitely pitiable, authentically tragic.

To achieve a portrait of such depth and resonance, the action follows Rudolf's journey to Mayerling by way of the claustrophobic, faction-ridden court of the Hapsburgs (Nicholas Georgiadis's settings are admirable in catching the enclosed and stuffy world of the Hofburg, as, too, a seedy tavern and the Vetsera house). Central to the development of the character is a sequence of duets for Rudolf with the women in his life, and in them MacMillan's mastery of the *pas de deux* has never seemed more complete. In none of them is there a suggestion of conventional romantic love: rather does each stress the isolated lovelessness that drives Rudolf deeper

Lynn Seymour (Mary Vetsera)
David Wall (Crown Prince Rudolf)
(1978)

into despair. We see him with his mother, the Empress Elizabeth, a role in which Georgina Parkinson (Gertrude to his Hamlet) superbly conveys a frigid reluctance to become involved with Rudolf's plight. The wedding night encounter with his new bride is illuminated by Wendy Ellis's beautiful sensitivity as a girl terrified and brutalised; earlier we find Rudolf flirting cruelly with his young sister-in-law at a wedding ball: Genesia Rosato showing promise of fine things here. We watch him take Stephanie to a louche tavern where he returns to a liaison with his mistress, Mitzi Caspar, a role exultantly taken by Laura Connor.

And recurring throughout the ballet is the woman who seems crucial to his unhappiness, the Countess Larisch: one-time mistress, now a procuress and evil genius, she is yet the only person who offers him any understanding or sympathy. As Larisch Merle Park gives a performance that uses her best qualities to the full: danced with dazzling bravura, acted with brilliant assurance, the role glitters with life as bright as the diamonds Larisch wears – it is a wonderful creation. To Lynn Seymour falls the role of Mary Vetsera, and she brings to it a luscious physical presence as a girl recklessly in love with the idea of love. In the duets for Rudolf and Mary, MacMillan is at his most persuasive as an erotic poet, exploring passion with images of extreme beauty – the final coupling at Mayerling marvellously combining lust and despair.

As a setting and explanation for this core of *pas de deux* MacMillan has provided big set pieces: a grand and magnificently organised set of waltzes at the Hofburg, a birthday party for Franz Joseph, and a boisterous tavern scene. At every moment in them the artists of the Royal Ballet are at their best: in secondary roles Michael Coleman, Stephen Beagley, Michael Batchelor and Derek Deane revel in the ardours of variations for a group of Hungarian officers, and Graham Fletcher makes a fine showing as a cab-driver used by Rudolf. And at the ballet's heart is David Wall. From his earliest performances as a very young and very gifted premier danseur Wall knew how to hold the stage. Now in his maturity he demonstrates a marvellous authority. He has the strength, both emotional and physical, for this unique role. Tireless throughout a most taxing sequence of *pas de deux*, assured in solos, he has entered into the soul of the Crown Prince: the degeneration of Rudolf's character is displayed with terrible inevitability.

His most remarkable moment, for me, is one of complete immobility. At a party in the Hofburg, Franz Joseph's mistress, the singer Katherina Schratt (Bernadette Greevy), entertains the courtiers with a song. Rudolf stands slightly apart, motionless and seething with emotion at his mother's behaviour and his own impotence: it is a measure of Wall's greatness in the role that we sense all Rudolf's sadness, the tears he dare not shed are plain to see.

The score for **Mayerling** is assembled from the music of Liszt, skilfully arranged by John Lanchbery. There are moments when it seems too fragmentary, but it everywhere sustains the danced action. Georgiadis' designs, as I have indicated, are most effective, and his costumes combine historical verisimilitude with balletic suitability. I have seen **Mayerling** twice – at Tuesday's gala and again on Wednesday at the official premiere – and it revealed far more of itself at a second viewing. At the risk of seeming a ticket-tout I would urge audiences to see it twice, the intricacies of plotting are not difficult, but the richness texture becomes even more rewarding when seen a second time. There are some cuts which will inevitably need to be made but these are slight, and ballet stands as a fascinating and innovative development with MacMillan, Wall and the entire cast meriting every praise. So, too, does IBM International, whose generosity made the ballet possible: industrial sponsorship of the arts in these hard time is of inestimable public benefit. ∎

Irek Mukhamedov

The Royal Ballet

Royal Opera House, Covent Garden

THE TRAGIC CIRCUMSTANCES surrounding the revival of **Mayerling** at Covent Garden inevitably make us more conscious of this ballet's merits. In 1978, freed from time-consuming duties as Director of the Royal Ballet, Kenneth MacMillan celebrated his release with a work of larger scale and deeper concerns than ever before. Seven years earlier, the full-length **Anastasia** looked at the collapse of the Romanov dynasty through the eyes of the young Grand Duchess, and focussed upon the matter of identity. In **Mayerling** we are shown a corruption of the Archduke Rudolf's identity that helped destroy the Hapsburg empire. And in doing this MacMillan brought off an astonishing feat, by surrounding his central characterisation – the most densely wrought and detailed male role created in this century's dance – with a series of female portraits no less psychologically apt.

For MacMillan, Rudolf's womanising is a key to his tragedy, sprung from his tormented relationship with his mother, exemplified by his brutality to his wife, and illuminated by his ambiguous relationship with Larisch, a mistress/procuress who is the only woman to comprehend his suffering. That she is the agent to bring Mary Vetsera to him is the final, fatal touch to their liaison. The fantasies central to Rudolf's psyche – love in death; sado-masochistic passion – find their terrible reality at Mayerling. Yet detailed as these female characters seem, they never overbalance the ballet's central concern with Rudolf. We see how complex was the ● ● ●

23rd November 1992

Irek Mukhamedov
(Crown Prince Rudolf)
Royal Ballet tour,
Bolshoi Theatre
(2003)

tight in focus, everywhere convincing, and some slight embellishments of steps are the choreographer's tribute to Mukhamedov's technique. From Viviana Durante an excellently judged Mary, conveying the sensuality just below the surface of social manners, and from Lesley Collier a perfect Larisch – worldly, watchful, and suddenly and touchingly gripped by her passion for Rudolf. Jane Burn, a young dancer new to us, was Stephanie, Rudolf's hapless bride. Her reading was delicate, urgently stated, if understandably careful as yet, but Sir Kenneth admired her abilities and she will grow with further performance.

On Saturday afternoon, another new cast was headed by Michael Nunn's Rudolf. Nunn fine in **The Judas Tree** as the innocent young man – gave a performance which combined physical elegance (beautiful line; lucid gesture) with an ideal sensitivity. He played the crucial "closet scene" with the Empress Elizabeth superbly: kneeling, with her hands pressed to his head, he said everything about the Rudolf who would behave with such frenzy as he goes to his bride. A nervous impetuosity informs this reading – rightly so – and it augurs brave things for the future.

In Gillian Revie, Nunn found a sensually vivid Mary: the dance was luscious, emotion exactly judged between sexual opportunism and fantasy. There was also a notably good Larisch from Genesia Rosato, and a completely understood Stephanie from Natalie McCann – showing us every nuance of incomprehension, distaste, and more than a hint of stuffiness. Company performance was excellent: I admired Matthew Hart's buoyant, musical account of Bratfisch, and Anthony Bourne's sensitivity in the same role; and also the bravura view of Mitzi Caspar from both Darcey Bussell and Leanne Benjamin. In Mayerling (as in so much of the MacMillan repertory) the Royal Ballet is seen as an ensemble of expressive dancers without peer. It is a message worth proclaiming. ∎

social and emotional fabric of the tragedy, and how superbly MacMillan has given its theatrical essence.

In the Royal Ballet performances this season, as in the past, we also see the grand sensitivity of the troupe to the roles he gave them. Most of the artists are making debuts, but the style and the power of playing by the entire troupe is magnificent. In Thursday's revival, Irek Mukhamedov was a Rudolf of entire truth. He understands the central anguish of the character, and he has mastered the physical outlines and the searing movement that must tell of that anguish. The reading was dark,

Royal Opera House, Covent Garden

FT

FINANCIAL
TIMES

**19th April
2007**

EDWARD WATSON is an exceptional dancer – the Royal Ballet has never before shown us an artist of such very different and distinctive powers. His physique is lean as a greyhound's. His line, that way in which a dancer's body displays and explores choreography, is as taut, as wiry and, at times, as nervously questioning as Egon Schiele's in probing character, in finding a truth about movement and dynamics, just as Schiele discloses personality or a state of mind.

In recent seasons Watson has made an indelible mark on his every role, be it as a chillingly scary teacher in **The Lesson**, as the manipulative brother in MacMillan's **My Brother, My Sisters**, or in the plotless (but somehow plot-full, in Watson's performances) developments of Balanchine's **Four Temperaments** or MacMillan's **Gloria**, or in the introversions of Wayne McGregor's **Chroma**. This season Watson has been cast as Rudolf in **Mayerling**, and I was knocked sideways by his second performance on Tuesday night. Here was the role as never seen before, a pale and haunted princeling whom we know at once is at odds with his world beneath a superficial elegance of manner, his actions marked by a neurotic bravado that ill masks the nervous terrors that drive him on.

Watson's physical line unfurls and drives through the dance like a scalpel, seeking Rudolf's every symptom of mania. The key incident is the closet scene with the Empress Elizabeth (superbly taken by Cindy Jourdain),

where Rudolf's anguished appeals are greeted with the mother's frozen inability to respond.

Watson's vulnerability here, and the final dreadful glance back at the Empress as Rudolf leaves for his wedding night, partake of the highest theatrical art: we know we are watching a prodigious dance-actor. Everything else, each terrifying twist and subterfuge of Rudolf's behaviour (and of MacMillan's dances, which seem new-minted by Watson) springs from this incident, and Watson has the psychic and physical strength to drive the role and the ballet to its terrible conclusion. Here is rare, heart-tearing, heart-lifting artistry and we are privileged to watch it. The company performances (Mara Galeazzi and Sarah Lamb ideally good as Mary Vetsera and Mme Larisch) were very fine. ∎

**Edward Watson
(Crown Prince Rudolf)
(2007)**

THAT THIS WORK is considered the *sine qua non* of classical ballet is only part of the story of **The Sleeping Beauty** and The Royal Ballet. Since it was staged in its entirety by them in 1939, under the title of **The Sleeping Princess**, it has represented the touchstone of the ensemble, the role of Aurora a rite of passage for company dancers and the whole undertaking a statement of intent and a demonstration of technical mastery by the entire company. Its pedigree which stretches back to pre-revolutionary Russia and the court of the Tsar adds to its lustre, but it is the success that it brought to The Royal Ballet in those early post-war years, making Margot Fonteyn world-famous and 'conquering' New York on the company's first tour, that gives it an aura which remains undimmed at Covent Garden. The decades since the war have seen The Royal Ballet wrestle to match up to the legend of its own past.

In Search of Beauty:

The Royal Ballet's quest for
the perfect production

Chapter 8

In Search of Beauty:

The Royal Ballet's quest for
the perfect production

Chapter 8

The Sleeping Beauty - 50 Years

FT

FINANCIAL
TIMES

With a performance of *'The Sleeping Beauty'* 50 years ago Covent Garden was re-born. Clement Crisp reports

FIFTY YEARS AGO tomorrow, on February 20 1946, the curtains of the Royal Opera House, Covent Garden, rose on a performance of **The Sleeping Beauty**. After six years of wartime service as a dance-hall – there had been a notice 'No Jitterbugging' on the proscenium arch – Covent Garden was reborn. Not with opera or those Ballets Russes troupes which had once ruled there, but with an English company: the Sadler's Wells Ballet.

It was a hugely significant evening. There were present the Royal Family, members of the government, what remained of the old habitués – whom the economist John Maynard Keynes called "the ancient hens of glory" – and those ballet-lovers who had given the Wells company their devotion. Keynes had masterminded the translation of the Wells ensemble to greater things, as he had inspired the creation of the Arts Council. The fostering of the arts in Britain implicit in this apotheosis of Ninette de Valois' company, gave an air of excitement to the event which quite effaced the slight odour of camphor from evening dress liberated from wartime storage.

Dame Ninette might have supposed, as she once told me, that her company would go back to the Wells after its tremendous, arduous wartime achievements, and "the Russians" come back to Covent Garden. But

the Ballets Russes were a spent force, and de Valois' company was strong in ballets and dancers, and – after a mere 15 years existence – a national ensemble.

So, with a grandly designed (by Oliver Messel) and staged **The Sleeping Beauty**, with Fonteyn as Aurora and Robert Helpmann as both Prince and Carabosse, with Constant Lambert (that genius) conducting, the Sadler's Wells Ballet entered into its inheritance. Nor was the evening a mere flash of brilliance. Later that week we also saw the noble Pamela May as Aurora, and then the fine-spun beauty of Moira Shearer, with Beryl Grey as a radiant Lilac Fairy, and our first Bolshoi dancer, Violetta Prokhorova Elvin, in the Bluebird duet. Here were riches, and we in the audience rejoiced. And went on rejoicing as our national ballet proved itself in the eyes of the world.

So, 50 years on, the curtain rises for a commemorative performance of **Beauty**. The situation is, I feel, less golden than such a jubilee merits. Since the first showing here of the present Anthony Dowell/Maria Björnson staging, I have reported on it with something like despair. No; not "something like", but with despair itself, the real and desolating thing, •••

19th February 1996

Poster (c.1946)
The Sleeping Beauty,
Sadlers Wells Ballet

as I look at the blustering wrong-headedness of sets and the mimsy vulgarity of costuming, and the toll they take on every civilised aspect of this noblest example of classic ballet.

But the staging is suggestive of a more serious malaise in ballet at Covent Garden. In 1946, if the general level of dancing was less gleaming than it now is – the Royal Ballet is a strong ensemble – there were ballerinas whose gifts were individual and splendidly varied. In Lambert we had a musical director of rarest talent. Ballets made by Ashton and de Valois gave the company a secure identity. (Within a couple of months of the Covent Garden debut, Dame Ninette had established a new young troupe at Sadler's Wells to serve as nursery) here was purpose and energy to what our national ballet was doing.

Even so, the success of these years set precedents later to become dangerous. The public came to think of "ballet" as an Opera House art concerned, at best, with full-length work. The Royal Ballet duly proved that it could produce both the big ballets and the dancers capable of sustaining them.

And, with increasing malignity, the idea has taken hold that if it has not got three acts, it is not a proper ballet.

So a deadly blanket of evening-long stagings lies over Britain, and performance schedules – of the Royal and Birmingham Royal troupes, of English National, Scottish, London City, Northern Ballet – reveal a dire catalogue of such productions. Titles are what matter, recognisable labels for the dwarfish or feeble, promising much and delivering clichés and swan-feathers.

248

At Covent Garden, despite an evident desire to face the problem, runs of **Swan Lake** or **Manon** are seat-fillers for a theatre debilitated by lack of funds, and mind-numbers for dancers and audience. Fearsome prices and a predictable repertory are the best way of killing an audience's interest and ballet's creative future. (My formative dance-going was built, in the 1940s and '50s, on cheap seats and a constantly fresh repertory. It is impossible, financially or aesthetically, to be thus educated – and excited – today).

The Royal Ballet now has no resident choreographer, no music director. It can offer (like many another troupe wanting to seem "modern") neurotic tussles by William Forsythe. It neglects too many ballets, by Ashton, de Valois, Cranko, MacMillan, which are central to its identity, and creations by Fokine, Massine, Nijinska, Balanchine, Tudor, which are the inheritance of 20th-century ballet. Quite soon the Royal Ballet will be unfamiliar with its own ancestry and unable properly to understand what is its rightful persona. The public must learn again to trust our national ballet, and not turn to it for the deadliest received ideas about what classical dancing means.

The moment has come to consider with great seriousness the Royal Ballet's future. In 1997 the Opera House closes for refurbishment.

A new general director will take over. The view given by BBC TV's *The House* is of an establishment in some disarray, and the ballet company's record in recent years is no inducement to change that opinion. The crass decoration of **Beauty**; a disastrous **Don Quixote**; the redressing of Ashton ballets; **Cyrano** and **Mr Worldly-Wise**, (now known as **Mr Deadly Dull**); too few performances; young creators pitched on to a large stage rather than nursed in a smaller ensemble – the Royal Ballet needs a permanent chamber group for experiment – are matters for concern.

We know the company is victim of financial difficulties that rack the Opera House, and that closure will present even further difficulties. We sense that brave decisions must be made to restore the Royal Ballet's public image and secure its future. Ingres said: "The task is not to invent but to continue". Ballet companies, like their dancers, are born with genetic traits, and these must be recognised. The Royal Ballet's future can be understood in what its rich and not-too-distant past tells us. A first move should be to jettison the present **Beauty** – no matter what the loss of face and funds – and to ensure a staging that does justice to what was once the company's signature ballet. Then the Royal Ballet might start to find itself again. ∎

FT

FINANCIAL
TIMES

Royal Opera House, Covent Garden

13th January 1969

THERE HAS BEEN TIME since Andrew Porter's initial review of the new **Sleeping Beauty** for first impressions to cool down – or gain in enthusiasm. I am sorry to have to report that after three viewings my own regrets at the staging, or more precisely, my mistrust of its decoration, have not altered. This is not simply a nostalgia for the style of the old Messel settings, which came in for a good many knocks in their time, but distress at the miscalculation in the period at which the ballet has now been set. The idea of a return to Perrault's world (and that seen through the Victorian distortion of Gustave Doré's illustrations to the tales) may have seemed attractive, but Perrault was himself intent on reviving the mediaevalism of old folk-tales, and Vsevolozhsky, who devised the ballet and supervised its realisation very thoroughly, cut and adapted Perrault to make little more than a scenario for what he called "a magical fantasy": in effect a typical *ballet féerie* of the period.

The music was to comprise melodies "in the style of Lully, Bach and Rameau" and the scenery was "to be in the style of Louis XIV". But put back a further two hundred years in this new production, dimmed and dampened by pale, faded colours, by greys and browns, placed on dancers in costumes that efface themselves against the sets, and Petipa's clear-cut, faceted choreography loses in sharpness.

There seems a "credibility gap" between the dances and their surroundings, even between the music and the stage action; the armour and faintly barbaric dress of the King and his court in the Prologue; the scullions and peasantry of the first act, and the short dresses of Aurora's friends, all result in a mixture that is less than convincing either as drama or as fairy-tale fantasy. It was one of the many merits of the Kirov's noble staging – so effortlessly right in style – that it offered a clear distinction between the enchantments of the fairies and the bold grandeur of a real palace through which the courtiers strolled.

But at the Royal Opera House majesty and magic are at a premium; the court's splendour has been minimised, domesticated, so that Aurora's birthday celebrations take place in the backyard of a castle; the architecture is low-keyed and low-scaled, tubby and pallid like the costumes, when it should soar elegantly: it presses in on the dance-area, affording neither the space nor the light in which Petipa's diamonds can flash. And here we come to the serious problem of adjustment for the dancers, who have had, surely, to reshape and rethink their interpretations to suit the muted tones, the lowered emotional temperature of the production. I have seen two fine and experienced Auroras – Antoinette Sibley and Merle Park – and neither seemed to me as effective or as touching as heretofore. On the first night Sibley and Anthony Dowell led the performance; Sibley evidently realised that she had to dominate both costume and

scenery by sheer presence, and she very nearly succeeded.

She danced forcefully and well, and showed all her customary youthful élan, balancing prodigiously in the Rose Adagio, but her girlish brightness was dimmed. The "old" Messel decor gave the dances room to breathe and flower; the airy improbability of the settings never gloomed over the dances, absorbing

their radiance, and though there is no true artistic precedent for the short tutu, it increases the feeling of lightness and allows the dancer's body to be seen fully extended; the new knee-length dresses stunt the ballerina, and every other female dancer. Anthony Dowell was almost extinguished in a dark-toned costume against the sombre browns and blacks of the Hunting Scene, and how regrettable are the cuts here; they shorten • • •

Antoinette Sibley (Aurora), design, Henry Bardon: costumes, Lila de Nobili and Mstislav Doboujinsky (1969)

the scene to make room, I surmise, for the new 'Awakening' *pas de deux*, but they endanger an important transition in the ballet's structure. The hunt is no longer an elaborate and far from uninteresting Court party, a reminder of Louis XIV's passion for the chase, but simply a depressing picnic. Dowell danced magnificently throughout the evening, and he alone of the three Princes I have seen gives an exultant joy to the final *pas de deux*.

The second cast, Merle Park and Rudolf Nureyev, were also somewhat at odds with the decoration, though by the time I caught up with their performance, both had had time to cope with some of the problems of the setting. Park is so exciting a technician, so fluent and fast and at ease with the choreography, that my only regret is that she does not make the Aurora of the first act more innocently youthful. Her princess is a very assured young woman, overawed neither by the occasion nor by her suitors – though the production makes a very nice Kirov-style difference between the princes, and Park "points" her dancing to each in turn. Her vision scene was lyrical, imponderable, the Awakening *adagio* wonderfully soft-grained, and the Wedding duet effortlessly brilliant. Nureyev did a great deal technically and dramatically – it is a bold and beautiful touch to finish the big third act variation on a soft, dying cadence – and he alone has complete mastery in the Hunting Scene.

The third cast, Vyvyan Lorrayne and Robert Mead, was the least experienced, and Lorrayne's Rose Adagio is still tentative, but the costume suits her – she carries its heavy shape with real distinction – and on her best form, in the last act, she suggests that her warm, opulent manner can make an appealing Aurora. Mead seemed, not surprisingly, subdued by the gloom of the Hunting Scene, but in the last act he impressed not only by his dancing, which has gained in attack and force, but by the excellent way he judged his technical effects, and by his nobility of presence.

The company performances have been dutiful, though hardly inspired by the novelty of the proceedings; in the splendid new solo for the extra fairy at the Christening, Georgina Parkinson is fine, as, too, Laura Connor on one occasion: here is a young dancer of remarkable quality. Monica Mason is brilliant in the Finger Variation, which has happily copied the Kirov version by including *pas de chat* on point, which gives even more edge and bite to the solo; three Lilac Fairies, Deanne Bergsma, Ria Pen and Vergie Derman, have all been good, with Miss Derman slightly to be preferred for sheer presence; and of the pairs of Bluebirds, my own welcome is for Wayne Sleep and Lesley Collier on Saturday matinée: whole-hearted and never less than dazzling. Elsewhere, freaked-out wigs and mediaeval clobber evidently take some getting used to, but as a final query, are we to assume that the woad-tinted Fairy Cavaliers of the prologue are piebald? Rather after the fashion of Edward Lear Jumblies. "Their hands are pink and their faces blue". ∎

The Royal Ballet

Royal Opera House, Covent Garden

FT
FINANCIAL
TIMES

A MAGICAL FANTASY – thus I. A. Vsevolozhsky, director of the Imperial Theatres and guiding spirit in the creation of **The Sleeping Beauty** as librettist and designer of the costumes, wrote to Tchaikovsky when he commissioned the score. **Beauty**, is of course, several things: the supreme achievement of Petipa's genius; the pinnacle of 19th century ballet; a ballet féerie designed to delight a court audience and pay discreetly flattering homage to the Tsar, whose servants the artists of the Imperial Ballet were. For us it is the signature work of the Royal Ballet – symbol of the company's maturity in the 1946 staging, testimony to the international standing of the troupe at the triumphant New York opening in 1949.

The 1946 staging was decorated by Oliver Messel, and after the austerities of the war it looked supremely opulent. Five years ago a new production, with designs by Henry Bardon and Lila de Nobili – *à la manière de Doré* – was a brave attempt at re-thinking the piece; but it lacked airiness, space in which Petipa's inventions could breathe; and hence the new production by Kenneth MacMillan with designs by Peter Farmer, given at a gala in the presence of Her Majesty the Queen last night to pay tribute to the American Friends of Covent Garden whose generosity has paid for this much-needed revision.

The result is entirely worthwhile. This new staging is Vsevolozhsky's magical fantasy, with steps restored, some choreography renewed,

other sections embellished. **The Beauty** has been re-awakened, and the whole staging is a re-assertion of MacMillan's love and understanding of the classic tradition of which he is a product. To detail the various innovations must wait until later viewings of the production; suffice it to say that the spirit of this great ballet is honoured throughout, MacMillan has done his homework – **Beauty** is a well-documented ballet – and both the spirit of the piece, and its choreographic structure have been honourably displayed.

It is the special merit of Peter Farmer's settings that they give ample room for the dances. Each act of the ballet is conceived in one colour: the Prologue is almost entirely blue – the most difficult shade to bring off on stage – and in amid the soaring arches of King Florestan's palace, which suggest a properly magical setting for a fairy-tale, the arrival of the fairy godmothers had been staged with extraordinary skill as they enter down mysterious flights of stairs hidden from our eyes.

For Act 1 we are in a garden setting which, at first viewing, seems too ingratiatingly pretty, but here – as throughout the evening – I was conscious of the care taken that nothing should obscure the impact of the dances. In the Prologue the Fairy variations glittered diamond-sharp against the indigo darkness of the palace; with Aurora's appearance we could see the majesty of Petipa's inventions plain, and Antoinette Sibley was in superb •••

16th March 1973

form as the young princess, and later as the vision, and ultimately and most brilliantly as the bride.

Carabosse – Alexander Grant, tremendous here as throughout the evening – is placed on stage under the guise of a courtier and the spell is cast, and the Lilac Fairy intervenes, with a real feeling for the magical element that sustains the whole action of the piece. In this scene, as at every point during the action, there is a concern for dramatic credibility; MacMillan has re-worked small incidents that have become dully traditional, and the action is carried forward with a nice appreciation for period style. The first two acts are set in a suitably fantastic and improbable realm of fairy enchantment; but with the hunting scene we enter a world which, as Vsevolozhsky intended, has some historical reality. The whole development of the staging moves from the imaginary, dream-like setting of Aurora's youth, into the clarity and formal elegance of the age of Louis XIV in which she must awake from Carabosse's enchantment.

The Prince Florimund is Anthony Dowell, princely in style and technique; his journey to Aurora's palace – with its use of a panorama as demanded by Tchaikovsky's music – is true theatrical magic, and the celebrations of the final act are grand and beautiful. Further comment must wait until the **Beauty** enters the repertory next week: until then a welcome for the production, and for the excellence of the company's performance. ∎

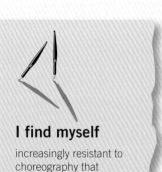

I find myself

increasingly resistant to choreography that imagines itself a clause in the United Nations Charter.

A Land
22nd July, 1993

The Sleeping Beauty

Royal Opera House, Covent Garden

THE QUESTION of authenticity in the Royal Ballet's classic stagings is one so vexed that it would be unwise to say that the new present-ation of **The Sleeping Beauty** is faithful to anything other than its producers' views on how the piece should be shown to the public. That those producers are Dame Ninette de Valois and Sir Frederick Ashton presupposes a great understanding of how the ballet was first mounted for the Sadler's Wells company in 1939 by Nicholas Sergueyev, régisseur at the Mariinsky Theatre, and charged there with supervising productions between 1904-17. But Sergueyev's version, like Diaghilev's celebrated 1921 staging, was already an emendation of the Petipa Ur-text, and Sergueyev's production for International Ballet during the 1940s was different again. What we are now seeing is a revision of the much loved and admired presentation that Dame Ninette supervised for our national company's entry into Covent Garden in 1946. And, significantly, we are given a decorative style in David Walker's new designs that may be supposed to hark back to the manner of Oliver Messel, whose sets and costumes retain in the public imagination an aura of rightness that no later décors (Henry Bardon in 1968; Peter Farmer in 1973) have had.

The initial merit of this new production can be seen in the way the solos and ensembles have been transmitted to the dancers by de Valois and Ashton: the cleanness of execution, the nuances of phrasing, are evidence of care and loving thought. The ensembles have, in

The Royal Ballet

FT
FINANCIAL
TIMES

the main, the openness, the light-reflecting brilliance of design that we now associate with Petipa. This is particularly good in the Prologue and the first act, where the Fairy *ballabili*, the sequences for Aurora and her friends, demonstrate a beautiful symmetry. Aurora's dances – marvellously clear; academically pure; amazing at each viewing – are exceptionally well refurbished; throughout the first two acts the logic and precision of

patterning and structural development (so vital in Petipa) are most happy.

But there are textual problems, and innovations – or the retention of later accretions – suggest an unnecessary compromise between what was known to be old and right (or right enough) and novelty. **Beauty** is, in fact, better documented than most of the old ballets, though Petipa's minutely detailed • • •

17th October
1977

The fairies
design, David Walker
(1977)

production notes and his requests to Tchaikovsky for precise musical effects and through Siloti's piano transcription identifying stage action with music. Sad, then, to lose the small, vivid scene in which Carabosse tears out Catalabutte's hair and feeds it to her minions, for this is dramatically reverberant in that Catalabutte appears in Act 1 wearing, in Petipa's words, "an absurd wig because his hair has never grown again".

More serious is the decision to retain Ashton's 'Awakening' *pas de deux*. As performed in Peter Wright's Gothick version of 1968 this accorded with the style of the production. Now, undeniably beautiful as it is, it supplants the grand moment when Aurora and her Prince should be formally affianced: drama departs as the newly awakened courtiers trail off stage, and the emotional force of the last act *grand pas* has been weakened. That Aurora has to wear a drifting nightdress to dance it is ludicrous, especially in a ballet "about" ballerinas in tutus than anything else. The producers have also decided to truncate the great Act 3 duet by allowing those damnable Ivans to usurp the coda. The Ivans are not Perrault characters; they have no place in a French court of the 18th century – least of all with three nursemaids from Petrushska who have now infiltrated the proceedings – and the hero and heroine are left, so to speak, hanging in mid-emotional air: these facts seem to me to be argument enough for immediate Ivan-suppression. The opening of a later cut in the score (the presto at the end of the Mazurka finale) to give Aurora and her Prince a whizzing moment of virtuosity is neither artistic nor technical amends.

Other alterations seem to me to be beneficial. There is an attractive new version of the Garland Dance: we have lost – and no regrets – Red Riding Hood, and have gained Hop o'my Thumb from the MacMillan version: the Florestan trio is back with Ashton's pentahedral "sapphire" variation in place of the second girl's solo; the fifth Fairy in the Prologue has the "finger" variation as Nijinska amended it and de Valois knew and danced it with Diaghilev, and Laura Connor does it brilliantly.

There remains, though, the matter of the designing. Each of the two previous productions foundered in public affection on their decor, and David Walker, I would hazard, has been presented with the unenviable task of trying to recapture the "feel" of the Messel 1946 design. It seems to me that he has failed to do this. Messel's work, architecturally flimsy though it may have looked, had an over-all imaginative force that sustained the staging and brought a logic to its development. Walker's designs are stylistically uncertain. **Beauty's** 120-year span was intended to evoke, without too much fantasy, the world of the French court in the 17th and 18th centuries, and this is never apparent in Walker's design. The Prologue is successful in an airy soaring-pillared way, though its garden prospect is feeble; for Act 1 we are apparently in the buildings to a Kent or Hawksmoor palace, and the Vision scene's grotto is a pantomime view of Sanquirico, an uncompromising flight of awakened courtiers trail off steps left undisguised to permit entrances. The Awakening set is the most effective: poetic, and suggestive of a castle facade framed by columns and vast draperies – here magic and reality mingle happily. The final act is placed in an early Bibiena head-on perspective a palace, with none of the relief that can come from the *scena per angolo* to lead the eye away to imagined spaces beyond the claustrophobic confrontation with colonnades and arches.

The same faults of style can be seen in the costumes. The progress of time, central to the action, is not mirrored in any clear development in dress. The very well-designed, naturalistic court costumes in the Prologue include an abberrant Catalabutte got up in the full and preposterous fig of a stage costume of the period of Louis XV, with feathers and tonnelet, looking like a cross between Gaëtan Vestris and Prince Ras Monolulu. It must be re-designed. The four princely suitors for Aurora are inanely booted like Principal Boys in pantomime; the nymphs of the Vision scene look tubby in their heavy costumes: the courtiers for the last act Polacca would fit into a ballet set in the late 19th century, and the men's hats make them look hydrocephalous. There is a good deal of decorative fuss on all the costumes (not least Aurora's little-girl puffed sleeves), and the profusion of pendant lace, frills, embroidery and winsome accessories runs counter to the grand simplicity of the dances: the Prologue fairies seem to be dancing "against" prettified fluster on their dress.

In the matter of dancing though, the staging is a triumph for the whole company. Leading the first performances on Friday night were Lesley Collier and Anthony Dowell. Collier danced with that winning bravura that is so happily hers: sensitive, radiantly assured and youthful, this was a reading in which the delicacy with which she treats small incidents was matched with a commanding ease in the grandest demands of the role. For Anthony Dowell, returned after a year's absence through injury, a hero's welcome, and heroic dancing, filled with classic authority, nobility of manner, and absolute mastery.

At Saturday night's performance Merle Park and David Wall took over the leading roles: Park bright, precise, musical; Wall ardent in acting, easy and dashing in dancing. Of the many other interpretations – of Lynn Seymour's Carabosse quivering with rage: Georgina Parkinson's lovely Countess and some magnificent ensemble and solo work – I shall hope to report later in the week. ∎

The Sleeping Beauty

The Royal Ballet

Royal Opera House, Covent Garden

FT

FINANCIAL
TIMES

'A Beauty Cursed'

**23rd January
1996**

WITH THE FIRST BARS of the overture to *The Sleeping Beauty*, the Opera House curtains part to reveal a gauzy front-cloth. It is painted with an incomprehensible shape – a deranged baroque pediment, perhaps, garnished with a book, sprigs of greenery and a shaft of light, and unevenly balanced on the last relics of a concertina. Through one of Covent Garden's miracles of lighting, we also glimpse a tinsel-bright King and Queen, ecstatic over a new-born baby. And thus, before the overture has finished, is encapsulated everything that is wrong with the Royal Ballet's production.

The Carabosse-curse on this staging – and no Lilac Fairy to alleviate it – is mistrust. Mistrust of Tchaikovsky: the two final acts of the ballet truncated, so that musical architecture and careful pacing of events are minimised, and such egregious vulgarities as thunderclaps are added to a score resonant with dramatic effects. (And in the Hunt scene there is a shift of key, caused by a brutish cut before the start of the Marquise's dance, which is a disgrace). Mistrust of Petipa, whose dances are cramped by obtrusive design, his patterns flattened, his skilled contrast between a "real" court and the fantasy of fairy-tale denied by staging and crass costuming. Mistrust of Beauty itself as a masterpiece hymning the harmonies of classicism as ballet understands it, so that the dizzying convolutions of Maria Björnson's vehement settings tear the eye away from dance towards the gratuitous caprices of ...

**...funereal
bathing
costumes,**

best suited for a quick dip after burying Grandmama.

L'Eveil
16th November, 2007

**Corps de ballet
design, Maria Björnson
(1996)**

The catalogue of miseries in the Anthony Dowell/Maria Björnson production is long and unrelieved. I sat through the staging twice on Saturday and at no moment could I believe in **Beauty** as the supreme achievement of classic dance. The coarse extravagance of costuming — too many of the women at the court of King Mistinguett wear gloves to the arm-pit; too many of the men are painted and wigged like shop-window dummies — and the incessant clamour of the design, deny dance and dancers. What should be assured in style looks flustered, indecisive. Small wonder that the interpretations I saw were less than convincing. The matinee was led by Muriel Valtat and William Trevitt, fighting to make their mark amid the encircling frockery and architectural posturing. In the evening, Viviana Durante and Bruce Sansom gave polished readings that sought to defy their surroundings.

I enjoyed two performances. At the matinee, Mara Galeazzi cut her variation in the last act quartet with diamond clarity. Later, Monica Mason reminded us of her grand and potent artistry as Carabosse. Mocking, sardonic, furiously focused, this is the only reading to confound my view that the staging thinks the wicked fairy is really Danny La Rue playing Miss Havisham. ▌

her graceless architecture. What should be sublimely ordered in choreography and in manner teeters as if its foundations were giving way. Le Nôtre is forgotten. Petersburg is denied. Vivienne Westwood rules.

Why is it necessary to trump Petipa and Tchaikovsky's aces in the christening scene by telling us during the overture of the baby Aurora's birth? The music is saying something else. How is it possible to fudge most of the important entrances — in a ballet built round stunning dramatic appearances — by damning dance and drama with a vast permanent oval which ruins our first view of Aurora and the magical arrival of the fairy godmothers and obliges them to step gingerly down a too steep staircase, and in the last act ranges a job lot of characters like spectators at a football match in a modern stadium? Is the justification for the Brobdingagian table which crowds the dance in the prologue merely the fact that it enables Carabosse to appear from under it? In a ballet which everywhere celebrates the triumph of noble decorum, grace, it is yet another example of the frantic unreason which makes this account of **Beauty** so lamentable.

Royal Opera House,
Covent Garden

FINANCIAL
TIMES

**11th March
2003**

ON SATURDAY NIGHT the Royal Ballet gave the first public performance of Natalya Makarova's new staging of **The Sleeping Beauty**. But, as we have come to recognise with an all-too-frequent sense of dismay, ballet first nights are often no more than final dress rehearsals. So it proved – again – with what is meant to be a splendid display-piece, endowed with magical, gauzy scenery and opulent costuming by Luisa Spinatelli. I find it hard to understand how an expensively refurbished opera house, blessed (we suppose) with the most modern stage technology, cannot cope with elaborate design and subtle lighting changes. I find it equally bizarre that the greatest of ballet-scores must be hustled along, trimmed of incident, played with its prologue and first act stuck crassly together, in order to avoid overtime. Were this to be done to operatic scores of comparable magnificence - Verdi or Wagner, perhaps – I can see administrative heads on spikes in Floral Street.

The staging, then, came to us under less than ideal conditions. It is, even so, welcome. The Royal Ballet has performed **The Sleeping Beauty** for 63 years. A first and distinctly demure version was shown at Sadler's Wells on the eve of war; in 1946 **Beauty**, in far grander form, re-opened the Opera House to lasting acclaim. But **Beauty**, for all that it is an international symbol of classic ballet, marks the apogee of Petersburg's glories in dance. The Royal Ballet has given it a home for decades, but its spirit is inescapably that of the city of its creation. So, who better than

Makarova – product of the ballet ensemble that created **Beauty** – to stage the piece anew, to re-assert its Petersburg virtues?

Makarova's staging offers, in essence, the production in which she grew up, its text established by Konstantin Sergueyev. Deeply conservative, a fine danseur and an inheritor (he was born in 1910) of the old regime's balletic traditions, a director of the Kirov troupe. Sergueyev loved and honoured his company's past. So the **Beauty** Makarova has now mounted must assume a double task: to present a work sanctified by a century of Mariinsky dedication, and to suggest to her dancers a manner that will best illuminate the choreography. It was a tribute to the Royal Ballet cast on Saturday night that the choreography received so spacious and dignified an exposition, that solos and ensembles looked so clear in shape, the dance, like the dancers, renewed.

That the ballet was renewed seemed harder to discern. Luisa Spinatelli's airy designs offer a sequence of ravishing gauzes whose lightness should admit of swiftest transformation, creating a world both credible (Louis XIV to Louis XV is the time-scale. Rigaud and Watteau the points of reference) and fantastic. Costuming is opulent, elegant, But Carabosse's curse lay on the stage-machinery: it slept, and it was clear that fudged transformations, murky lighting (the prologue was pea-soupish), were taking a toll on hoped-for magic. The use of dry ice to help illusion is a valued trick: the Opera House sought to imitate a passing ●●●

steam-train rather than vaporous mystery, and the Flying Scotsman roared through the action. All these dress-rehearsal bogeys eroded *Beauty's* effects, and I am reluctant to write about a staging which was presented in so slipshod a manner.

Be it said at once that the shape of the choreography is true, that the company has

gained from the rehearsal period in dignity of classic style, that *The Sleeping Beauty* is – if only just awakening – a beauty nonetheless. Makarova's one dubious innovation is the introduction of a tiny but loathsome cupid who acts briefly as a master of ceremonies. The role is played by a small boy, and, as ever with child performers, I think longingly of how Good King Herod dealt with such pests. There are, as at the Mariinsky, juvenile students in the Garland dance, and damned tiresome they are, too, in their spaghetti-footed trippings. The production's closing outburst of flashing coloured lights and fireworks is also an unnecessary attempt to trump Petipa's and Tchaikovsky's aces, and should be abandoned.

Of first-night interpretations, much praise to the ensemble; to Zenaida Yanowsky as a viciously serpentine Carabosse; to Marianela Nuñez, a Lilac Fairy radiant in technique and presence: to Donald MacLeary, happily returned to the stage as a Catalabutte foppish, perfect. The Aurora was Darcey Bussell, on less than best form. (She sustained an injury towards the end of the final *pas de deux*, and Marianela Nuñez replaced her in the coda). The role is not well suited to a tall dancer – the choreography presupposes the physical outlines, even the muscular speed, of a smaller artist – and despite fine moments, Bussell's reading did not move from *ingenue* sweetness to ballerina grandeur. Roberto Bolle was her cavalier: handsome, not well served by pallid and rather meagre outfits, and something less than princely in manner. Valery Ovsyanikov conducted with a loving understanding of the score. More anon. ∎

Luke Bloxam (Cupid) design, Luisa Spinatelli (2003)

260

Royal Opera House, Covent Garden

FT

FINANCIAL TIMES

18th May 2006

THERE IS A NEW FAIRY at the christening. She appears in the Royal Ballet's "reconstruction" of **The Sleeping Beauty** staging by Ninette de Valois, which opened the Royal Opera House in February 1946, and was revealed to us on Monday night.

It is Fairy Compromise, a less than magical being who has so often brought her dubious gifts to Royal Ballet Initiatives. She is notable for her sweetly adaptable nature and her ability not to look facts clearly in the eye, and above all not to make waves.

Ninette de Valois' 1946 production (which I saw from the very first and much admired, as did we all) was serious as to text, theatrically vital and an educative milestone for the company, which discovered that the "English" style, with its bright footwork, discreet lyricism, dramatic sincerity and decorous dance-manners was a passport to world renown.

So, with Fonteyn's miraculous central interpretation, with Constant Lambert's phenomenal musical and intellectual guidance, with Oliver Messel's magically evocative designs and with de Valois' own integrity and unerring belief, this **Beauty** won the world. It was not without faults – it tended at moments to be somewhat too "nice"– but it taught audiences everywhere of our honesty in classicism and it inspired that most gratifying of tributes, emulation. (There were, and are worldwide, gruesome attempts at "the classics" that owe their inspiration to

what de Valois had achieved with the 19th century masterpieces).

But no ballet company can leave well alone. New productions, fresh thoughts (almost all wrong-headed) inspired further Royal versions, even unto Natalia Makarova's recent brave attempt to open wider perspectives on to the Neva and the Winter Palace for a masterwork born in those very locations. And so the Royal Ballet offers us its "restoration" of the original de Valois staging as a birthday present to itself on its 75th anniversary. And, of course, dear Fairy Compromise has brought her corrupting gifts of Indecision and Mimsiness to the christening.

The Messel designs have been in part adapted and altered by Peter Farmer, who has provided a new Vision scene setting and transformation (beautifully painted) and has reworked some other elements. Messel's Bibiena vision is still there, but adulterated, and how I miss the gigantic spider's web that used to guard the sleeping court.

Costuming has been rethought and re-coloured, with gleaming fabrics and an uneasy whisper of flimsiness and debilitating prettiness. Whatever happened to the red velvet coat in which Prince Florimund made his first appearance, a figure vivid and commanding in an entry that has also gone by the board? (My memory goes back to Robert Helpmann's first appearance, and to Anton Dolin's return with Markova in 1948, the very incarnation ●●●

she and her partner

wore the uneasy expressions of people who sense that the oysters weren't as fresh as they ought to have been.

Nureyev Farewell
7th May, 1991

Alina Cojocaru (Aurora),
Marianela Nuñez (Lilac Fairy),
Johan Kobborg (Prince Florimund),
design, Peter Farmer,
after Oliver Messel
(2006)

of nobility as he took the stage. And, ancient joke, there used to be a red plush sofa near the gallery at Covent Garden that was named after one of the ballet company's then princes, who took the stage in rather portly fashion as Florimund in the Hunting scene).

And Fairy Compromise has insisted that ideas from previous stagings, and a new Garland Dance (very attractive) by Christopher Wheeldon, be also incorporated. And, for all-too-guessable reasons, Florimund has been allowed his solo in the Vision scene.
It is all very nice. And very nostalgic (in the sense that we corrupt our past by rosy

memories), very appealing (oh, the cheers and the rain of flowers at curtain fall) and woolly-minded.

Its merits are those of de Valois' determin-ation to show our national troupe accepting ballet's past and claiming a right to it. Its faults are that endemic prettiness with which British dancers approach the pinnacles of the academic ballet, believing that charm is all. Many of the solo performances looked to me below par.

The great joy of this first night was the dancing of Alina Cojocaru as Aurora, such grace and felicity in execution, and unaffected elegance in living in the music, were worthy of the greatest traditions of this ballet at Covent Garden. It was the performance of a wonderfully gifted ballerina. No less lovely, Marianela Nuñez as the Lilac Fairy, exhilarating in her account of the dances, radiant in manner as the very best interpreters must be. Johan Kobborg was a boldly drawn but faintly plebeian Florimund. Carabosse, taken by Genesia Rosato, is more like a petulant divorcée than the spirit of affronted malice that was the key to the role as Helpmann played it in 1946. And the *farandole* in the hunting scene must be restored: it is a vital indication of the real world that will be swept away by the Lilac Fairy's appearance. I shall hope to return to these matters after further performances. ▌

FOR ALL CLEMENT'S GREAT KNOWLEDGE and erudition, for all his enthusiasm for the great dancers of yesterday, today and tomorrow and for all his elegant and witty turns of phrase, there is nothing in his corpus of writing which is so delicious as his bad reviews. Over the years, companies, choreographers and performers have grown to fear a swingeing Crisp review and readers have taken guilty delight when his quill is at its sharpest. His comments are never intended to be cruel, but they invariably pierce the toughest artistic hide to hit their mark. Who, then, have been the recipients of his most pointed criticism? The following selection is of those unfortunate or unwise enough to rouse his artistic hackles. His comments are voiced in the wittiest of fashions, so that it is often difficult not to laugh out loud at their brilliance but, similarly, not to feel sorry for those poor souls that are the object of his displeasure. My own favourite among this bouquet of barbed wire has to be his 2001 Eurotrash Attack which has, rightly, passed into legend among critics.

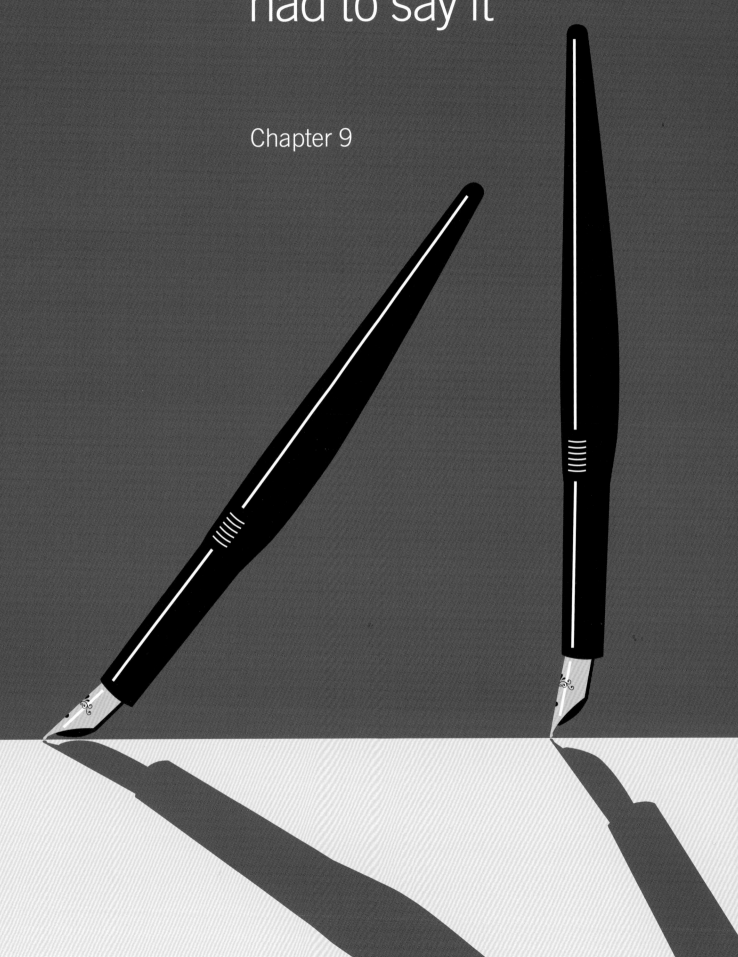

'Someone
had to say it'

Chapter 9

'Someone had to say it'

Chapter 9

Nijinsky, Clown of God

London Coliseum

FT
FINANCIAL
TIMES

5th May
1972

AS YOU COME OUT of the Coliseum and turn left, you face the Edith Cavell memorial, and there, incised in stone, is the word Fortitude – a quality you will need if you are to sit through Maurice Béjart's stupefying **Nijinsky, Clown of God**, which opened a two-week season last night.

As a compendium of vulgarity, posturing, and minimally interesting choreography, the piece has a certain weird interest; on any other terms – those of a serious study of Nijinsky as a tragic figure plummeting into madness – it is insufferable. Béjart has neatly cut the ground from under our critical feet by stating that the work is not a biographical reconstruction of Nijinsky's life, but rather an exploration of the thoughts and fantasies to be found in the diaries which he wrote at the onset of insanity. These diaries are, indeed, a pathetic document and we hear parts of them intoned in a portentous baritone, as if they were Holy Writ, but Béjart has so inflated their symbolism that, for me at least, he traduces even that aspect of Nijinsky's suffering.

The work is additionally loaded with excess intellectual baggage by turning Diaghilev into a God-figure (a lumbering puppet of the impresario is manoeuvred over the stage) and casting Nijinsky in the first part as an Adam who, on discovering his Eve, is chased from the Paradise of the Ballets Russes. In the second part he is shown as the Christ-figure of Nijinsky's madness, is crucified (a sequence of abysmal bad taste involving a

troupe of sylphides and a group of puppets representing high finance), and is finally allowed to die – though not before a scampering clown, who has haunted the action with staggering persistence, gives him a pink rose.

I feel it beyond my powers to detail the sequence of events as they whirl past in this fantasmagoria. Certain passages stand out with a horrid clarity in the first half, which lasts an interminable hour. We see a vulgar mélange of Nijinsky's greatest roles – Faun, Spectre of the Rose (Paolo Bortoluzzi, and superb), Golden Slave and Petrushka, in travesties of the original costumes, dancing travesties of the original choreography – while an electronic score by Pierre Henry sits at odds with chunks from Tchaikovsky's sixth symphony.

Suzanne Farrell appears, in successively shorter skirts and remarkably dull choreography, as the woman in Nijinsky's life; Death also appears; so does a lady bearing a lightly sequined Cox's orange pippin as the Serpent. It is all, as you may gather, highly significant, and – to me – desperately pretentious. Clowns, nymphs and whores (I quote the programme), society ladies straight from the Ascot scene in *My Fair Lady*, and a Fred Karno version of the French army all add their distinctive and inexplicable touches, and at the last the hero declines into madness, which, considering what has gone before, is not surprising. •••

The performances by the artists of the Ballet du Vingtième Siècle are totally committed, and Jorge Donn as Nijinsky gives a thrilling interpretation, tireless, deeply moving at all times, and – which is the greatest tribute – convincing. But the ballet itself is sheer kitsch: solemn, heavy with "meaning", and under its surface vitality (which is ill-enough organised), hollow and unrewarding. ∎

Suzanne Farrell
(La Jeune Fille en Rose)
(1972)

Cullberg Ballet

Playhouse Theatre, Edinburgh

FT

FINANCIAL
TIMES

**25th August
1999**

THE BASIS FOR MATS EK'S version of *Giselle* – first offering in the Cullberg Ballet season at the Playhouse – is that an old ballet can be modernised for today's audiences. This is so wrong-headed, and the result so ill-conceived, that it is difficult to understand the hosannas that have variously greeted the staging. The ballets of the 19th century are windows on to a past which is as frail, artistically, as any endangered piece of nature today, and as deserving of care and conservation. Clever-dick producers who mess with these works, decoding, exploiting and deconstructing them for their own crass ends, are no better than the vandals who pillage archaeological sites or despoil a natural habitat with buildings. The old ballets respond to loving conservation. They live again – and gloriously so – through sensitivity to their style and ambiance, and through the genius of great dancers. We have but to look at Petersburg's view of *Giselle* or *La Bayadère* to know this.

What the new Visigoths proclaim is a spurious relevance for the drama – as if we watched *Giselle* for its narrative – with no thought to original step or score. So the shades of Freud or Lenin are invoked, the drama is crudely titivated while the choreography is jettisoned and the "new" version hits the stage. Thus Ek's *Giselle*. We find bunkered politicising (rich versus poor) and Adam's pretty score used like a doormat. The new choreography is little more than awkward romping, and the intriguing

dramatic fabric of the original is torn to shreds and remade as a shroud for Gautier's delightful tale. Giselle galumphs in a state of advanced unease with a small group of cross peasantry armed with pitchforks. The aristos are few but over-dressed as a Spanish dancing team. The countryside is a verdant female torso. Giselle is betrayed and goes mad, but does not die. Instead she finds herself in the local loony-bin where Myrtha is matron, and the other inmates are the ci-devant wilis. Dawn finds Albrecht (who is afflicted with a white tail-suit worthy of Liberace) stark naked. Happily Hilarion, who has also survived the night's fun and games, finds a blanket to cover his confusion. The curtain falls. It should never have risen on a work whose dance-text is leaden, dependent upon heavy-footed and coarse-grained performance which clatters over the score like the tramp of the invading vandals. The members of the Cullberg company give this *Giselle* the sort of interpretations it deserves. ∎

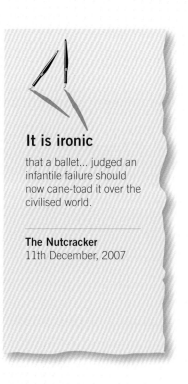

It is ironic

that a ballet... judged an infantile failure should now cane-toad it over the civilised world.

The Nutcracker
11th December, 2007

Compagnie M

Mother Teresa and the Children of the World

FT
FINANCIAL
TIMES

Peacock Theatre, London

11th February 2003

'The torments of the damned'

I HAD NOT EXPECTED to see Marcia Haydée come on stage on her knees, wiping the floor. That, at the Peacock Theatre, is part of the week's bad news, and it is owed to Maurice Béjart. Ever ready to take on Big Names, from Nijinsky to Che Guevara, his victim is now Mother Teresa. A life spent in the service of outcasts in an Indian slum might be difficult enough, and beatification a proper recognition. But Béjartian canonisation is the dread reward here, with an entourage of graduates from Béjart's Rudra School in Lausanne, grinning, spinning, expert in the flashy physicality that marks the Master's style, talking, singing, registering emotion rather after the fashion of Olive Oyl. *Libera nos, Domine.*

Mother Teresa and the Children of the World is an 80-minute-no-interval parade of pietistic tosh, pinned on to the robes and *obiter dicta* of the saint of the Indian poor. The piece begins with the 15 young of this new Compagnie M lying on the ground, while

Marcia Haydée
with graduates of Maurice Béjart's
Ecole-Atelier Rudra
(1972)

dismal Indian dronings fill the air. The Curse of the Prawn Curry, thought I. Not so! This is prelude to a catalogue of damply emotional scenes in which Haydée progresses over the stage, feeding her horde with rice (stage looks very messy after this), acting as ballet-mistress (one of the many things you did not know about Mother T. was her years at the barre), wearing an expression of rather taut sanctity, and telling us about the Need for Love. At one moment she kneels – praying, I hoped, about the Need for Choreography. Meantime the galvanic young of the ensemble indulge in those cheap tricks that are the common currency of Béjartian style, and – worst of all – show us how sincere they can be. I thought them, one and all, perfectly frightful.

The piece is, of course, a sanctimonious stinker. Its message about Love is blearily well-intentioned and insulting in its vagueness. Mother T's phrase "Let us suffer joyfully" – brightly echoed by her gang – is, of course, what we should be telling the starving millions in the Sudan, or those infants whose life is spent picking over city rubbish tips in quest of subsistence. It should brighten their day no end. (The price of your ticket to the Peacock might do something for them: the evening will do nothing for you). Haydée has a solo – to the funeral march from the *Eroica* – which has a faintly Isadora-ish (late Isadora-ish) air to it. For all her great artistry, it is ill-advised. Another Teresa – of Avila – prayed to know something of the torments of the damned. This loathsome entertainment is a good place to start. ∎

La Dame aux Camélias

Compagnie Jean Gaudin

The Place, London

26th April 1991

THE PROGRAMME LEAFLET begins, of course, with a meaty quotation from Roland Barthes, and follows it with a message from the mastermind of the evening telling us that it is not the quotation that influenced him but the way of thinking. Yes, it is the French new dance back at The Place – the Compagnie Jean Gaudin – and yes, the heart plummets as the evening gets under way, and **La Dame aux Camélias** is given the rounds of the kitchen.

A few observations from a victim of this enterprise may suggest something of its flavour. There is a large wooden trellised set, emblazoned (ask not why) with the Pétainist motto *Travail, Famille, Patrie*. There is a round red velvet seat with ambulant tendencies on which the performers perch and journey about the stage area (and how I wish it had done the decent thing and taken them off to Heathrow).

There are two men and three women involved: I could identify Marguerite and Armand, but the slightly Spanish girl, and the tall chap in the ill-cut jacket, mauve skirt and sensible shoes, did not really ring true as Dumas characters. There was a great deal of dialogue in French, much of it whispered, all of it of transcendent tedium, with the cove in mauve as chief chatterbox. He had a heavy English accent and kept his hands very busy above his waist and shoulders with ever such graceful gesticulation.

Fragments of a squally Callas recording of *La Traviata* are played when the chit-chat dies down, and two of the girls suggest the falsities of La Vie by bursting into mocking laughter from time to time. There are references to sniffing cocaine. M. Gaudin's "choreography" is more concerned with production than steps, and is banal.

The evening amounts to a confused, pretentious, ill-conceived and drearily executed gloss on its original, and receives the support of the *Association Française d'Action Artistique*. It is singularly lacking in artistic action, and I do not find it does any good to the fair name of French contemporary creativity. It is, though, yet another example of the perfectly dreadful things the French are perpetrating under the impression that this is modern dance.

The programme-sheet provides an idiosyncratic translation of the spoken text. The key to the affair reads: "Oh, I feel like an indistinct heap tonight". A heap of what only General Cambronne could tell. ∎

...the whistlings
and borborygmi of what must be marine gastro-enteritis of a particularly virulent kind.

Ocean
24th May, 1994

Mikhailovsky Ballet

Spartacus

FT

FINANCIAL
TIMES

London Coliseum

**25th July
2008**

BY HEAVEN YOU WILL NEED fortitude if you sit through the Mikhailovsky Ballet's view of **Spartacus**, which opened the troupe's first British season on Tuesday night. We know this ballet from Yury Grigorovich's masterly creation for the Bolshoi Theatre, and from Leonid Jacobson's early version in St Petersburg.

Grigorovich's choreography combines monumental power and narrative directness: we understand what happens, and why, and suffer with the destruction of the hero's dreams. The Mikhailovsky staging, made this year at its home theatre in St Petersburg, is by Gyorgy Kovtun, who has revised and complicated the scenario, with design by Vyacheslav Okunev and the Khachaturian score boasting an outbreak of choral singing. The production looks as if millions of roubles have been thrown at it, and it resembles nothing so much as an ice-show rejected by a Las Vegas casino as being too gaudy. It sets the art of ballet back by 100 years.

Everything about this **Spartacus** is loud: the score, played with unrelenting energy by the Mikhailovsky's orchestra, beats at our eardrums; emotions, basic to a degree near idiocy, are shouted. The costuming is garish, making much of gold thread and shiny fabric. The dramatic action relies upon a crowded stage – we are promised 200 people on call, and there they all are, busy as can be, emoting, singing, parading, dancing (in a manner of speaking), and generally rhubarbing in approved fashion. There are gladiators, Roman soldiery racing across the stage holding swords as if to skewer the chap in front, and female gladiators behaving in the same cheery way. And there are named characters: Spartacus (Denis Matvienko, fighting a losing battle in every sense of the phrase) has Valeria (Irina Perren) as his rather blank beloved and Crassus (Marat Shemiunov) has a mistress Sabina (Anastasia Matvienko) whose proclivities are expressed in a chronic case of six o'clock legs.

It is all sound and fury and inanity. Of dramatic tension, emotional sense, choreographic imagination, nary a trace could I see. It is, alas, a brash, interminable bore. I hope for better things later in the season. ∎

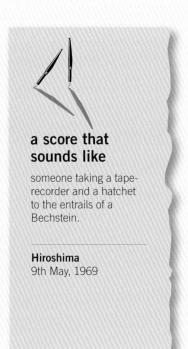

a score that sounds like

someone taking a tape-recorder and a hatchet to the entrails of a Bechstein.

Hiroshima
9th May, 1969

Denis Morozov (Crixus)
'It is all sound and fury and inanity'
(2008)

Damaged Goods

Appetite

FINANCIAL
TIMES

Festival Theatre, Edinburgh

24th August 1999

AFTER LENGTHY consideration on Sunday night – I had a desolating 85 minutes during which the fatuities of *Appetite* dragged their pointless way over the Festival Theatre stage – I decided that this production by Meg Stuart and Ann Hamilton was the worst thing I had ever seen during my service at the Edinburgh Festival. It could, indeed, be the worst evening I have ever spent as a dance-goer. (Worse than the Hungarian troupe which showed me *Gangrene*? Worse than the Argentinian danseuse getting into a coffin with a penguin? More exasperating than Yvonne Rainer screaming at a fur coat? Yes! Yes! Yes!)

Pretentiousness; gaseous programme notes; lumpen physicality; unrelenting dreariness; posturing non-dance; a minimal yet determinedly hideous "installation" owed to Hamilton; collaborative creativity (pah!) owed to Stuart and her six minions, poor things; unsavoury clatterings as accompaniment – these were all there in this apotheosis of Eurotrash.

Part Pina Bausch, part Belgian free-dance mopery – shades of Wim Vandekeybus and Anne-Teresa de Keersmaeker – and wholly awful, *Appetite* claims to be about the human body. This means that the performers play touchy-feely games, stuff themselves into clothes, or stuff clothes inside their clothes, stumble and group themselves to invisible purpose. They look awkward, psychotic, and damn foolish. The stage, as far as one may discern, is covered with toast. Miss Stuart's troupe goes under the name of Damaged Goods, which could not be more apposite.

There is no point in considering this tosh any further. But there is good reason to question its presence as an official offering at the Festival. We know that dance has made an increasingly undistinguished showing in Edinburgh over the past decades – a fact owed to the cost of transporting major important companies, but also suggesting a lack of concern about what is of value and what is modishly transitory. (Why no Paul Taylor or Baryshnikov or Cunningham in his 80th year? No French dancers or Royal Danes? No Russians? No Chinese? No Royal Ballet or Kabuki or Noh or Indian or Balinese dance? No serious English new dance – Burrows, Hawkins, Siobhan Davies, Brandstrup? No galas of stellar dance?) In showing *Appetite* I think the festival is betraying an audience which expects to trust its offerings. *Appetite* is a dismal imposture which does damage to the idea of new and adventurous dance, and to the festival as a place of serious artistic values. ∎

Sabotage Baby

Barbican Theatre,
London

FINANCIAL TIMES

5th October 2001

THE BARBICAN MANAGEMENT very kindly placed notices outside its theatre warning patrons of the noise levels in Tuesday night's appearance by the Batsheva Dance Troupe from Tel-Aviv. They would have done better to alert us to the appalling nature of the evening's offering – Ohad Naharin's **Sabotage Baby**. The 'music" was actually very jolly. It was provided by *Orkater*, a Dutch ensemble which manufactures din from a complex of machines and gizmos that lurk at the back of the stage. Peter Zegveld and Thijs van der Poll (the musician/machinists) busy themselves furiously amid this deranged gamelan, which is a cross between the Titfield Thunderbolt and Da Vinci's prototype for a Teasmade. Crazed tootlings, fearful borborygms, the occasional twang, fill the air, while Naharin's hapless cast lumber about, by turns lethargic or frenetic.

The staging is, of course, both incomprehensible and regrettable. The cast wears dun-coloured outfits that hang depressingly to the ground - the dancers look like the Sodom and Gomorrah League of Health and Beauty, and behave in suitable fashion. Angst is their favoured sport, together with writhing and despairing journeys across the Barbican stage. Seek not for reason, or even imaginative felicity. This is a piece that has been produced in glum association with Nederlands Dans Theater and has all the trademarks of gloom and introspection, while sense flew out of the window long ago.

The choreography – such a big word for such a tiny effect – is predictably anxious and unrewarding. As the evening wears suicidally on, four figures on stilts, sporting teeny feathered knapsacks and expressions of direst menace, totter above the common herd (and few herds have looked more common than these straining performers). I hoped they might have come from some pest-control agency.

A closing sequence offers the uninviting spectacle of the cast's buttocks, generously displayed. Strictly for fans of cellulitis. The two musicians are great fun, not least when singing in close harmony and making Spike Jones-ish clatter while a heavily made-up Chinese maiden is manhandled by five chaps in black velvet monks' habits with gold lamé linings. Of course. This parlous event marks the beginning of the 23rd Dance Umbrella season. It can only, please Heaven, get better – and Mark Morris is due soon. ∎

The Queen began the evening

with a teeny plastic ship poised on top of her wig. So sweet, so fitting, and probably meant to be the Titanic.

Sleeping Beauty
12th June, 2000

Cullberg Ballet

**Fluke
Home and Home**

FINANCIAL
TIMES

Playhouse Theatre, Edinburgh

**14th August
2003**

'The costuming
verges on the suicidal'
Fluke (2002)

AT LAST the Edinburgh Festival has come up with a performance ideally suited for the blaze of gloom, the 40-watt effulgence, the Romanian orphanage charm of the Playhouse Theatre. On Monday night the Cullberg Ballet from Sweden – better named the Strindberg Fun-Dance Troupe, since ballet is far, far from anything on offer – opened a brief season.

It is an ensemble that proposes a movement theatre which ranges from manic caperings to therapy for the seriously disturbed. Its relationship with the real world, let alone the real world of academic dance, seems to me tenuous. Neither language (the "ballet" of the title) nor execution (lumpen flappings and flailings; an earnest quest for sanctuary among the dull structures of the set) convey the slightest artistic merit to me. We face a theatre of obscurantism, neurotic activity having a quaint trust in the dead hand of surrealism, and the Limburger-cheese whiff of angst.

The dreary procedures of the two items which feature in this programme are dreadfully predictable. Johan Inger's **Home and Home** was much shorter that Mats Ek's **Fluke** but the latter was no more than its clone afflicted with elephantiasis. The performers suffered, were frenetically gay or neurotically glum (Inger's men wore frocks, and a bit of sympathy had better go to the lad in the red plastic dress, who may well attract rather special devotees; Ek's were mostly depressing in white) and behaved with unbridled psyches. Real music – Bach was treated abominably: the rest of the scores were nugatory.

We are given a view of life best identified by a celebrated actor. Objecting to a wig for a costume drama, she remarked: "It's like looking at the world through a yak's arse". I have no patience with any of it, least of all the chat and shouting while the cast shies itself on bits of the set.

The costuming verges on the suicidal. The evening lasts forever. My one star is awarded for the good lighting. ∎

Pauline de Groot Ensemble

Sadler's Wells

FT

FINANCIAL
TIMES

**19th February
1980**

IT USED TO BE SAID that dance was the only theatre art in which not one foolish word was heard all evening – at least from the stage. Alas, no longer. The Dance Umbrella season has brought a babble of inanities from some performers, and none which I think more tiresome than Pauline de Groot's Dutch ensemble on Friday night. In company with two other female dancers, with two male musicians who were barefoot, and with a stage decorated only by a loaf of bread, Miss de Groot showed us her **Stepping Stones** whose 11 incidents purport to be "the search for the next step in the lives of three women and two men".

The search brought the ladies on stage, chanting and slumping over each other. Thereafter we saw one flailing around with a good deal of energy – continuous turning, unless one is a dervish, is not the most inspirational of activities – and Miss de Groot in a patchwork dress heavily accoutred with old saucepans. She, in turn, spun round, which allowed the pans to clatter while she emitted disconsolate cries. This may have been a request for help with the washing-up. We heard a commentary upon a flight of aeroplanes. The ladies divided the loaf rather brutally – perhaps the Dutch like very thick sandwiches – and all the while one of the musicians banged a variety of percussion instruments (we appreciated his need for bare feet when he gripped a miniature drumstick with his toes) and his companion went to work on a saxophone, and I wondered if

there should be a Society for the Prevention of Cruelty to Musical Instruments.

One of the dancers rotated, and talked to us about mountains, Time and Space: the New Dance crowd are well up to tackling Big Themes, rather like gnats deciding to sing Der Ring des Nibelungen. And it was all over. The programme, which carries a heavyweight message about her art from Miss de Groot, also bears the minatory words "There will be no interval" which seems to me the modern equivalent of "Abandon hope all ye who enter here". As a specimen of Advanced Nincompoopery, **Stepping Stones** is a collector's item. As dance, I find it a non-starter, a dull *rechauffé* of Merce Cunningham's more abstruse moments, idiosyncratic and self-indulgent, with none of Cunningham's discipline, wit, nor one iota of his choreographic skill. The programme, a mine of information I would rather not have acquired, also announced that the Dutch Government provided financial support for the work. The least they can do is to offer danger money to critics having to watch it. ∎

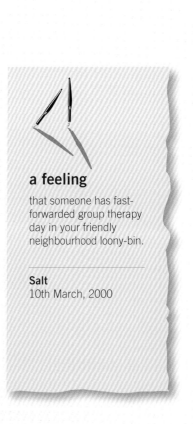

a feeling
that someone has fast-forwarded group therapy day in your friendly neighbourhood loony-bin.

Salt
10th March, 2000

Cleopatra

FINANCIAL
TIMES

Sadler's Wells

5th April 2001

WATCHING HOUSTON Ballet's *Cleopatra*, with which the company began a week's visit to Rosebery Avenue on Tuesday night, was rather like time-travelling. There we were, back in the dear dead days as the 19th century ended. Music by Rimsky Korsakov. Scenery that at best might have been copied from one of Alma Tadema's exercises in academic fakery, and at worst had served for a staging of **Thais** in Marseilles in 1895. A dramatic manner that semaphored emotion in Capital Letters to the attendant throng. (There is a precious film, circa 1906, showing the Moscow ballerina, Geltzer, being roguish with flowers and drapery, while Tikhomirov lusts carefully after her fair white body. They would recognise this Houston territory at once).

Of such are the delights, far too conducive to the giggles, of this balletic curiosity. Ben Stevenson, Houston's director and choreographer of this romp, is far too astute and able a creator not to have seen the dangers implicit in the staging. I suspect that it might have worked as a piece of archaeology – a revival of one of those ancient dance extravaganzas which Diaghilev and his cohorts drove from the stage with the early Ballets Russes seasons – but played earnestly, as here, it is an Ancient Egyptian hoot, recognisable as *My Mummy done Ptolemy,* and with those blessed sand-dancers Wilson, Keppel and Betty as presiding divinities.

The action lurches from the Nile (Cleopatra bathing, sent packing by young Ptolemy, meeting Caesar – cue carpets – and Antony)

to Rome, where conspirators do their fell deeds, which include dancing too energetically, and Calpurnia has a nightmare, played with the abandon of Mrs Vincent Crummles on a bad night. It is all there in the scenario, obligingly run up by D.L. Groover. It is rather less all there in Stevenson's dances – charming for Cleo's hand-maidens, who strike hieroglyphic poses with the best will in the world – and in the characterisations. Lauren Anderson is the Serpent of Old Nile, and hardly compelling. Antony (Dominic Walsh) is too close to Ernie Wise in one of his historical dramas for comfort. Caesar (Timothy O'Keefe) dies at some considerable length – and the ghost of Kenneth Williams could be heard saying "Infamy". Young Ptolemy and Pothinus are having a raging affair, with temper-tantrums and cussed lifts as part of the fun. There is an orgy – more discreet than one might have supposed – and three Roman soldiers in red who have the shifty air of men who know that there is not much one can do with a Hitler salute. Gesture, of a kind, is allowed to run amok. Cleopatra's barge got a round of applause. The big duet for Antony and Cleopatra is set to a bombinating arrangement of the Song of the Indian Guest from Sadko, and may soon become a Tune on Classic FM. (John Lanchbery, who elsewhere makes a clever patchwork of Rimsky scores seems to have gone overboard here). There is an asp, apparently caught in the orchestra pit, and the mime often evokes – how apt – Gippy Tummy. ∎

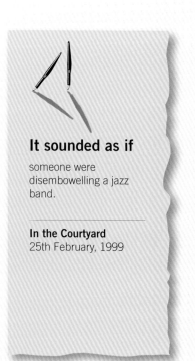

It sounded as if

someone were disembowelling a jazz band.

In the Courtyard
25th February, 1999

Companhia de Dança Deborah Colker

Barbican Theatre, London

FT
FINANCIAL TIMES

1st May 2006

THERE MIGHT HAVE BEEN, in this great metropolis, a theatrical evening more tiresome, more gapingly foolish than Deborah Colker's **Knot**, which lurked last week in the rat-maze of the Barbican and now tours the regions, but – *miserere me* – I do not want to know about it.

Colker, with her troupe of Brazilian performers, has been several times before to the Barbican. The trick she brings on each visit is an enormous set: a huge wheel for **Rota**; that Brobdingnagian dolls' house for **Casa**. This time it is ropes, lots of ropes, dangling in bunches or hanging loose like a baby forest, and then a vast Perspex fish-tank in which the performance goes belly-up.

And there, frankly, the event ends. Colker manipulates her cast in a movement language that suggested to me the manner of a chicken that has just laid a hand-grenade – with, shall we say, some difficulty. (And the little but tedious solo she gives herself at the start of the event's second part conveyed the chicken's feelings on surveying what she had wrought). **Knot** purports to be about sexual angst, lust (it's nice for a boy to have a hobby), and copious and platitudinous programme notes detail Colker's fourth-form *pensées* on life and erotic behaviour. There is also a good deal of tying up in the ropes. (Bondage freaks are in for a disappointment here, too, unless their fancy is for skimpily dressed women hanging about like unlit chandeliers: "Sorry, darling, I'm a bit caught up at the moment"). As with those other Colker affairs, there is

minimal and predictable movement, no development or emotional force to the action (or rather, inaction), witless costuming and an exasperating accompaniment. This hits a nadir of vulgarity in the use of the slow movement of Ravel's *G* major piano concerto (given in an anonymous but gluey and indulgent performance), with Colker offering us the miserable prospect of her cast trailing through her rope-forest. The piece is 85 minutes long, including an interval, and wins every prize for pretentiousness, inadequacy and chutzpah. The programme indicates that the troupe has a "philosophy teacher". I hope he enables the cast to accept rampant mediocrity with a decent resignation of spirit. ∎

'…ropes, lots of ropes, dangling in bunches or hanging loose like a baby forest' (2006)

279

NDT 2

FINANCIAL
TIMES

Sadler's Wells

**12th May
2007**

"IF THIS IS TO BE BORNE, then anything is to be borne!" Confucius's comment when faced with eight rows of dancers in a friend's house came to mind as Nederlands Dans Theater's second troupe began a week's visit to Rosebery Avenue. Here are all the portentous signs of Euro-dance, that amalgam of the heavy-footed, the doom-eager (Martha Graham's phrase) and the damned exasperating activities of performers locked in a routine of introspective, impenetrable activity. Why the good Dutch do not rise up against it, as they did against the Spaniards, I cannot fathom.

There is a world of dancing out here in the free world where movement is light, clear, musically responsive, even – perish the thought – life-affirming and comprehensible. Meanwhile, the poor Dutch must endure the factitious gloom, the gut-wrenchings and cussed posturing of the Nederlands Dans ensembles.

The three urgent invitations to therapy that are on offer at the start of this NDT2 visit come from Jiri Kylián (with **Sleepless**, whose little outbreaks of aggression and dismal gropings are performed with blankest determination by three couples); from Ohad Naharin (whose **Spit** is a culling of frenetic moments from no fewer than four works of his manufacture); and from Paul Lightfoot and Sol Leon, now as inseparable in name as Rimsky and Korsakov (whose **Sleight of Hand** is nailed to part of Philip Glass's second

symphony and richly deserves its fate). Here is the theatre of obscurantism, of tiny cells of activity that flare and burn out like matches, of dancers as awkward automata, of music (when there is music rather than electronic racket) maltreated, cheapened. Kylián uses Mozart (what I suspect may be the music for glass harmonica) put through the wringer to enable his six performers to indulge in predictable games with somehow lumpy-looking bodies in now-you-see-it-now-you-don't antics. Naharin's offering of unrelated and tiresome romping (five chaps are best served as they leap over the stage and daub themselves with a muddy substance from a bucket) has a hectoring, buttonholed-by-a-world-bore manner.

The Lightfoot and Leon piece brings, as I have seen before with this couple, fascinating design. Here an inky stage features two figures on hidden stilts, looming over the action while the cast go through the mysterious (but not as mysterious as all that) rites that are shown to us in grim arabesques and twitches of movement.

It is, as my companion noted, "just another anxious night with the Dutch". I remembered Gerard Manley Hopkins: "What hours, oh what black hours/Have we spent this night! What sights, you, heart, saw". ∎

**...the Royal
Ballet's version,**

which now has an air
of national service in
inimical territory...

Sleeping Beauty
13th February, 1987

"What hours, O what black hours we have spent
This night!' what sights, you, heart, saw"
Sleepless
(2006)

Rosas Dance Troupe

Mikrokosmos

FINANCIAL
TIMES

Gardner Centre, Brighton

21st May 1997

'Bartók taken to the cleaners'

WHO ARE THESE ghastly people, and why are they infesting an innocent and unprotesting stage? This, I have little regret in saying, is my reaction to the activities of Anne Teresa de Keersmaeker and her Rosas dance troupe. Keersmaeker is the darling of Belgian modern dance, and present incumbent of the dance chair at the Théátre Royal de Ia Monnaie. Her trump card is the ace of gloom, and her dance pieces are anxious, lumpen, and boast a fit-where-it-touches musicality. A past visit to London brought an assault on Mozart that should have seen her condemned to the hulks. The Brighton Festival showed her on Monday night at the Gardner Centre in a small outrage entitled **Mikrokosmos**.

It is a decade old, and does not wear its years with any grace – but then, grace is not what Keersmaeker is about. Her dances are exercises in a curious loping, body-slamming, provocative disgruntlement, and suggest nothing so much as a half-term frolic in a reformatory.

To go into as little detail as is decently possible, I record that the stage is dressed with a few old red cinema seats, a clever arrangement of rows of Sansevieria – a boring succulent known as "Mother-in-law's Tongue" – and two pianos on a raised platform behind. In the first part, the fine pianists – Laurence Cornez and Stephane Ginsburgh – play seven of Bartók's piano duets, while Martin Kilvady and Samantha van Wissen indulge in a courtship ritual too tedious to contemplate. The dancers quit the stage, and the pianists offer us a commanding but lengthy – and how lengthy only its victims can know – performance of some pages from Gyorgy Ligeti. Splendidly played; monolithically dull.

Some 50 minutes have now elapsed since these Olympic Games of Angst began. The Duke Quartet now appears to give a very well-judged performance of Bartók's fourth string quartet, which music must have offended Keersmaeker in unfathomable but deeply wounding ways, because she takes vicious revenge. She brings on four dancers, in black shifts and boots, having the air of delinquents who have gained access to banned substances. The manner is of teenage misrule. Skirts are cheerily raised to reveal white knickers. They crouch, click heels, and romp in aggressive, faux-naif fashion. These are the Balthus Babes, and unless your taste runs to such juvenile charms but then, this is a Belgian company – the effect is vastly off-putting. Poor Bartók is taken to the cleaners. The score is a marvel, here degraded for public delectation, and nowhere more so than in the miraculous "night-music" movement where a spindle-shanked mademoiselle trudges over the stage, her little chums galumphing after her. I longed for war to break out, or the Last Trump to sound. Alas, vain hope. The pots of Sanse-vieria weren't looking in tip-top condition by the end of the evening, and I felt as if I'd just done 10 rounds with Frankenstein's Monster. Come to think of it, I had. ∎

i Said i

Rosas Dance Troupe

Barbican Theatre, London

FINANCIAL TIMES

10th September 2001

I SUPPOSE WE MUST be at war with Belgium. How else to explain the vicious attack on the Barbican's public by the Brussels-based troupe Rosas under the command of Anne Teresa de Keersmaeker on Thursday night? The weapon was de Keersmaeker's staging of *i Said i*. (Incomprehensible in every sense). This was unprovoked exposure to Eurotrash dance – as horrible in its way as napalm – and I report on the event with scars still fresh. We were subjected to the terrible devices of "physical theatre", that bastard term, for two and a half hours, without interval, battered by platitudes, shouting, clutter, fearful noise and even more fearsome posturing and capering. There must, surely, be something in the Hague Convention that forbids such sense-rotting tosh. I urge reprisals: a bombardment with episodes of the revived Crossroads or exposure to Tracy Emin's bed installation might be a good starter.

The details of the evening are more than wearisome, they are tasteless and offensive. Ten dancers (7f, 3m). A braying saxophonist and a scratch DJ, plus a piano trio. Part of a Brahms symphony massacred by distortion. A bare stage to be littered with blocks of newspapers, dozens upon dozens of plastic bowls, chairs, sticky tape and de Keersmaeker's thin dances (bits of Béjart; strands of faux Cunningham), somewhat akin to Tourette's Syndrome in movement. Interminable talking. There is a text, from Peter Handke's self-accusation, used as a substitute for the General Confession in Anglican worship. ("I played with thoughts of suicide", said one performer as the evening dragged on, and I knew how she felt). The cast behave badly, notably a Japanese girl who bays at the audience in her native tongue and reveals aspects of aggressive psychotic behaviour. Much time is spent piling the stage with rubbish, then clearing it. There is nudity (but nothing to intrigue anyone owning a bathroom mirror), dismal clothing and for a moment the cast "sleep rough". They dance rough, speak rough, behave rough. One tall, rangey girl deploys fascinating line (she resembles Siobhan Davies in elegance and clarity of movement). This is Eurotrash *in excelsis*, dedicated to alienation, anger, self-indulgence, intellectual pretension (physical pretension, too) and a denial of discipline or control of effect. Not theatre. Not dance. Merely the nursing of grudges, the distortion of skill, of aspiration. Of theatrical art. To hell with it, say I: let's retaliate with Pets Hospital or a bombardment of rap music and TV cookery programmes. ∎

There is also a score by Carl Davis that sounds at best like hung-over Massenet.

Private City 21st March, 1987

Wim Vandekeybus

Blush

FINANCIAL TIMES

Sadler's Wells

10th February 2004

THIS UNSAVOURY AFFAIR at Sadler's Wells by Wim Vandekeybus lasts two hours. Without an interval. Two leaden-footed hours of gabble, screaming, bumper-car collisions between bodies (Vandekeybus's trademark, and one he uses with numbing re-iteration), ill-conceived sexual shenanigans, and the late-1960s blare of rock from a quartet of bores at the back of the Wells' stage, grossly over-amplified. An evening, as you may gather, of the most delicate charm and civilised manners. It makes no sense that I could discern, save as a harking back to the more tiresome clatter and neurotic scab-picking of 20 years ago when dance was mutating into a form of physical theatre of which Vandekeybus was then an intriguing protagonist in his native Belgium. I admired his early work for its directness of message and its anarchic energies.

Blush, with its film and coarse stage effects (the dancers build lightweight blocks into idiot structures and then destroy them: a man capers about in the buff; women scream, climb poles, address the audience and make damn nuisances of themselves while the men engage in fatuous argument) is a retreat from that earlier theatrical power into dreariest and most self-indulgent non-communication. At one happy moment, albeit rather late in the evening (about six hours too late it seemed to me), a girl appears with a buzzing chainsaw and I hoped for mayhem – or at least some opportune maiming – but no, she (like Vandekeybus) just played with it and made no effect.

This frightful show tours the country and, so says the press release "is funded by the Arts Council England". Heads should roll. Serious and valuable dance in England is under-funded, and there are European troupes who should be seen here – but not this obscurantist tosh. **Blush** plays Glasgow and Newcastle this week. I am sure there are chores at home to keep you out of harm's way. ∎

'It makes no sense
that I could discern'
Blush
(2005)

FOR CLEMENT, DANCERS DIVIDE into the incompetent, the proficient, the talented and the truly gifted. He has seen tens of thousands, the majority well-intentioned and striving to give of their best, but those whom he has admired have been few. For him, it has been something akin to the recognition of a spark of the divine, and every time the curtain has risen, it has been, for him, with an inner hope of seeing it ignite before him. It is a question of inner artistic intelligence which will give movement meaning and purpose, allowing the dancer to bring shifts of weight and emphasis, of light and dark which illuminate and leave the observer moved and changed. The dancers I have chosen here have done so to Clement, and for them his admiration is boundless, for they have made him feel himself in the presence of greatness. Choreographer Kenneth MacMillan died backstage at Covent Garden during the first night of the 1992 revival of *Mayerling*, and Clement's review of that night is included here. It is not an outpouring of grief – that is not Clement's way – but rather a tribute to his late friend's genius and the life inherent in performance; no more potent a testament could have been made.

'These I have loved'

"...inner artistic intelligence giving movement meaning and purpose"

Chapter 10

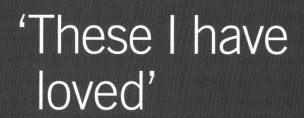

'These I have loved'

"...inner artistic intelligence giving movement meaning and purpose"

Chapter 10

La Fille mal gardée

Royal Opera House, Covent Garden

FINANCIAL TIMES

**14th April
1977**

WHAT IS SO THRILLING about Baryshnikov is not his physical prowess, prodigious though that is, but his uncompromising use of a superlative technique as the servant of a no less remarkable artistry. Audiences may gasp to see him soar and spin as few other dancers can; they are also made aware of the fact that his performances are no mere displays of transcendental ability, but wonderfully conceived views of character or choreography.

In Ashton's **La Fille mal gardée**, which he danced for the first time on Saturday afternoon, everything in his reading of Colas was bright, true, fresh. The great moments of the cornfield duet were stunning, not just because of the way Baryshnikov takes to the air – the upward surge of his body quickly finding the central image of the leap and then lingering, opening out in the pose and sustaining it for our delight – but because they seemed a spontaneous and happy expression of Colas' feelings.

Spontaneity, indeed, is one of the chief qualities of this Colas. Baryshnikov comes to the role partly prepared, as it were, by his knowledge of the American Ballet Theatre version of the old ballet; certainly nothing in this debut could be faulted as an interpretation of a highly rewarding part. Time and again, as some particularly happy piece of stage business seemed newly invented, I thought: "Why has no-one ever done that before?" – from the mock heart-beats as he held the lover's knot of ribbon to

his breast during his first scene with Lise, to the sparky vivacity of his impersonation of a horse a few minutes later.

Baryshnikov brings a greater sense of fun to Colas than any other interpreter I have seen, but he does not play with the role. His view of the young farmer is sincere – but high-spirits, joy in love, are essential to the character, and Baryshnikov revels in them. In the final *pas de deux* he moves his raised arm back more quickly than anyone else, and one feels the eagerness of Colas' happiness; his frantic search for cover when Simone returns after the second act mime-scene starts with a hand-to-head moment of mock horror which suggests that he is really rather enjoying the whole business.

The beautifully "open" quality of his style, with no image blurred, shapes Colas' solos to perfection. Their impulse, as well as their logic, is clear. Up in the air Baryshnikov enters an element in which, like a swimmer, he can disport himself. Dancing seems for him, as for how few others, the most completely natural method of expression. Character and step are one, and when such a temperament has been refined and focused by Kirov training, then we can but marvel.

Yet of all the marvels of the afternoon, one of the most potent for me was the brief pose in which Colas stands in very open fourth position, one arm raised while the other holds the end of a bunch of silk ribbons, in its •••

harmony and phenomenal counterbalancing of line, Barishnikov's greatness was as clear as at any more pyrotechnical moment.

Everywhere Baryshnikov is musical. He enters a musical phrase as if eager to savour it, and he sustains the dances for exactly its length; there are no fudged or truncated endings when dancer and music seem to part company. The one slight disappointment in his performance was an uneven start to the first solo with the staff: he seemed at odds with the tempo and the steps. In all else, this was a glorious interpretation. ∎

Lesley Collier (Lise),
Mikhail Baryshnikov (Colas)
in rehearsal for
La Fille mal gardée
(1977)

Three Russian Preludes

London Coliseum

'True Lord of the Dance'

HOT ON THE JIGGING HEELS of the witless **Lord of the Dance** show, the Coliseum is showing us a real Lord of the Dance in Mikhail Baryshnikov. He is in London this week with his White Oak collective – gifted modern dancers in intriguing modern dance pieces – and though we welcome the chance to see his colleagues and the works they bring, the point of the show is inevitably Baryshnikov.

I once, in the sort of idle game that devotees occasionally play, compiled a list of "the greatest male dancers I've seen" with two American colleagues. My candidates included such glorious and obvious names as Babilée, Bruhn, Solovyov, but the ultimate and crowning laurels had to go to Baryshnikov. The exercise might seem a mere and pointless laundry-list, but it identified what Baryshnikov was in his classical days – a sublime virtuoso of noblest style; a dance actor of rare perceptions; an almost flawless artist. (The "almost" a sop to the idea of artistic hubris).

The astonishing fact now is that, in his post-classical period, when time and knee-injury have precluded the grand challenges of the academic style, Baryshnikov remains a dancer of supremest gifts, sublime integrity. He is what he ever was: a genius of the dance.

Mikhail Baryshnikov
White Oak Project

23rd August 1996

He is 48 years old – was it really 26 years ago when he soared and hung glorious over the stage of the Festival Hall? – and his art and his physical command of movement are still uniquely great. For this week at the Coliseum he offers two solos. Mark Morris's **Three Russian Preludes** is set to Shostakovich piano preludes – music both allusive and dense. Baryshnikov, dressed for the office in shirt and tie, trousers and waistcoat, is a man living out fantasies, puppet games, sudden jokey ideas and small tragedies.

The piece is very Russian – glimpses of Chekhov or Gogol are there – and the dance sets him moving through micro-second incidents, tiny moods. Concentrated, dancing with the most wonderful control and ease, Baryshnikov is the very spirit of the music. ∎

Natalia Makarova

Giselle

FINANCIAL
TIMES

Royal Festival Hall

**5th August
1970**

Natalia Makarova (Giselle)
Kirov Ballet
(1970)

IN THIS IMPERFECT WORLD we must hail perfection and treasure it, and for me Natalia Makarova's Giselle is as near perfection as I hope to see. Bold words, but not a sudden affectation: four years ago, when the Kirov were at Covent Garden, we saw what was a first sketch of the role from this exquisite dancer. It promised greatness then, and last night we were privileged to see the realisation of that promise. And this despite surroundings that could well defeat any interpretation. Within the narrow confines of the Festival Hall stage, with Hugh Stevenson's back-cloths borrowed from Festival Ballet, plus two superior dog-kennels for the cottages in Act I, and dead, blank lighting, Makarova proved totally thrilling. We forget the inadequacies of the production and the surroundings as soon as the delicate creature that is Makarova's Giselle makes her first appearance.

Everything that the Kirov stands for is revealed in this performance – grandeur of style, beautiful technique as the utterly expressive servant of a characterisation, completely meaningful dancing. This Giselle is a nervous, fragile being in Act I, springing joyously into her lover's arms, moving with a lightness that seems barely to skim the ground. Madness comes as a complete dislocation of the personality, fraught with terrible memories: Makarova recalls the flower test by tearing with claw-like hands at imagined petals, and gazes, hypnotised, at the sword before seizing it; the reprise of her dance with Loys is done with outstretched arms and head held back, the whole body telling of her mental agony. It is heart-rending and beautiful.

In Act II we are treated to a display of flawless dancing, the very essence of lyricism and wonderfully in accord with Gautier's concept of a spirit floating and bounding through the night as the weight of the earth that has covered the corpse is forgotten. Marvellous at every moment, Makarova's interpretation transcends the staging to become the very incarnation of the Romantic ballet.

Her Albrecht was Soloviev; there is no point in discussing his impeccable dancing, which even on this stage can soar to majestic effect. Dramatically his reading is of the simple, sincere kind, strongest in the second act, where he manages an ardent and convincing grief. Acting honours must go to Anatoly Gridin as the ideal Hilarion, and were all this not enough, we also had Mikhail Baryshnikov with Bolshakova in the peasant *pas de deux*. At the risk of repeating myself, I must comment again upon the phenomenal abilities of Mr Baryshnikov, whose dancing is not only thrilling to watch but serves also a text-book example of beautiful placing and effortless technical grace. ∎

Natalia Makarova
London Festival Ballet

London Coliseum

FT

FINANCIAL
TIMES

**18th July
1986**

THERE ARE CERTAIN great dance artists whose interpretations have altered our perceptions about what performance may attain in communicative power, through that grand and self-immolatory incandescence which marks the art of the *monstre sacré*. So it has been with Makarova since her first appearances in London with the Kirov Ballet just 25 years ago. Even then, as a debutante Giselle, she showed how the controls provided by the finest classic schooling might focus the fire of her temperament and cause it to burn brighter.

Across the years, and especially since her decision to stay in the West in 1970, Makarova's performances have shown that special intensity that can hush an auditorium until the final curtain releases the cathartic explosion of cheers and applause: she has ever held us by the phoenix-rite through which she sacrifices herself in a role, which is reborn before our eyes. Her Giselle and Odette/Odile, her Juliet, Tatiana, Manon, are unassailable testimony to this.

It is the unique combination of temperamental impetuosity and rigorous academic control of means which brings to Makarova's dancing its especial quality; at what may seem the most abandoned and impulsive moments, the instrument remains a Stradivarius in the hands of a master, the dance keeps its formal rectitude whatever the effusions of feeling it expresses.

So it was at Wednesday night's Royal Gala by Festival Ballet, when Makarova made her only London appearance this season (a disgraceful fact which rebounds no credit to British ballet companies) as Tatiana in Cranko's **Onegin**. It is a role which she made her own, from the dreaming girl of the first scene to the beautiful and mature woman who racks herself with grief as she rejects Onegin's love. It is a portrait whole, ablaze with emotion.

We see Tatiana fall in love with Onegin and pinpoint the very moment, at the end of her first duet with him. In the letter scene Tatiana's body bends reed-like in his arms before great gusts of passion. As he returns her letter, she is broken with sorrow: her solo in the party scene (ravishing in its speed and lightness and clarity) is an appeal for understanding, and a mirror of her despair.

The final scene, after 10 years have passed, is one of the supreme displays of dance acting in my experience, as Tatiana fights against Onegin's love and, in the process, dragging herself from him, seems to tear herself in half, falling back on him only to find fresh strength to reject him.

In all this, with Alexander Sombart a fine Onegin and a princely partner, Makarova deployed the full panoply of her art. It was a performance, as always with this ballerina, in which the truth of the role was told in the most sensitive and vividly expressive terms, and there is no other dancer today able ●●●

so generously or gloriously to achieve this theatrical miracle.

Were this to have been a London farewell, then Makarova has left us with no least sign of diminished powers. Her art is more potent than ever, and at the performance's end it received a happy accolade through the presence of the Princess of Wales, who gave Makarova the *Evening Standard* award for her contribution to ballet in 1985.

But not to see Makarova dance again is unthinkable. Our ballet companies have a duty to their public, to the art of dancing itself, to provide a suitable repertory for a ballerina of this magnitude. Otherwise they are cheating their audiences and diminishing ballet itself. ∎

The Princess of Wales presents *The Evening Standard* award to Natalia Makarova following her performance in *Onegin* London Coliseum (1986)

Lynn Seymour
The Royal Ballet

Royal Opera House,
Covent Garden

FINANCIAL
TIMES

IN WHAT DOES GREATNESS in a ballerina reside? In a physical instrument that is, of itself, beautiful, and entirely obedient to the demands of a role; in the power to embody emotion, and communicate it fully; in musicality. All these, certainly, and then in something mysteriously more – hard to define, and easy to appreciate – in which the dancer is metamorphosed, and becomes the character she dances. All of these qualities are Lynn Seymour's, and in last night's revival of **Romeo and Juliet** she proclaimed her greatness yet again, and in so doing transcended even her own exceptional past performances in the role.

Juliet lives in Seymour's interpretation, fully and utterly, the part is hers. Made for her, inspired by her physique and temperament, it is shaped and led by her lyricism and her complete identification with the dance, and has been so since its creation. With maturity, and in this magnificent year in which she has returned to dancing with a technique burnished to virtuosity and all traces of past ill-health swept away, she seems more completely Juliet than ever before. Last night, with David Wall as her ardent Romeo, she gave the first act a youthful radiance and impetuosity that was marvellous to behold.

The awakening and parting with Romeo at the beginning of Act 3 found her body pouring out an unbroken cantilena of passion which stilled into a terrible isolation as the young girl suddenly realises her plight.

Then the great run to Friar Laurence, a surge of energy that made all one has read (and seen in photographs) of Pavlova or Isadora seem gloriously real. There follows the terrible interview with her parents and Paris. Struggling in his embrace, she can escape to the window, and, captured again, she is held with one arm raised as if to fend him off.

As he moves away, she maintains the pose, then stands still – hand to mouth, lost in a dream – before the slight bow that tells of her acceptance of him. Dance-acting of this calibre is not to be seen every day, or every decade, and Seymour gives her performance such passionate intensity, and such lyric beauty of expression, that one can but be grateful for the privilege of seeing so phenomenal an artist in her prime. ∎

**25th July
1975**

**Lynn Seymour (Juliet),
David Wall (Romeo)
Royal Opera House
(1976)**

Lynn Seymour
London Festival Ballet

Onegin

FT

FINANCIAL
TIMES

London Coliseum

**25th July
1988**

LYNN SEYMOUR'S RETURN to classic ballet is a matter for great rejoicing. After injury and some traumatic times in the late 1970s, she retired from dancing at what should have been the peak of her powers. Since then she has made occasional stage appearances – most recently in an Italian production of **Cinderella** and in the mimed role of L S Lowry's mother in **A Simple Man**.

Now, seven years after we had given up hope that we might ever again see her artistry at full stretch, she appeared as Tatyana in Cranko's **Onegin** in Saturday's closing performance of Festival Ballet's Coliseum season. The inevitable question in the minds of Miss Seymour's legion of admirers must have been whether a full-length ballet, in which she had never previously danced, was the best choice for this phoenix-like rebirth.

We should have trusted Miss Seymour's judgment and her dance genius. From curtain rise, with Tatyana reclining, lost to the world in her romantic novel, the role was hers. As the action developed, as Onegin (Alexander Sombart: brooding in presence, impeccable as partner) becomes the focus of her dreams, Miss Seymour's movement blossomed. For devoted Seymour-watchers, here was what

we had been missing for nearly a decade: the ideal line of leg and the ravishing feet, the deliquescence of arms, and the harmonies of *contraposto* as gesture opened out from the trunk. A swirling pirouette into Onegin's arms became a symbol of impetuous physical devotion; the flawless musicality held every moment in balance with the score; the hands, surest guide to what a Seymour character feels or intends, signalled emotion, spoke.

And, of course, Miss Seymour's mastery of dramatic playing took us to the heart of Tatyana's sufferings. She is incapable of lying in performance, as she is incapable of a graceless movement, so that the progress from provincial girl to mature Petersburg aristocrat, was exquisitely judged. In the last scene, where the storm of Onegin's passion broke about her and nearly broke her, Miss Seymour rivalled any of her greatest interpretations in power of feeling and integrity of means.

There had earlier been uneven moments in setting out the choreography, but the sensitivity and clarity of Miss Seymour's art was everywhere thrilling. The final tearing of Onegin's letter took all her strength; the piteous gathering up of its fragments as the ballet ended, was the price paid for that strength. Sublime art, profound understanding, great dancing. ∎

**Lynn Seymour (Tatyana),
Ivan Liska (Onegin)
London Festival Ballet
(1988)**

296

Kenneth MacMillan

FT
FINANCIAL TIMES

1st October 1992

ONE OF THE MOST INFLUENTIAL as well as the most challenging of modern choreographers, MacMillan sought throughout his career to extend the boundaries of classical dancing so that it might reflect the psychological climate of his time. He gave ballet, and especially the repertory of the Royal Ballet, a new seriousness, and an emotional honesty rare in an art which he found to be often no more than "window-dressing" when he started his career as a young dancer with the Sadler's Wells Ballet.

I met Kenneth MacMillan at the time of his first professional ballet, **Danses Concertantes**, in 1955, and thereafter our friendship was an abiding joy for me. His creative career was charted with sympathy and admiration in these pages: Andrew Porter offered most perceptive appreciation of his work from the very first, and as his successor in the 1970s I also hoped to convey the significance of the innovations, the intense perceptions, that marked MacMillan's choreography. There was an understanding between us, though, that MacMillan never discussed his work: criticism was unguided by anything save an interest in the way he extended the boundaries of classic dance as an expressive language for the theatre.

As a choreographer he was, in his most searching works, custodian of a gift, his genius, which took possession of him. He made what he made because he had to. Superb theatre-craft was consciously his and an unfailing ability to shape new and stimulating movement, but the creative drive was deep-seated and mysterious. Talking about **The Judas Tree** after its premiere, he said to me "I sometimes don't understand all that I've put into a ballet until I've seen it on stage three or four times".

Standing in silence in the Opera House on Thursday night, sharing the tangible sense of shock that affected the audience, I remembered so much about MacMillan. His marvellous ability to grasp the new; his iron integrity; his humour, and his delight in the improbable and the ludicrous; his faultless eye for a dancer and his lifelong devotion to the classic dance. And, centrally, his great joy in his family life. His profound and compassionate understanding of the human condition gave his choreography abiding truth. His creations gave a new maturity to ballet in our time. They are a vital part of our national heritage, and of the dance of our century. ∎

Sir Kenneth MacMillan died from a heart attack backstage at the Royal Opera House during a performance of *Mayerling*. Jeremy Isaacs, the general director of the Royal Opera House, informed the audience, asking they rise and bow their heads and leave the theatre in silence.

THERE IS NO NEED to paraphrase what Clement has written about Alicia Markova. For him, she represented what it was to be a ballerina and an artist. He became a good and personal friend of Dame Alicia, with whom he would talk frequently and, more importantly, listen. He listened to her stories from her childhood, her training, her time with Diaghilev's Ballets Russes, her international stardom, her contribution to the establishment and development of ballet in the United Kingdom and her own unwavering dedication to her art. In many ways, for him, she encapsulated the story of classical dancing in the twentieth century and he admired and loved her for both who and what she was. She has been, I feel, the benchmark against which he has measured all other performers, and when he has seen dancers on stage, her image has always lain in his consciousness.

Alicia
Markova

"her image has always lain
in his consciousness"

Chapter 11

Alicia Markova

"her image has always lain
in his consciousness"

Chapter 11

Giselle

Royal Festival Hall, London

23rd July 1958

MANY BALLERINAS are content to make some success of Giselle through a straight-forward presentation of the role, whose range of dynamics, both dramatic and technical, are as considerable as anything in the repertoire.

Only the three truly great Giselles of our time, Ulanova, Markova and Chauviré, seem to have achieved complete authority in the part. Ulanova's is the supremely dramatic realisation in which the light of genius illuminates the portrayal. Chauviré, whose interpretation we are fortunately to see at Covent Garden next month, is the exponent of the pure French school, beautifully danced and mimed. Last night the Festival Ballet presented Markova as Giselle, and through her physique and temperament, we are shown the Romantic era in her portrait.

In Act I she is an innocent seen by a poet of the 1830s, gentle, fey, not long for this world; and in Act II she is the perfect Wili, the night-dancer amid the Gothick gloom, air-borne and intangible. Her very personal dance-quality is perfectly in keeping with period. All her movements are informed by a delicacy and a kind of crystalline precision; each one has a clarity and a completeness that are among her unique attributes as a dancer. Each phrase is effortless, every movement in the air shows her to be weightless. Her beautiful feet, supple and articulate as her hands, perform their tiny miracles, barely skimming the ground in Act II, while in her justly celebrated mad-scene her delicately

etched features express the tragedy with extreme economy. Most remarkable, the whole characterisation is perfectly harmonious, the peasant girl of the first act foreshadows the ghost of the second, and this unity of mood makes the love-duet of Act II all the more poignant.

Festival Ballet's production is as carefully considered as ever, the story is presented with clarity and a respect for period feeling, and Mme Markova has the benefit of Mr John Gilpin's noble Albrecht. ∎

Alicia Markova (*Giselle* Act II), Sadler's Wells Ballet, The Royal Opera House (1948)

Markova at 90

FINANCIAL
TIMES

1st December 2000

I CANNOT BELIEVE that Alicia Markova celebrates her 90th birthday today. When we sit talking, Markova summoning up ballets and dancers with gesture or step, she remains what she has ever been for me during the 30 years of our friendship: an ageless, vivid and still lovely woman.

A turn of the head, the profile balanced by the line of neck and those "keep-sake" shoulders, and Giselle and a dozen other of her roles are suddenly there again, potent as when she danced them. We were talking lately about **L 'Après-midi d'un faune**, and she started to show me the choreography as she knew it from her Diaghilev days: the ballet was at once more alive than in recent dutiful performances at Covent Garden. And she recalled how, chez Diaghilev, the men in the company stood in the wings calling "This way, this way" to guide the nymphs, since the choreography did not allow the danseuses to see the wing-space.

Markova has been working for 80 of her 90 years, as ballerina, teacher, director, university professor. I still say to her: "Work, work! There's more to be done!" – more to explain and show from the storehouse of a prodigious memory and prodigious experience.

No other ballerina of the 20th century had creations from Fokine, Nijinska, Massine, Balanchine, Ashton, Tudor. It is a roll-call that tells something of her genius, and her artistic lineage.

The story of her life is well-known: Diaghilev's "little English daughter"; the young ballerina who helped launch English ballet; the international star whom a New York critic called "the greatest dancer in the world". (Markova's response was typical: "That's all very well, but I'm the one who has to live up to it").

I first saw her dance in 1948, when she returned with her partner Anton Dolin to Covent Garden. I fell at once under the spell of her artistry, her unfailing technical elegance, her dramatic power, her mystery. "Who Markova is, nobody knows" said New York's finest critic: it was the role that mattered.

Looking at film of her Giselle recently, I was bowled over – even more than as a young balletomane – by her musical felicity in phrasing, the prestissimos that came out of nowhere, the imponderable flights into the air, her emotional force. Her dancing has been a touchstone for me, for many others; her friendship has been a combination of masterclass and time-travel, the past brought to life, art explained. I have come to understand something of what made her so astounding on the stage: the temperament that could hold a crowded stadium on an in-held breath; the dedication to dance, so that nothing else mattered save the use to which she put a God-given talent; the quest for 'purity in expression'; the phenomenal musical understanding.

302

I remember how, visiting an art gallery a few years ago with her, a woman came up and said "Isn't that Markova? I saw her dance!" As for so many thousands more, Markova had touched her life, unforgettably, gloriously. It is what she still does. Happy birthday, my dear friend. ▌

Dame Alicia Markova
(c. 1960s)

Alicia Markova: A Sketch for a Portrait

The Journal of the Society for Dance Research
Vol. 24, No. 2

FINANCIAL TIMES

1st December 2006

IN 1948, Alicia Markova and Anton Dolin returned to Britain to dance for the first time since the outbreak of war in 1939. Then, contracts with the Ballets Russes companies to whom they were bound, obliged them to work away from their native land. These war-time years had been marked by a massive change in the fortunes of the Sadler's Wells Ballet for which they had vitally danced in its earliest Vic-Wells period; and these years had also seen the great developments in their own careers as principal dancers with, variously, the Ballets Russes de Monte Carlo, American Ballet Theatre, the Original Ballet Russe of Colonel de Basil, and their own Markova-Dolin troupe. In 1948 Dolin, flawless partner, vivid dramatic artist, was 44 years old, still an elegant presence on stage, and essential to Markova's art as sustaining figure in many ballets. Markova was 37, adored, hailed by John Martin in New York as 'possibly the greatest dancer who has ever lived'. (When a friend asked her how it felt to be given this unlikely accolade, Markova observed: 'That's all very well, but I'm the one who has to live up to it'). Markova and Dolin's return to the Sadler's Wells troupe, now established as a national ballet and installed at the Royal Opera House, Covent Garden, was eagerly awaited. The old hands, the pre-war ballet-goers, were more than fascinated to see how this celebrated partnership would seem after a decade away. To the more recent devotees, like my very young self, the chance to see such legendary figures was tremendously important. They came, trailing their clouds of glory from Diaghilev's time onwards, their achievements well-known, their artistic collaborations with Fokine, Massine, Nijinska, Balanchine, Robbins, de Valois, Ashton, Tudor – all of whom had made roles for them – seeming of prodigious lustre.

They came, we saw, were conquered. They made a first appearance at a gala, dancing the **Don Quixote** *pas de deux*. Markova told me that this came too soon after their return to England, and she still had not found her 'land legs' after a stormy Atlantic crossing. Their real return was marked in performances of **Giselle**, **Swan Lake** and **The Sleeping Beauty** (the first time they had danced this full-length version). Dolin was in all things the perfect cavalier. (After 56 years, I still recall his entrance as the Prince in **Sleeping Beauty**. Red-coated, he took the stage with an exquisitely stated nobility. Years later, I mentioned this to Markova and she replied: 'Of course! He had seen Pierre Vladimirov when he was in the Diaghilev staging of **The Sleeping Princess** (in 1921) and he learned from him how to walk like a prince in the grandest traditions of the Mariinsky Ballet.' (Vladimirov had been a celebrated *danseur noble* in St. Petersburg).

Markova, too, learned a lesson from **The Sleeping Princess**. Even as a very young dancer she was enraptured by the artistry of Vera Trefilova, purest of the Imperial ballerine of her time, who was one of the Auroras in **The Sleeping Princess**, and whom Arnold Haskell called 'The Ingres of the dance', so formally perfect her style. Markova noted that in the last act *pas de deux*, when, in the final bars of the entree, Aurora must rise from the ground on point, her hand in that of her Prince, Trefilova unlike the other illustrious ballerine in the production, rose with exceptional slowness (and exceptional clarity – and strength, too). This moment Markova adopted in performance: the effect is far more elegant in defining Aurora's identity. It also (very discreetly) identifies the dancer's prowess. I have only seen one other ballerina (and that in Russia) who has opted for this poised, lovely move into the succeeding pose.

In 1948, audiences were eager above all to see Markova and Dolin in **Giselle**. Markova's interpretation had been hailed from the time of her first performance of the role with the infant Vic-Wells Ballet on 1 January 1934, that night of pea-souper fog and triumph for her. It was a role which she had subsequently danced to an acclaim that was a tribute both to her incomparable lightness and clarity in dancing and to her phenomenal control over an audience. Her fragile figure emerging from the cottage in Act One, the effortless way in which she produced marvels of technical dancing (pirouettes which appeared as if by magic), the emotional force of her every action, the inevitability of her playing as it culminated in the mad-scene: these were the marks of dramatic and dance genius. Her second act was imponderable, Dolin there as both dramatic frame for her art and the perfect complement to her dancing as he

seemed to draw her out of the night air. Again, uncanny speed, and effortless legato. And, as marvellous as anything else, her musical sensitivity, her skill in phrasing dance along the music's lines, giving colour, fascination, grace to the least step because she had that rare gift of being able to shape movement within a musical or dance phrase, lightening it with tiny accelerando or quick accents. There is a film (cruelly abbreviated) of Markova and Dolin in **Giselle** made in 1952: study this and you see how peerless and potent was Markova's art. (I recall that she and I were working with a television company on a programme about her favourite roles. We had been shown part of this **Giselle** film for her approval; as we motored back from the studios, she turned to me and said: 'Not bad for a 42 year old woman, who had got up at five in the morning to film that!' Not bad indeed!) Public eagerness to see Markova and Dolin led to regional tours with an ensemble, and then, in 1950, to the creation of a company that Markova named Festival Ballet (the Festival of Britain was imminent). One of the most notable aspects of the troupe was Markova and Dolin's understanding of what the public should see, and want to see. The repertory was dominated by traditional classics (a fine **Giselle**; a worthy **Nutcracker**) and by honourable revivals of those Ballets Russes masterpieces that both artists had danced, and which had proved their worth and their drawing power over the previous three decades. These were sensible decisions – though it was not the easiest of matters to train a new • • •

ensemble to deal with ballets that are so
difficult to realise well (as we know to our
cost today). Markova and Dolin also knew
that great names, great dancers, were essential
to realise these ballets and to win a public.
Thus, during the early 1950s we were shown
the late and golden performances by Alexandra
Danilova and Massine, by Riabouchinska,
with choreography by David Lichine, and
interpretations from Yvette Chauviré and Mia
Slavenska and, later, Tamara Toumanova, and
by the notable English dramatic ballerina
Paula Hinton. Dolin also encouraged and
guided performances by the wonderfully
gifted John Gilpin and Belinda Wright, and
nurtured other young artists from the
company's ranks. And Markova danced, with
that phenomenal grace and lightness which
were hallmarks of her art.

Her Sugar Plum Fairy in **Nutcracker** was made
of spun sugar, so light and so transparent in
technique. (She is one of the only two
dancers – the other was the Kirov Ballet's

noble stylist Zhanna Ayupova in a staging in
Nice – whom I have seen make the *double
gargouillades* in the ballerina's variation seems
crystal clear. There is a film-clip made in
1942 of Markova in this solo, her feet faster
than the camera can catch them).

Markova decided to leave Festival Ballet at the
end of the 1952 season and thenceforward
became a guest artist with companies round
the world. She danced for the Marquis de
Cuevas in Paris, giving her only performances
as Bournonville's sylphide, a role for which
she had every gift, and which she learned in
Copenhagen from Hans Brenaa. She was in
all balletic things a stickler for correct text,
and Cyril Beaumont recognised this, writing
that, unlike many dancers, Markova handed
on the text of a ballet exactly as she had
received it. She had a phenomenal memory
for choreography and a no less prodigious
understanding of style: not her own style
(though this she understood with entire
assurance: she knew exactly how to achieve

an effect on stage), but the dance style as it had been created for a specific ballet. She knew what her choreographers (and they were a list of the greatest masters of the twentieth century from Fokine and Nijinska and Massine, to Balanchine and Ashton and Tudor) had asked of her, and she understood every nuance of their manner, and was fascinated by it. She was happy to pass this knowledge on to worthy heirs: I recall that she unlocked the very subtle role of the Girl in Blue in **Les Biches** – which Nijinska had staged for her – for Natalia Makarova. Dancers and producers who disregarded her knowledge evinced no more than a raised eyebrow or a shrug: ignorance of their art was their own sad problem. When she saw a dancer bungling one of her former roles she would pose the plaintive question: 'Why didn't you ask me? It's really so easy!'

Markova as a dancer was that being beloved of all ballet troupes, a bankable name. On Monday night in any provincial town, rain or shine, the name Markova on the evening's bill meant a capacity house. She was known far beyond the realms of the usual ballet public, and I can cite two instances: twenty years ago we were together in Manchester, where Markova had been staging **Les Sylphides** (a ballet which Fokine had asked her to dance and had taught her), and we got into a taxi after a rehearsal. At once the driver turned round and said 'You're Alicia Markova, aren't you?' He got the expected reply, but something more negative when he asked me 'And would you be Anton Dolin?' Years later, we were visiting The Queen's Gallery. As we passed through the entrance hall, a woman turned to me and said 'Isn't that Markova?' I replied that indeed it was, and with eyes brimming with emotion she said 'I saw her dance Giselle: it was the most wonderful thing in the world'. Until she retired in 1963, Markova continued to enthral her public. Her style remained true, she made sure that choreography remained true, and the public still saw her artistry at its truest. Dancing was lightly yet faithfully offered, with phrasing of angelic ease, extraordinary in its musical

finesse. On film you can see how she made tiny accents give variety, savour, to the simplest *enchaînement*, and how she was mistress of a *rubato* within a phrase or even within the sweep of a single extension, flicking the initial impulse, then making an infinitesimal *rallentando*, then – right on the musical and emotional beat – finishing the movement.

You can see how she times a gesture, offering a hand or bending that exquisite head, beautifully placed on those sloping shoulders, so that it achieves maximum theatrical effect-iveness, legible to everyone in her audience, unhurried, purposeful, vivid. It was the same gift that Ulanova had as Giselle: small wonder that they so admired each other. Years and years later, when we talked or lunched, Markova would sometimes want to show me a step or a moment from a ballet, often something long-lost, like **Le Pas d'acier** or the 'correct' (as she had been taught it by some illustrious ballerina or coach) variation in one of the classics – 'they used to have their own special vocabulary of steps, you know, but now dancers muddle them all up and the choreography has lost its individuality' – and the same mystery, the same sense of perform-ing life, was there. She was incapable of cheating on what she had learned, had danced, had garnered from experiences that dated back to the 1920s, and I remembered that she had been taught the second act adagio in **Swan Lake** by Mathilde Kshessinskaya, the first Petersburg ballerina to dance it, within a year of its creation at the Mariinsky Theatre in 1895. Such artistic lineage cannot be bettered.

We met properly, became friends, in 1973, when Markova returned finally to London after her years directing the ballet ensemble at the Metropolitan Opera House, New York, and then serving as Distinguished Professor in the theatre faculty of the University of Cincinatti. I urged her to write her memoirs, although there were already books about her and in *Giselle and I* she had discussed with exceptional insights the nature of the role and her approach to it. Now I was eager • • •

that she set down further aspects of her life, and we worked together on this, my promptings leading her to talk and reveal how clear was her memory in its detail, and how profound her understanding of her art. The phrase 'Well, dear, it was like this…' served as a prelude to some extraordinary revelations about a ballet or a dancer or a tour, or how some ballerina had behaved. 'Felia Doubrovska was finally cast as the Firebird (with the Diaghilev company) and she wanted to have a pedicure. Everyone told her not to do so, but she was determined to have it, and, of course, she finished the performance with her shoes soaked in blood, because her toe-nails were too short. You have to have toe-nails for that kind of point-work'.

Her vanities were about her career, in the sense that she had worked with every major choreographer of her time, and that she had been taught and coached by the greatest of masters, from Cecchetti and Nicholas Legat to Egorova and Spessivtseva. In New York in 1940, she had hired a studio for daily class, and discovering that Spessivtseva, whom she revered, was in New York, she asked her if she would care to share the studio – Vincenzo Celli, a favoured student of Cecchetti, was on hand to give counsel. Spessivtseva agreed. Markova had known her from Diaghilev times and had watched her performances in 1932 in London during her Camargo Society season, when Markova danced the second act of **Swan Lake**, and Spessivtseva appeared as Giselle (and had said to Markova: 'This ballet will be good for you'). Most extraordinary was the fact that Spessivtseva shared with Markova her own daily class which she had known with Yekaterina Vazem in St. Petersburg. Vazem (1848-1937) was celebrated for her brilliant style – she was the first Nikiya in Petipa's **La Bayadère** – and was known as a very demanding teacher. Keith Lester, who had danced with Spessivtseva in South America during the 1930s, had told me how taxing were these exercises and how dedicated Spessivtseva was to them. Markova watched, learned, related this also to those classes in Paris with another Mariinsky ballerina,

Lyubov Egorova, which, during the 1930s, she had shared with Alexandra Danilova, who was also a product of Petersburg training.

Here, for her, was another vital link with ballet's past, with the greatest of Petersburg's dance traditions, in which she had been reared by Cecchetti and Legat. Her sense of history, of the significance of a step or an *enchaînement*, of the vital importance of preserving a step or a phrase as it had been passed down to her, was part of the armour which protected her own dance and stage identity. A decade ago, I took Lyudmila Semenyaka, exquisite product of the Vaganova School, pupil of those illustrious Petersburg/ Leningrad ballerine, Natalya Dudinskaya, Galina Ulanova and Marina Semyonova, to tea with Markova. Within a couple of moments they were chattering like girls about steps and how they must be performed. 'I always dance Pavlova's variation,' said Semenyaka, and Markova knew exactly what it was. Semenyaka, reared in the hallowed traditions of Petersburg, spoke thereafter with reverence of 'Alicia Arturovna'. Markova said, 'She's like a young sister to me'.

Markova was the repository of extraordinary knowledge about her art. She did not offer it to everyone, but if a dancer was intelligent, had some sense of history, her guidance was invaluable. Markova had gained enormously from the friendship of Cyril Beaumont who, early on, lent her books about dancers and history; Arnold Haskell was also a vital educative force in the intellectual life of the child Markova, her days dedicated to the theatre rather than the schoolroom. Markova could reveal exceptional facts, traditions, insights. She had a faultless eye for technique: I remember a conversation between her and Makarova when they talked about technical problems, both agreeing that it was futile to try to master an awkward *enchaînement* by constant repetition in the studio. Far better to think about it analytically, about its technical requirements, and only then to return to the physical work, when the problem would be solved. Markova had used this same approach during her Ballets Russes de Monte Carlo days, when she and Alexandra Danilova discussed what they called 'Waterloos' – those cussed moments in choreography which must be mastered. I recall sitting with Markova during a performance of the Shades scene from **La Bayadère** and watching a celebrated ballerina muddle the pirouettes in Nikiya's solo. The solo was falling apart. 'She's not using her eyes properly' was Markova's comment.

Markova was proud of her feet. They were small (size 2 shoe) and flawless even into her 90th year. Agnes de Mille, in her brilliant book of memoirs, *Portrait Gallery*, writes about Markova with great sympathy and admiration. She notes that many dancers' feet are as gnarled and knobbly 'as the Ace of Clubs', and she describes how Markova protected her feet from injury or bruising by the most careful preparation and tender care.

Markova had danced hard and tirelessly during her twenties and thirties, giving an exhausting eight performances a week for the two-year life of the Markova/Dolin Ballet, on 40-week tours during which she had to dance a leading role (these included Giselle, Odette / Odile, and Aurora) each night. This cruel schedule she sustained, as she sustained the lengthy tours of the Ballets Russes de Monte Carlo round America, and the extensive touring schedule and major seasons with Ballet Theatre. Her feet were cosseted, and remained beautiful. Even when she was 90 years old she would remove her shoes and show me steps, the feet still mobile, still like the 'little hands' that Cyril Beaumont praised, and still exceptionally strong.

I knew that part of Markova's power as an artist was her entire single-mindedness, especially about the artist who was Alicia Markova. She was an astounding case-study in dedication, in almost obsessive concern with an art that had claimed her as a child. It was as a child that she knew ballet's inexorable discipline, its rewards (she had been, after all, a child and an apprentice star in the greatest ballet-troupe of her time: the Diaghilev

Ballets Russes) and its complexities. She had a sense of her own destiny, and through family circumstance, of her own duties as an artist, even of the isolation that great talent brings. This induced in a highly observant child an exceptional focus upon her career and on her own identity as a dancer. With Diaghilev she was protected, every decision made for her: all she had to do was to dance, to listen and learn, to watch and learn, to dance and learn, to treasure what she saw and danced and heard and learned. At the age of 18 she was as rare a being in Western ballet as can be imagined. And at this moment she lost everything through the death of Diaghilev and the immediate collapse of his ballet troupe. No future. No hope. Nowhere to work. Nothing to work on. No artistic sustenance, and it has to be realised that Markova was, because of her five years with Diaghilev, preternaturally sophisticated in artistic taste. She had worked with such figures as Matisse and Stravinsky, knew (by theatrical association) the artistic milieu of the Diaghilev circle, danced to, and understood, scores by Prokofiev, Ravel and Poulenc. She knew how ballets must be lit (she spent mute hours in darkened theatres watching Diaghilev bring a stage-set to life through lighting). She had worked with great conductors, great dancers, great choreographers, and was, for a girl in her teens, exceptionally aware of the demands of the art she practised. Silent she may have been, and in many ways innocent of the world of young girls, but she watched, felt, understood a great deal of the life of the Diaghilev troupe, knew Europe from uncomfortable train travel across its length and breadth, from Barcelona to Budapest, from Edinburgh to Rome. She also knew the prodigy's protected dedication to an art.

All this was to temper the fine blade of her personality and of her talent. Her sense of entire desolation when she returned to London and the desert of its balletic scene in 1929 following Diaghilev's death, was only to be lifted when Marie Rambert and Ninette de Valois offered her work as • • •

they launched their enterprises. Markova was a prodigious gift to them; they were, in turn, a great gift to her. Her life had purpose, artistic rewards (Ashton, de Valois, Tudor making ballets for her) and then the classics, justified by her truest dance identity as a classical ballerina, and a justification for it. In 1934 *Swan Lake* and *Giselle* were staged by de Valois' Vic-Wells Ballet for her and because of her. It is at this time that Markova became the self-reliant figure, the young woman accepting responsibility for her gifts and for her destiny, who was the Markova of the next 70 years. (Once, I asked her about the very early days of her return to London: 'Who gave you daily class at that time?' 'Oh, my dear,' came a smiling reply, 'they couldn't give me class, but I could have given them class!') She was adored by the British public, and when she left the Vic-Wells Ballet in 1935, it was generally thought that the troupe would collapse. But Markova understood that, at the age of 24, she must dance far more than the Vic-Wells twice-weekly schedule allowed, and more widely than the repertory permitted. The Markova/Dolin Ballet, during its two years, was rewarding, exhausting, necessary to confirm her talent, her identity. When injury obliged her to quit, and Massine urged her to return to her Ballets Russes roots with his newly formed Ballets Russes de Monte Carlo, Markova, aged 27, was ready to face a larger world audience than she had known since Diaghilev, was also faced with competition and challenges (from other ballerine, from a different yet familiar repertory), and was faced with survival as 'Markova' in a tough and difficult milieu. Her strengths were her marvellous talent, a few friends (Danilova the chief among these), and her own ability to fight her corner. She was, as I came to know her later, steely in her determination that her identity, her roles, could not be eroded or minimised. Her weapons, as Ninette de Valois had already realised and later described, were her skill in making people (managers, colleagues) appreciate her worth and the value of her art, on absolute terms and on sheer box-office arithmetic. She might seem insistent upon

her own decisions and, as Massine once said, behave like the 'Chinese water torture', but if she did not protect her roles and her position as a principal ballerina, then who would? The Monte Carlo Ballets Russes, seething with intrigue, made her determination and her personality the steelier. She was a willing and generous colleague, but she was not to be crossed: her stage identity was herself, and all the sacrifices she had made to create it, to justify her wonderful talent, were not to be thrown away to gratify some lesser artist or to minimise her own artistry. Talking about these years to me, she spoke with a kind of resignation about certain dancers who had treated her with less than consideration. One might have deliberately missed a lift and injured her. Another might have intrigued to be given the first night of *Giselle* in an important New York season (death-threats were the order of the slightly hysterical day) but Markova circumvented these annoyances, and I felt sorry for the artists who had tried to cross her.

What fascinated me always with Markova as I worked with her, got to know her better, was the fact that she always kept something in reserve. There was always another fact, an anecdote ('I don't know why she fell out of the window'), another fascinating and unexpected detail, another name, another piece of choreography remembered (and how angry she was at a late and ludicrous 'reconstruction' of *Le Chant du Rossignol* – 'not a step right, and they've even got the designs wrong') to be produced for my amazement and delight. She always had something extra in the bank, as a reassurance for herself. Her ability to pull surprises out of her artistic hat was typified for me by her ravishingly beautiful and wholly unexpected Juliet in Tudor's *Romeo and Juliet* (a score by Delius was at some performances conducted by Sir Thomas Beecham, who much admired Markova's musicality: his tempi, which Markova adored, made the ballet fourteen minutes longer!) Equally astounding, because so unexpected, was her vivid Gypsy Zemphira in Massine's *Aleko*, where Chagall painted a tree of life on the white bodice of

Markova's costume. (She had earlier been decorated by Matisse, the artist painting on her leotard before she appeared in Massine's **Rouge et Noir** in 1939).

Her career, when she stopped dancing, did not diminish Markova as a person. She had unfailing grace, a delight in lending her name and her presence to balletic associations and clubs, and she taught and coached, loving especially working with children. She did not coach as much as she could have done – my feeling is that companies or dancers were either too much in awe of her, and not willing to make the time she expected for her serious coaching, or too ignorant of what she knew – but I cherish the fact that, when she was 90, Dominique Delouche and I persuaded her to guide some young artists of the Paris Opéra Ballet in certain of her greatest roles for the camera. Delouche had chronicled the lives and art of many celebrated dancers – Yvette Chauviré, Serge Peretti, Nina Vyrubova, Serge Lifar, Violette Verdy, Maximova and Vasiliev among them – in films of great distinction and passion for the art of ballet itself. They are precious records. I urged him to make a film about Markova, warning him, too, that she was 90 and inevitably somewhat frail, and very cautious about working. For a year we cajoled and urged. Over lunch one day she signed the contract, and Dominique then performed marvels. She travelled to Paris by Eurostar, was greeted at the Gare du Nord like a queen, was installed at the Hotel Scribe, and bright talents among the Opéra young awaited her, with Élisabeth Platel (the Opéra Ballet's leading étoile), whom Markova knew and greatly admired, as guide, assistant and, as it turned out, pupil too. Delouche did not quite know what to expect (his book about his films – *Corps Glorieux* – is the happiest of records of his work and contains a loving description of filming with Markova in the documentary which he called *Markova, la Legende*). He was astonished at the verve and the exceptional charm of Markova's coaching. Happy with these beautiful young artists, she blossomed, demonstrated, remembered, with all her natural grace and with all the power of her artistry. The young responded with enthusiasm; Élisabeth Platel watched and helped, and was happy to learn, too. It is for me as, surely, for any balletomane, a most rewarding and heart-lifting record of a great ballerina passing on the fruits of a prodigious career and of prodigious artistry. I called Markova my university. I was, I am proud to think, in some ways her pupil. She taught me infinitely much. I adored her. ∎

Photograph
Credits

Index

315